Classics of Strategy and Counsel

The Collected Translations of
Thomas Cleary

CLASSICS OF STRATEGY AND COUNSEL

VOLUME ONE

The Art of War
Mastering the Art of War
The Lost Art of War
The Silver Sparrow Art of War

VOLUME TWO

Thunder in the Sky
The Japanese Art of War
The Book of Five Rings
Ways of Warriors, Codes of Kings

VOLUME THREE

The Art of Wealth
Living a Good Life
The Human Element
Back to Beginnings

CLASSICS OF STRATEGY AND COUNSEL

VOLUME ONE

The Art of War
Mastering the Art of War
The Lost Art of War
The Silver Sparrow Art of War

SHAMBHALA
Boston & London
2000

Shambhala Publications, Inc.
Horticultural Hall
300 Massachusetts Avenue
Boston, MA 02115
www.shambhala.com

9 8 7 6 5 4 3 2 1

FIRST EDITION
Printed in the United States of America

⊗ This edition is printed on acid-free paper that meets
the American National Standards Institute z39.48 Standard.
Distributed in the United States by Random House, Inc.,
and in Canada by Random House of Canada Ltd

LIBRARY OF CONGRESS CATALOGING-IN-PUBLICATION DATA
Classics of strategy and counsel : the collected translations of Thomas Cleary.
p. cm.
Includes bibliographical references.
Contents: v. 1. The art of war—Mastering the art of war—The lost art of war—The
silver sparrow art of war—v. 2. Thunder in the sky—The Japanese art of war—The
book of five rings—Ways of warriors, codes of kings—v. 3. The art of wealth—
Living a good life—The human element—Back to beginnings.
ISBN 1-57062-750-9 (set)—ISBN 1-57062-727-4 (v. 1)—ISBN 1-57062-728-2 (v. 2)
—ISBN 1-57062-729-0 (v. 3)
1. Military art and science.   2. Strategy.   3. Management.   I. Cleary, Thomas F.,
1949–
U104.C484 2000
355.02—dc21
00-030765

CONTENTS

THE LOST ART OF WAR

THE SILVER SPARROW ART OF WAR

PUBLISHER'S NOTE

The works contained in The Collected Translations of Thomas Cleary were published over a period of more than twenty years and originated from several publishing houses. As a result, the capitalization and romanization of Chinese words vary occasionally from one text to another within the volumes, due to changes in stylistic preferences from year to year and from house to house. In all cases, terms are rendered consistently within each text.

THE ART OF WAR

Sun Tzu

TRANSLATOR'S PREFACE

The Art of War (Sunzi bingfa/Sun-tzu ping-fa), compiled well over two thousand years ago by a mysterious Chinese warrior-philosopher, is still perhaps the most prestigious and influential book of strategy in the world today, as eagerly studied in Asia by modern politicians and executives as it has been by military leaders and strategists for the last two millennia and more.

In Japan, which was transformed directly from a feudal culture into a corporate culture virtually overnight, contemporary students of *The Art of War* have applied the strategy of this ancient classic to modern politics and business with similar alacrity. Indeed, some see in the successes of postwar Japan an illustration of Sun Tzu's dictum of the classic, "To win without fighting is best."

As a study of the anatomy of organizations in conflict, *The Art of War* applies to competition and conflict in general, on every level from the interpersonal to the international. Its aim is invincibility, victory without battle, and unassailable strength through understanding of the physics, politics, and psychology of conflict.

This translation of *The Art of War* presents the classic from the point of view of its background in the great spiritual tradition of Taoism, the origin not only of psychology but also of science and technology in East Asia, and the source of the insights into human nature that underlie this most revered of handbooks for success.

In my opinion, the importance of understanding the Taoist element of *The Art of War* can hardly be exaggerated. Not only is this classic of strategy permeated with the ideas of great Taoist works such as the *I Ching (The Book of Changes)* and the *Tao-te Ching (The Way and Its Power)*, but it reveals the fundamentals of Taoism as the ultimate source of all the traditional Chinese martial arts. Furthermore, while *The Art of War* is unmatched in its presentation of principle, the keys to the deepest levels of practice of its strategy depend on the psychological development in which Taoism specializes.

The enhanced personal power traditionally associated with application of Taoist mental technology is in itself a part of the collective power associated with application of the understanding of mass psychology taught in *The Art of War*. What is perhaps most characteristically Taoist about *The Art of War* in such a way as to recommend itself to the modern day is the manner in which power is continually tempered by a profound undercurrent of humanism.

Throughout Chinese history, Taoism has been a moderating force in the fluctuating currents of human thought and action. Teaching that life is a complex of interacting forces, Taoism has fostered both material and mental progress, both technological development and awareness of the potential dangers of that very development, always striving to encourage balance between the material and spiritual sides of humankind. Similarly, in politics Taoism has stood on the side of both rulers and ruled, has set kingdoms up and has torn kingdoms down, according to the needs of the time. As a classic of Taoist thought, *The Art of War* is thus a book not only of war but also of peace, above all a tool for understanding the very roots of conflict and resolution.

TRANSLATOR'S INTRODUCTION

Taoism and The Art of War

According to an old story, a lord of ancient China once asked his physician, a member of a family of healers, which of them was the most skilled in the art.

The physician, whose reputation was such that his name became synonymous with medical science in China, replied, "My eldest brother sees the spirit of sickness and removes it before it takes shape, so his name does not get out of the house.

"My elder brother cures sickness when it is still extremely minute, so his name does not get out of the neighborhood.

"As for me, I puncture veins, prescribe potions, and massage skin, so from time to time my name gets out and is heard among the lords."

Among the tales of ancient China, none captures more beautifully than this the essence of *The Art of War,* the premiere classic of the science of strategy in conflict. A Ming dynasty critic writes of this little tale of the physician: "What is essential for leaders, generals, and ministers in running countries and governing armies is no more than this."

The healing arts and the martial arts may be a world apart in ordinary usage, but they are parallel in several senses: in recognizing, as the story says, that the less needed the better; in the sense that both involve strategy in dealing with disharmony; and in the sense that in both knowledge of the problem is key to the solution.

As in the story of the ancient healers, in Sun Tzu's philosophy the peak efficiency of knowledge and strategy is to make conflict altogether unnecessary: "To overcome others' armies without fighting is the best of skills." And like the story of the healers, Sun Tzu explains there are all grades of martial arts: The superior militarist foils enemies' plots; next best is to ruin their alliances; next after that is to attack their armed forces; worst is to besiege their cities.*

Just as the eldest brother in the story was unknown because of his acumen and the middle brother was hardly known because of his alacrity, Sun Tzu also affirms that in ancient times those known as skilled warriors won when victory was still easy, so the victories of skilled warriors were not known for cunning or rewarded for bravery.

This ideal strategy whereby one could win without fighting, accomplish the most by doing the least, bears the characteristic stamp of Taoism, the ancient tradition of knowledge that fostered both the healing arts and the martial arts in China. The *Tao-te Ching,* or *The Way and Its Power,* applies the same strategy to society that Sun Tzu attributes to warriors of ancient times:

> Plan for what is difficult while it is easy, do what is great while it is small. The most difficult things in the world must be done while they are still easy, the greatest things in the world must be done while they are still small. For this reason sages never do what is great, and this is why they can achieve that greatness.

Written over two thousand years ago during a period of prolonged civil warfare, *The Art of War* emerged from the same social conditions as some of the greatest classics of Chinese humanism, including the *Tao-te Ching.* Taking a rational rather than an emotional approach to the problem of conflict, Sun Tzu showed how understanding conflict can lead not only to its resolution, but even to its avoidance altogether.

The prominence of Taoist thought in *The Art of War* has been noted by scholars for centuries, and the classic of strategy is recognized in both philosophical and political works of the Taoist canon. The level of knowledge represented by the upper reaches of *The Art of War,* the level of invincibility and the level of no conflict, is one expression of what Taoist lore calls "deep knowledge and strong action."

The Book of Balance and Harmony (Chung-ho chi/Zhongho ji),

---

*Note again the similarity of Sun Tzu's advice to medical wisdom: to foil the enemies' plots is like keeping healthy so as to be resistant to disease; to ruin their alliances is like avoiding contagion; to attack their armed forces is like taking medicine; to besiege their cities is like performing surgery.

a medieval Taoist work, says, "Deep knowledge of principle knows without seeing, strong practice of the Way accomplishes without striving. Deep knowledge is to 'know without going out the door, see the way of heaven without looking out the window.' Strong action is to 'grow ever stronger, adapting to all situations.' "

In terms of *The Art of War*, the master warrior is likewise the one who knows the psychology and mechanics of conflict so intimately that every move of an opponent is seen through at once, and one who is able to act in precise accord with situations, riding on their natural patterns with a minimum of effort. *The Book of Balance and Harmony* goes on to describe Taoist knowledge and practice further in terms familiar to the quest of the warrior.

> Deep knowledge is to be aware of disturbance before disturbance, to be aware of danger before danger, to be aware of destruction before destruction, to be aware of calamity before calamity. Strong action is training the body without being burdened by the body, exercising the mind without being used by the mind, working in the world without being affected by the world, carrying out tasks without being obstructed by tasks.
>
> By deep knowledge of principle, one can change disturbance into order, change danger into safety, change destruction into survival, change calamity into fortune. By strong action on the Way, one can bring the body to the realm of longevity, bring the mind to the sphere of mystery, bring the world to great peace, and bring tasks to great fulfillment.

As these passages suggest, warriors of Asia who used Taoist or Zen arts to achieve profound calmness did not do so just to prepare their minds to sustain the awareness of imminent death, but also to achieve the sensitivity needed to respond to situations without stopping to ponder. *The Book of Balance and Harmony* says:

> Comprehension in a state of quiescence, accomplishment without striving, knowing without seeing—this is the sense and response of the Transformative Tao. Comprehension in a state of quiescence can comprehend anything, accomplishment without striving can accomplish anything, knowing without seeing can know anything.

As in *The Art of War*, the range of awareness and efficiency of the Taoist adept is unnoticeable, imperceptible to others, because their critical moments take place before ordinary intelligence has mapped out a description of the situation. *The Book of Balance and Harmony* says:

> To sense and comprehend after action is not worthy of being called comprehension. To accomplish after striving is not worthy of being called accomplishment. To know after seeing is not worthy of being called knowing. These three are far from the way of sensing and response.
>
> Indeed, to be able to do something before it exists, sense something before it becomes active, see something before it sprouts, are three abilities that develop interdependently. Then nothing is sensed but is comprehended, nothing is undertaken without response, nowhere does one go without benefit.

One of the purposes of Taoist literature is to help to develop this special sensitivity and responsiveness to master living situations. *The Book of Balance and Harmony* mentions the "Transformative Tao" in reference to the analytical and meditative teachings of the *I Ching*, the locus classicus of the formula for sensitivity and responsiveness. Like the *I Ching* and other classical Taoist literature, *The Art of War* has an incalculable abstract reserve and metaphorical potential. And like other classical Taoist literature, it yields its subtleties in accord with the mentality of the reader and the manner in which it is put into practice.

The association of martial arts with Taoist tradition extends back to the legendary Yellow Emperor of the third millennium B.C.E., one of the major culture heroes of China and an important figure in Taoist lore. According to myth, the Yellow Emperor conquered savage tribes through the use of magical martial arts taught him by a Taoist immortal, and he is also said to have composed the famous *Yin Convergence Classic (Yinfu ching/Yinfu jing)*, a Taoist work of great antiquity traditionally given both martial and spiritual interpretations.

Over a thousand years later, warrior chieftains overthrowing the remnants of ancient Chinese slave society and introducing humanistic concepts of government composed the classic sayings of the *I Ching*, another Taoist text traditionally used as a basis for both martial and civil arts. The basic principles of the *I Ching* figure prominently in Sun Tzu's science of political warfare, just as they are essential to individual combat and defense techniques in the traditional martial arts that grew out of Taoist exercises.

The next great Taoist text after the *Yin Convergence Classic* and *I Ching* was the *Tao-te Ching*, like *The Art of War* a product of the era of the Warring States, which ravaged China in the middle of the first millennium B.C.E. This great classic represents the prevailing attitude toward war that characterizes Sun Tzu's manual: that it is destructive even for the victors, often counterproductive, a reasonable course of action only when there is no choice:

> Those who assist a leader by means of the Tao do not use arms to coerce the world, for these things tend to reverse—brambles grow where an army has been, bad years follow a great war.
>
> Weapons are inauspicious instruments, not the tools of the enlightened. When there is no choice but to use them, it is best to be calm and free from greed, and not celebrate victory. Those who celebrate victory are bloodthirsty, and the bloodthirsty cannot have their way with the world.

In a similar way, *The Art of War* pinpoints anger and greed as fundamental causes of defeat. According to Sun Tzu, it is the unemotional, reserved, calm, detached warrior who wins, not the hothead seeking vengeance and not the ambitious seeker of fortune. The *Tao-te Ching* says:

> Those who are good at knighthood are not militaristic, those who are good at battle do not become angry, those who are good at prevailing over opponents do not get involved.

The strategy of operating outside the sphere of emotional influence is part of the general strategy of unfathomability that *The Art of War* emphasizes in characteristic Taoist style: Sun Tzu says, "Those skilled in defense hide in the deepest depths of the earth, those skilled in attack maneuver in the highest heights of the sky. Therefore they can preserve themselves and achieve complete victory."

This emphasis on the advantage of enigma pervades Taoist thinking, from the political realm to the realms of commerce and craft, where, it is said, "A good merchant hides his treasures and appears to have nothing," and "A good craftsman leaves no traces." These sayings were adopted by Zen Buddhists to represent their art, and the uncanny approach to the warrior's way was taken up both literally and figuratively by Zen Buddhists, who were among the foremost students of the Taoist classics and developers of esoteric martial arts.

Writings on both the civil and military aspects of political organization are found throughout the Taoist canon. *The Book of the Huainan Masters (Huainanzi/Huai-nan-tzu)*, one of the great Taoist classics of the early Han dynasty, which followed the dramatic end of the Warring States period, includes an entire chapter on Taoist military science that takes up the central theme of the practice of *The Art of War:*

> In martial arts, it is important that strategy be unfathomable, that form be concealed, and that movements be unexpected, so that preparedness against them be impossible.
>
> What enables a good general to win without fail is always having unfathomable wisdom and a modus operandi that leaves no tracks.
>
> Only the formless cannot be affected. Sages hide in unfathomability, so their feelings cannot be observed; they operate in formlessness, so their lines cannot be crossed.

In *The Art of War*, Sun Tzu writes, "Be extremely subtle, even to the point of formlessness. Be extremely mysterious, even to the point of soundlessness. Thereby you can be the director of the opponent's fate."

Both Sun Tzu and the masters of Huainan, a group of Taoist and Confucian sages gathered by a local king, recognize a level of wisdom where conflict does not emerge and victory is not visible to the ordinary eye, but both books are, after all, written in recognition of the difficulty and rarity of this refined attainment. Like Sun Tzu's art of war, the strategy of the masters of Huainan provides for actual conflict, not only as a last resort, but also as an operation to be carried out under the strictest conditions, with appropriate leadership:

> A general must see alone and know alone, meaning that he must see what others do not see and know what others do not know. Seeing what others do not see is called brilliance, knowing what others do not know is called genius. Brilliant geniuses win first, meaning that they defend in such a way as to be unassailable and attack in such a way as to be irresistible.

The rigorous conditions of Taoistic military action are paralleled by those of Taoist spiritual practice. Metaphors of peace and war are widely used in manuals of Taoist meditation and exercise. One of the most basic principles of Taoist practice, deriving from the teachings of the *I Ching,* is the mastery of "emptiness and fullness," which has both physical and psychological implications.

Given an entire chapter in *The Art of War,* the mastery of emptiness and fullness is fundamental to the physical accomplishment of Taoist fighting arts like Absolute Boxing, and to the organizational, or sociopolitical, aspect of the arts of both civil and military government. Explaining the understanding of emptiness and fullness as the Way to certain victory, the masters of Huainan say:

> This is a matter of emptiness and fullness. When there are rifts between superiors and subordinates, when generals and officers are disaffected with each other, and dissatisfaction has built up in the minds of the troops, this is called emptiness. When the civilian leadership is intelligent and the military leadership is good, when superiors and subordinates are of like mind, and will and energy operate together, this is called fullness.
>
> The skilled can fill their people with energy to confront the emptiness of others, while the incompetent drain their people of energy in face of the fullness of others.
>
> When welfare and justice embrace the whole people, when public works are sufficient to meet national emergencies, when the policy of selection for office is satisfactory to the intelligent, when planning is sufficient to know strengths and weaknesses, that is the basis of certain victory.

The political basis of military strength, or the social basis of the strength of any organization, is a teaching that is also rooted in the *I Ching.* In *The Art of War* this is given premier importance, as the first item in the first chapter, on strategy, involves examining the Way of an adversary group—the moral fiber, the coherence of the social order, the popularity of the government, or the common morale. Under the right conditions, according to Sun Tzu, a small group could prevail over a large group; and among the conditions that could make this possible were justice, order, cohesion, and morale. This is another pivot of Chinese thought that is also highlighted by the masters of Huainan in the context of military strategy:

> Strength is not just a matter of extensive territory and a large population, victory is not just a matter of efficient armaments, security is not just a matter of high walls and deep moats, authority is not just a matter of strict orders and frequent punishments. Those who establish a viable organization will survive even if they are small, while those who establish a moribund organization will perish even if they are large.

This theme is also emphasized by another of the great military strategists of old China, Zhuge Liang of the third century C.E., who followed the teachings of Sun Tzu to become legendary for his genius:

> The Tao of military operations lies in harmonizing people. When people are in harmony, they will fight naturally, without being exhorted to do so. If the officers and soldiers are suspicious of each other, warriors will not join up; if loyal advice is not heard, small minds will talk and criticize in secret. When hypocrisy sprouts, even if you have the wisdom of ancient warrior kings you could not defeat a peasant, let alone a crowd of them. This is why tradition says, "A military operation is like a fire; if it is not stopped, it will burn itself out."

Zhuge's status as a practical genius is so great that his writings, his designs, and writings about him are actually included in the Taoist canon. Like *The Art of War* and the Taoist classics, Zhuge's philosophy of warfare approaches the positive by way of the negative, in the Taoist fashion of "nondoing":

> In ancient times, those who governed well did not arm, those who were armed well did not set up battle lines, those who set up battle lines well did not fight, those who fought well did not lose, those who lost well did not perish.

This echoes the idea of combat as a last resort, the ideal of winning without fighting offered by *The Art of War*, following the teaching of the *Tao-te Ching*. Zhuge Liang also quotes the classic admonition from this revered Taoist text, "Weapons are instruments of ill omen, to be used only when unavoidable," but he too shares the Taoist historical consciousness that the age of original humanity was already gone, and like Sun Tzu he was personally involved in a time of raging civil war. Zhuge's work in the Taoist canon therefore contains both rational views and practical teachings for political and military security that follow closely on those of ancient Sun Tzu:

> The administration of military affairs means the administration of border affairs, or the administration of affairs in outlying regions, in such a way as to relieve people from major disturbances.
>
> This administration is done by authority and military prowess, executing the violent and rebellious in order to preserve the country and keep the homeland secure. This is why civilization requires the existence of military preparedness.
>
> It is for this reason that beasts have claws and fangs. When they are joyful, they play with each other, when angry they attack each other. Humans have no claws or fangs, so they make armor and weapons to help defend themselves.
>
> So nations have armies to help them, rulers have ministers to assist them. When the helper is strong, the nation is secure; when the helper is weak, the nation is in peril.

Here Zhuge follows Sun Tzu directly, as he does in his emphasis on leadership and its popular basis. In Sun Tzu's scheme, both civil and military leadership are among the first conditions to be scrutinized. Zhuge follows Sun Tzu and the masters of Huainan in seeing the strength of leadership based at once on personal qualities and on popular support. In Taoist thought, power was moral as well as material, and it was believed that moral power manifested itself both as self-mastery and as influence over others. To explain the strength of a national defense force, Zhuge writes:

> This in turn depends on the generals entrusted with military leadership. A general that is not popular is not a help to the nation, not a leader of the army.

A general who is "not popular" is one who, according to another way of reading the characters, "denies the people." Sun Tzu emphasizes the unity of wills as a fundamental source of strength, and his minimalist philosophy of warfare is a natural outgrowth of the central idea of common interest; on the basis of this principle, Zhuge Liang again quotes the *Tao-te Ching* to express the ideal of the sage warrior concerned for the body of society as a whole—"Weapons are instruments of ill omen, to be used only when it is unavoidable."

Zhuge also follows *The Art of War* closely in his emphasis on avoiding action without strategy as well as action without need:

> The way to use weapons is to carry out operations only after having first determined your strategy. Carefully examine the patterns of the climate and terrain, and look into the hearts of the people. Train in the use of military equipment, make patterns of rewards and punishments clear, observe the strategy of opponents, watch out for dangerous passes enroute, distinguish places of safety and danger, find out the conditions of both sides, be aware of when to advance and when to withdraw, adapt to the timing of circumstances, set up defensive measures while strengthening your attack force, promote soldiers for their ability, draw up plans for success, consider the matter of life and death—only when you have done all this can you send forth armies entrusted to generals that will reach out with the power to capture opponents.

Speed and coordination, central to success in battle according to Sun Tzu's art of war, also derive not only from strategic preparedness, but from the psychological cohesion on which leadership depends; Zhuge writes:

> A general is a commander, a useful tool for a nation. First determining strategy then carrying it out, his command is as though borne afloat on a torrent, his conquest is like a hawk striking its prey. Like a drawn bow when still, like a machine starting up in action, he breaks through wherever he turns, and even powerful enemies perish. If the general has no foresight and the soldiers lack impetus, mere strategy without unification of wills cannot suffice to strike fear into an enemy even if you have a million troops.

Mentioning Sun Tzu's classic as the ultimate manual for successful strategy, Zhuge concludes his essay on military organization by summing up the main points of *The Art of War* as he incorporated them into his own practice, centering on those aspects of the training and mood of warriors that derive from Taoist tradition:

> Have no hard feelings toward anyone who has not shown you enmity, do not fight with anyone who does not oppose you. The

effective skill of an engineer can only be seen by the eyes of an expert, the operation of plans in battle can only be set in action through the strategy of Sun Tzu.

Following Sun Tzu, Zhuge emphasizes the advantages of unexpectedness and speed, capable of reversing otherwise insurmountable odds:

Planning should be secret, attack should be swift. When an army takes its objective like a hawk striking its prey, and battles like a river broken through a dam, its opponents will scatter before the army tires. This is the use of the momentum of an army.

As mentioned before, among the main points of emphasis in Sun Tzu's art of war is objectivity, and his classic teaches how to assess situations in a dispassionate manner. Zhuge also follows Sun in this, stressing the advantage of carefully calculated action:

Those who are skilled in combat do not become angered, those who are skilled at winning do not become afraid. Thus the wise win before they fight, while the ignorant fight to win.

Here Zhuge quotes *The Art of War* directly, adding Sun Tzu's warnings about the consequences of poor planning, wasteful actions, and wasteful personnel:

A country is exhausted when it must buy its supplies at high prices, and is impoverished when it ships supplies long distances. Attacks should not be repeated, battles should not be multiplied. Use strength according to capacity, aware that it will be spent with excessive use. Get rid of the worthless, and the country can be peaceful; get rid of the incompetent, and the country can be profited.

Finally Zhuge goes on in the tradition of the *Tao-te Ching*, *The Art of War*, and *The Masters of Huainan* to give victory to the unfathomable:

A skilled attack is one against which opponents do not know how to defend; a skilled defense is one which opponents do not know how to attack. Therefore those skilled in defense are not so because of fortress walls.

This is why high walls and deep moats do not guarantee security, while strong armor and effective weapons do not guarantee strength. If opponents want to hold firm, attack where they are unprepared; if opponents want to establish a battlefront, appear where they do not expect you.

This idea of knowing while being unknown, repeated again and again as a key to success, is one of the strongest links between Taoist meditation and *The Art of War*, for the secret to this art of "invisibility" is precisely the interior detachment cultivated by Taoists for attaining impersonal views of objective reality. Certain of the philosophical teachings of early Taoism are commonly used in practical schools as codes for exercises used in personal cultivation.

Understanding the practical aspect of Taoist philosophical teachings helps to cut through the sense of paradox that may be caused by seemingly contradictory attitudes. That Sun Tzu calmly teaches the ruthless art of war while condemning war may seem contradictory if this fact is seen outside the context of the total understanding of the human mentality fostered by Taoist learning.

The simultaneous appreciation of very different points of view is a powerful Taoist technique, whose understanding can resolve contradiction and paradox. The model of the paradox of *The Art of War* can be seen in the *Tao-te Ching*, where both ruthlessness and kindness are part of the Way of the sage.

"Heaven and earth are not humanistic—they regard myriad beings as straw dogs; sages are not humanistic—they regard people as straw dogs," wrote the philosopher of the *Tao-te Ching*. A horrified Western Sinologist working in the 1950s, shortly after the truce in Korea, wrote that this passage had "unleashed a monster," but to a Taoist this statement does not represent inhumanity but an exercise in objectivity, similar to Buddhist exercises in impersonality.

In modern terms, this sort of statement is no different from that of a psychologist or sociologist making the observation that the attitudes, thoughts, and expectations of entire nations are not arrived at purely by a multitude of independent rational decisions, but largely under the influence of environmental factors beyond the control of the individual or even the community.

As Sun Tzu's classic attests, the place of such an observation in the art of war is not to cultivate a callous or bloodthirsty attitude, but to understand the power of mass psychology. Understanding how people can be manipulated through emotions, for example, is as useful for those who wish to avoid this as it is for those who wish to practice it.

Seen in this light, *The Art of War* is no more a call to arms than a study on conditioning is a recommendation for slavery. By so thoroughly analyzing the political, psychological, and material factors involved in conflict, Sun Tzu's professed aim was not to encourage warfare but to minimize and curtail it.

An impersonal view of humanity as not the master of its own fate may be necessary to liberate a warrior from emotional entanglements that might precipitate irrational approaches to conflict; but it is not, in the Taoist scheme of things, held to justify destructive behavior. The counterbalance to this view is also found in the *Tao-te Ching*, prefiguring Sun Tzu's teachings in *The Art of War:*

> I have three treasures that I keep and prize: one is kindness, second is frugality, and third is not presuming to take precedence over others. By kindness one can be brave, by frugality one can reach out, and by not presuming to take precedence one can survive effectively. If one gives up kindness and courage, gives up frugality and breadth, and gives up humility for aggressiveness, one will die. The exercise of kindness in battle leads to victory, the exercise of kindness in defense leads to security.

In his classic Master Sun likens military action to a "fire, which burns itself out if not stopped," and if his strategy of success without conflict was not always attainable, his strategy of hyperefficiency could at least minimize senseless violence and destruction. In Taoist terms, success is often gained by not doing, and the strategy of *The Art of War* is as much in knowing what not to do and when not to do it as it is in knowing what to do and when to do it.

The art of not doing—which includes the unobtrusiveness, unknowability, and ungraspability at the core of esoteric Asian martial arts—belongs to the branch of Taoism known as the science of essence. The arts of doing—which include the external techniques of both cultural and martial arts—belong to the branch of Taoism known as the science of life. The science of essence has to do with state of mind, the science of life has to do with use of energy. Like a classic Taoist text, it is in true balance of these two that *The Art of War* is most completely understood.

In more modern times, the definitive Taoist statement on this subject is immortalized in *Journey to the West (Hsi-yu chi/Xiyou ji)*, one of the Four Extraordinary Books of the Ming dynasty (1368–1644). Drawing on earlier Taoist sources from wartime China under the duress of Mongol invasions, this remarkable novel is a classic representation of the result of what in Taoist terms would be called studying the science of life without the science of essence, material development without corresponding psychological development, or in Sun Tzu's terms having force without intelligence.

The central figure of this novel is a magical monkey who founds a monkey civilization and becomes its leader by establishing a territory for the monkeys. Subsequently the monkey king overcomes a "devil confusing the world," and steals the devil's sword.

Returning to his own land with the devil's sword, the monkey king takes up the practice of swordsmanship. He even teaches his monkey subjects to make toy weapons and regalia to play at war.

Unfortunately, though ruler of a nation, the martial monkey king is not yet ruler of himself. In eminently logical backward reasoning, the monkey reflects that if neighboring nations note the monkeys' play, they might assume the monkeys were preparing for war. In that case, they might therefore take preemptive action against the monkeys, who would then be faced with real warfare armed only with toy weapons.

Thus, the monkey king thoughtfully initiates the arms race, ordering pre-preemptive stockpiling of real weapons.

If it seems disconcerting to read a thirteenth-century description of twentieth-century politics, it may be no less so to read a book as old as the Bible describing tactics in use today not only by guerrilla warriors but by influential politicians and corporate executives. Following the disillusionist posture of the *Tao-te Ching* and *The Art of War*, the story of the monkey king also prefigures a major movement in modern scientific thought following the climax of the Western divorce of religion and science centuries ago.

The monkey king in the story exercised power without wisdom, disrupting the natural order and generally raising hell until he ran into the limits of matter, where he was finally trapped. There he lost the excitement of impulsive enthusiasm, and he was eventually released to seek the science of essence, under the strict condition that his knowledge and power were to be controlled by compassion, the expression of wisdom and unity of being.

The monkey's downfall finally comes about when he meets Buddha, whom the Taoist celestial immortals summon to deal with the intractable beast. The immortals had attempted to "cook" him in the "cauldron of the eight trigrams," that is, to put him through the training of spiritual alchemy based on the Taoist *I Ching*, but he had jumped out still unrefined.

Buddha conquers the monkey's pride by demonstrating the insuperable law of universal relativity and has him imprisoned in "the mountain of the five elements," the world of matter and energy, where he suffers the results of his arrogant antics.

After five hundred years, at length Guanyin (Kuan Yin), the transhistorical Buddhist saint traditionally honored as the personification of universal compassion, shows up at the prison of the now repentant monkey and recites this telling verse:

> Too bad the magic monkey didn't serve the public
> As he madly flaunted heroics in days of yore.
> With a cheating heart he made havoc
> In the gathering of immortals;
> With grandiose gall he went for his ego
> To the heaven of happiness.
> Among a hundred thousand troops,
> None could oppose him;
> In the highest heavens above
> He had a threatening presence.
> But since he was stymied on meeting our Buddha,
> When will he ever reach out and show his achievements again?

Now the monkey pleads with the saint for his release. The saint grants this on the condition that the monkey devote himself to the quest for higher enlightenment, not only for himself but for society at large. Finally, before letting the monkey go to set out on the long road ahead, as a precaution the saint places a ring around the monkey's head, a ring that will tighten and cause the monkey severe pain whenever a certain spell invoking compassion is said in response to any new misbehavior on the part of the monkey.

The Art of War has been known for a hundred generations as the foremost classic of strategy; but perhaps its greatest wizardry lies in the ring of compassion that Master Sun slips over the head of every warrior who tries to use this book. And as history shows, the magic spell that tightens its grip is chanted whenever a warrior forgets the ring.

The Structure and Content of The Art of War

The Art of War, permeated with the philosophical and political thought of the *Tao-te Ching*, also resembles the great Taoist classic in that it is largely composed of a collection of aphorisms commonly attributed to a shadowy, semilegendary author. Certain Taoists regard the *Tao-te Ching* to be a transmission of ancient lore compiled and elaborated by its "author," rather than a completely original work, and the same may very well be true of *The Art of War*. In any case, both classics share the general pattern of central themes recurring throughout the text in different contexts.

The first book of *The Art of War* is devoted to the importance of strategy. As the classic *I Ching* says, "Leaders plan in the beginning when they do things," and "Leaders consider problems and prevent them." In terms of military operations, *The Art of War* brings up five things that are to be assessed before undertaking any action: the Way, the weather, the terrain, the military leadership, and discipline.

In this context, the Way (Tao) has to do with civil leadership, or rather the relationship between political leadership and the populace. In both Taoist and Confucian parlance, a righteous government is described as "imbued with the Tao," and Sun Tzu the martialist similarly speaks of the Way as "inducing the people to have the same aim as the leadership."

Assessment of the weather, the question of the season for action, also relates to concern for the people, meaning both the populace in general as well as military personnel. The essential point here is to avoid disruption of the productive activities of the people, which depend on the seasons, and to avoid extremes of weather that would handicap or harm troops in the field.

The terrain is to be sized up in terms of distance, degree of difficulty of travel, dimensions, and safety. The use of scouts and native guides is important here, for, as the *I Ching* says, "Chasing game without a guide leads one into the bush."

The criteria offered by *The Art of War* for assessment of the military leadership are traditional virtues also much emphasized in Confucianism and medieval Taoism: intelligence, trustworthiness, humaneness, courage, and sternness. According to the great Chan Buddhist Fushan, "Humaneness without intelligence is like having a field but not plowing it. Intelligence without courage is like having sprouts but not weeding. Courage without humaneness is like knowing how to reap but not how to sow." The other two virtues, trustworthiness and sternness, are those by which the leadership wins both the loyalty and obedience of the troops.

The fifth item to be assessed, discipline, refers to organizational coherence and efficiency. Discipline is very much connected with the virtues of trustworthiness and sternness sought after in military leaders, since it uses the corresponding mechanisms of reward and punishment. A great deal of emphasis is placed on the establishment of a clear system of rewards and punishments accepted by the warriors as fair and impartial. This was one of the main points of Legalism, a school of thought that also arose during the Warring States period, stressing the importance of rational organization and the rule of law rather than personalistic feudal government.

Following a discussion of these five assessments, *The Art of War* goes on to emphasize the central importance of deception: "A military operation involves deception. Even though you are competent, appear incompetent. Though effective, appear ineffective." As the *Tao-te Ching* says, "One with great skill appears inept." The element of surprise, so important for victory with maximum efficiency, depends on knowing others while being unknown to others, so secrecy and misdirection are considered essential arts.

Generally speaking, the toe-to-toe battle is the last resort of the skilled warrior, who Sun Tzu says should be prepared but should nevertheless avoid confrontation with a strong opponent. Rather than trying to overwhelm opponents directly, Master Sun recommends wearing them down by flight, fostering disharmony within their ranks, manipulating their feelings, and using their anger and pride against them. Thus, in sum, the opening statement of *The Art of War* introduces the three main facets of the warrior's art: the social, the psychological, and the physical.

The second chapter of *The Art of War*, on doing battle, stresses the domestic consequences of war, even foreign war. Emphasis is on speed and efficiency, with strong warnings not to prolong operations, especially far afield. Considerable attention is devoted to the importance of conservation of energy and material resources. In order to minimize the drain of war on the economy and population, Sun Tzu recommends the practice of feeding off the enemy and using captive forces won over by good treatment.

The third chapter, on planning a siege, also emphasizes conservation—the general aim is to gain victory while keeping as much intact as possible, both socially and materially, rather than destroying whoever and whatever stands in the way. In this sense Master Sun affirms that it is best to win without fighting.

Several tactical recommendations follow in pursuit of this general conservative principle. First of all, since it is desirable to win without battle, Sun Tzu says that it is best to overcome opponents at the outset by foiling their plans. Failing that, he recommends isolating opponents and rendering them helpless. Here again it would seem that time is of the essence, but the point is made that speed does not mean haste, and thorough preparation is necessary. And when victory is won, Sun stresses that it should be complete, to avoid the expense of maintaining an occupation force.

The chapter goes on to outline strategies for action according to relative numbers of protagonists versus antagonists, again observing that it is wise to avoid taking on unfavorable odds if possible. The *I Ching* says, "It is unlucky to be stubborn in the face of insurmountable odds." Furthermore, while the formulation of strategy depends on prior intelligence, it is also imperative to adapt to actual battle situations; as the *I Ching* says, "Coming to an impasse, change; having changed, you can get through."

Master Sun then makes note of five ways to ascertain victory, pursuant to the theme that skillful warriors fight only when assured of winning. According to Sun, the victors are those who know when to fight and when not to fight; those who know when to use many or few troops; those whose officers and soldiers are of one mind; those who face the unprepared with preparation; and those with able generals who are not constrained by government.

This last point is a very delicate one, as it places an even greater moral and intellectual responsibility on the military leadership. While war is never to be initiated by the military itself, as later explained, but by the command of the civilian government, Sun Tzu says an absentee civilian leadership that interferes ignorantly with field command "takes away victory by deranging the military."

Again the real issue seems to be that of knowledge; the premise that military leadership in the field should not be subject to interference by civilian government is based on the idea that the key to victory is intimate knowledge of the actual situation. Outlining these five ways to determine which side is likely to prevail, Sun Tzu states that when you know both yourself and others you are never in danger, when you know yourself but not others you have half a chance of winning, and when you know neither yourself nor others you are in danger in every battle.

The fourth chapter of *The Art of War* is on formation, one of the most important issues of strategy and combat. In a characteristically Taoist posture, Sun Tzu here asserts that the keys to victory are adaptability and inscrutability. As the commentator Du Mu explains, "The inner condition of the formless is inscrutable, whereas that of those who have adopted a specific form is obvious. The inscrutable win, the obvious lose."

Inscrutability in this context is not purely passive, does not simply mean being withdrawn or concealed from others; more important, it means perception of what is invisible to others and response to possibilities not yet discerned by those who look only at the obvious. By seeing opportunities before they are visible to others and being quick to act, the uncanny warrior can take situations by the throat before matters get out of hand.

Following this line of thought, Sun Tzu reemphasizes the pursuit of certain victory by knowing when to act and when not to act. Make yourself invincible, he says, and take on opponents only when they are vulnerable: "Good warriors take their stand on ground where they cannot lose, and do not overlook conditions that make an opponent prone to defeat." Reviewing these conditions, Sun rephrases some of his guidelines for assessment of organizations, such as discipline and ethics versus rapacity and corruption.

The topic of the fifth chapter of *The Art of War* is force, or momentum, the dynamic structure of a group in action. Here Master Sun emphasizes organizational skills, coordination, and the use of both orthodox and guerrilla methods of war. He stresses change and surprise, employing endless variations of tactics, using opponents' psychological conditions to maneuver them into vulnerable positions.

The essence of Sun Tzu's teaching on force is unity and coherence in an organization, using the force of momentum rather than relying on individual qualities and talents: "Good warriors seek effectiveness in battle from the force of momentum, not from individual people."

It is this recognition of the power of the group to even out internal disparities and function as one body of force that sets *The Art of War* apart from the idiosyncratic individualism of the samurai swordsmen of late feudal Japan, whose stylized martial arts are so familiar in the West. This emphasis is one of the essential features that has made Sun Tzu's ancient work so useful for the corporate warriors of modern Asia, among whom *The Art of War* is widely read and still regarded as the matchless classic of strategy in conflict.

The sixth chapter takes up the subject of "emptiness and fullness," already noted as fundamental Taoist concepts commonly adapted to martial arts. The idea is to be filled with energy while at the same time draining opponents, in order, as Master Sun says, to make oneself invincible and take on opponents only when they are vulnerable. One of the simplest of these tactics is well known not only in the context of war, but also in social and business maneuvering: "Good warriors get others to come to them, and do not go to others."

Conserving one's own energy while inducing others to dissipate theirs is another function of the inscrutability so highly prized by the Taoist warrior: "The consummation of forming an army is to arrive at formlessness," says Master Sun, for then no one can formulate a strategy against you. At the same time, he says, induce opponents to construct their own formations, get them to spread themselves thin; test opponents to gauge their resources and reactions, but remain unknown yourself.

In this case, formlessness and fluidity are not merely means of defense and surprise, but means of preserving dynamic potential, energy that could easily be lost by trying to hold on to a specific position or formation. Master Sun likens a successful force to water, which has no constant form but, as the *Tao-te Ching* notes, prevails over everything in spite of its apparent weakness: Sun says, "A military force has no constant formation, water has no constant shape. The ability to gain victory by changing and adapting according to the opponent is called genius."

The seventh chapter of *The Art of War*, on armed struggle, dealing with concrete field organization and combat maneuvers, recapitulates several of Sun Tzu's main themes. Beginning with the need for information and preparation, Sun says, "Act after having made assessments. The one who first knows the measures of far and near wins—this is the rule of armed struggle." The *I Ching* says, "Be prepared, and you will be lucky."

Again expounding his characteristic minimalist/essentialist tactical philosophy, Sun Tzu goes on to say, "Take away the energy of opposing armies, take away the heart of their generals." Echoing his teachings on emptiness and fullness, he also says, "Avoid keen energy, strike the slumping and receding." To take full advantage of the principles of emptiness and fullness, Sun teaches four kinds of mastery essential to the uncanny warrior: mastery of energy, mastery of the heart, mastery of strength, and mastery of adaptation.

The principles of emptiness and fullness also display the fundamental mechanism of the classic yin-yang principles on which they are based, that of reversion from one to the other at the extremes. Master Sun says, "Do not stop an army on its way home. A surrounded army must be given a way out. Do not press a desperate enemy." The *I Ching* says, "The sovereign uses three chasers, letting the game ahead escape," and "if you are too adamant, action is unlucky, even if you are right."

The eighth chapter of *The Art of War* is devoted to adaptation, already seen to be one of the cornerstones of the warrior's art. Master Sun says, "If generals do not know how to adapt advantageously, even if they know the lay of the land they cannot take advantage of it." The *I Ching* says, "Persist too intensely at what is currently beyond your depth, and your fidelity to that course will bring misfortune, no gain."

Adaptability naturally depends on readiness, another persistent theme of *The Art of War*. Master Sun says, "The rule of military operations is not to count on opponents not coming, but to rely on having ways of dealing with them; not to count on opponents not attacking, but to rely on having what cannot be attacked." The *I Ching* says, "If you take on too much without a solid foundation, you will eventually be drained, leaving you with embarrassment and bad luck."

In *The Art of War*, readiness does not just mean material preparedness; without a suitable mental state, sheer physical power is not enough to guarantee victory. Master Sun here defines the psychological dimensions of the victorious leader indirectly, by enumerating five dangers—to be too willing to die, too eager to live, too quick to anger, too puritanical, or too sentimental. Any one of these excesses, he affirms, create vulnerabilities that can easily be exploited by canny opponents. The *I Ching* says, "When waiting on the fringes of a situation, before the appropriate time to go into action has arrived, be steady and avoid giving in to impulse—then you won't go wrong."

The ninth chapter deals with maneuvering armies. Again Master Sun deals with all three aspects of the warrior's art—the physical, social, and psychological. In concrete physical terms, he begins by recommending certain obvious types of terrain that enhance the odds of victory: high ground, upstream, the sunny side of hills, regions with plenty of resources. Referring to all three dimensions, he then describes ways of interpreting enemy movements.

Although Master Sun never dismisses the weight of sheer numbers or material might, here as elsewhere there is the strong suggestion that social and psychological factors can overcome the sort of power that can be physically quantified: "In military matters it is not necessarily beneficial to have more, only to avoid acting aggressively; it is enough to consolidate your power, assess opponents, and win people, that is all." The *I Ching* says, "When you have means but are not getting anywhere, seek appropriate associates, and you will be lucky." Similarly emphasizing directed group effort, *The Art of War* says, "The individualist without strategy who takes opponents lightly will inevitably become a captive."

Solidarity calls especially for mutual understanding and rapport between the leadership and the followers, achieved through both education and training. The Confucian sage Mencius said, "Those who send people on military operations without educating them ruin them." Master Sun says, "Direct them through cultural arts, unify them through martial arts; this means certain victory." The *I Ching* says, "It is lucky when the rulers nourish the ruled, watching them and bringing out their talents."

The tenth chapter, on terrain, continues the ideas of tactical maneuvering and adaptability, outlining types of terrain and appropriate ways of adjusting to them. It requires some thought to transfer the patterns of these types of terrain to other contexts, but the essential point is in consideration of the relationship of the protagonist to the configurations of the material, social, and psychological environment.

Master Sun follows this with remarks about fatal organizational deficiencies for which the leadership is responsible. Here again emphasis is on the morale of unity: "Look upon your soldiers as beloved children, and they willingly die with you." The *I Ching* says, "Those above secure their homes by kindness to those below." Nevertheless, extending the metaphor, Master Sun also warns against being overly indulgent, with the result of having troops who are like spoiled children.

Intelligence, in the sense of preparatory knowledge, is also stressed in this chapter, where it is particularly defined as including clear awareness of the capabilities of one's forces, the vulnerabilities of opponents, and the lay of the land: "When you know yourself and others, victory is not in danger; when you know sky and earth, victory is inexhaustible." The *I Ching* says, "Be careful in the beginning, and you have no trouble in the end."

The eleventh chapter, entitled "Nine Grounds," presents a more detailed treatment of terrain, particularly in terms of the relationship of a group to the terrain. Again, these "nine grounds" can be understood to apply not only to simple physical territory, but also to "territory" in its social and more abstract senses.

The nine grounds enumerated by Master Sun in this chapter are called a ground of dissolution, light ground, ground of contention, trafficked ground, intersecting ground, heavy ground, bad ground, surrounded ground, and dying (or deadly) ground.

A ground of dissolution is a stage of internecine warfare or civil strife. Light ground refers to shallow incursion into others' territory. A ground of contention is a position that would be advantageous to either side of a conflict. Trafficked ground is where there is free travel. Intersecting ground is territory controlling important arteries of communication. Heavy ground, in contrast to light ground, refers to deep incursion into others' territory. Bad ground is difficult or useless terrain. Surrounded ground has restricted access, suited to ambush. Dying ground is a situation in which it is necessary to fight at once or be annihilated.

Describing the tactics appropriate to each type of ground, Master Sun includes consideration of the social and psychological elements of conflict, insofar as these are inextricably bound up with response to the environment: "Adaptation to different grounds, advantages of contraction and expansion, patterns of human feelings and condi-tions—these must be examined."

The twelfth chapter of *The Art of War*, on fire attack, begins with a brief description of various kinds of incendiary attack, along with technical considerations and strategies for follow-up.

Perhaps because fire is in an ordinary material sense the most vi-cious form of martial art (explosives existed but were not used mili-tarily in Sun Tzu's time), it is in this chapter that the most impassioned plea for humanity is found, echoing the Taoist idea that "weapons are instruments of misfortune to be used only when un-avoidable." Abruptly ending his short discussion of incendiary attack, Master Sun says, "A government should not mobilize an army out of anger, military leaders should not provoke war out of wrath. Act when it is beneficial to do so, desist if not. Anger can revert to joy, wrath can revert to delight, but a nation destroyed cannot be restored to existence, and the dead cannot be restored to life."

The thirteenth and final chapter of *The Art of War* deals with espi-onage, thus coming full circle to link up with the opening chapter on strategy, for which intelligence is essential. Again turning to the efficiency-oriented minimalism and conservatism toward which the skills he teaches are directed, Master Sun begins by speaking of the importance of intelligence agents in most emphatic terms: "A major military operation is a severe drain on the nation, and may be kept up for years in the struggle for one day's victory. So to fail to know the conditions of opponents because of reluctance to give rewards for intelligence is extremely inhumane."

Sun goes on to define five kinds of spy, or secret agent. The local spy is one who is hired from among the populace of a region in which operations are planned. An inside spy is one who is hired from among the officials of an opposing regime. A reverse spy is a double agent, hired from among enemy spies. A dead spy is one who is sent in to convey false information. A living spy is one who comes and goes with information.

Here again there is a very strong social and psychological element in Sun Tzu's understanding of the practical complexities of espionage from the point of view of the leadership. Beginning with the issue of leadership, *The Art of War* also ends with the observation that the effective use of spies depends on the leadership. Master Sun says, "One cannot use spies without sagacity and knowledge, one cannot use spies without humanity and justice, one cannot get the truth from spies without subtlety," and he concludes, "Only a brilliant ruler or a wise general who can use the highly intelligent for espionage is sure of great success."

Historical Background

The Art of War was evidently written during the so-called Warring States period of ancient China, which lasted from the fifth to the third century B.C.E. This was a time of protracted disintegration of the Chou (Zhou) dynasty, which had been founded over five hundred years earlier by the political sages who wrote the *I Ching*. The collapse of the ancient order was marked by destabilization of interstate relationships and interminable warfare among aspirants to hegemony in the midst of ever-shifting patterns of alliance and opposition.

A preface to *Strategies of the Warring States (Zhanguo ce/Chan kuo ts'e)*, a classic collection of stories about the political and military affairs of the feudal states of this time, provides a graphic description of the Warring States period:

> Usurpers set themselves up as lords and kings, states run by pretenders and plotters set up armies to make themselves superpowers. Increasingly they imitated one another in this, and their posterity followed their example. Eventually they engulfed and destroyed each other, colluding with larger territories and annexing smaller territories, passing years in violent military operations, filling the fields with bloodshed. Fathers and sons were not close to each other, brothers were not secure with each other, husbands and wives separated—no one could safeguard his or her life. Virtue disappeared. In later years this grew increasingly extreme, with seven large states and five small states contesting each other for power. In general, this was because the Warring States were shamelessly greedy, struggling insatiably to get ahead.

The great humanist philosopher and educator Confucius, who lived right on the eve of the Warring States era, spent his life working against the deterioration in human values that marked the fall of his society into centuries of conflict. In the classic *Analects of Confucius*, the imminent dawn of the Warring States period is presaged in a symbolic vignette of Confucius' encounter with a ruler whom he tried to advise: "Lord Ling of the state of Wei asked Confucius about battle formations. Confucius replied, 'I have learned about the disposition of ritual vessels, but I have not studied military matters,' and left the next day."

This story, as if representing the disappearance of humanity ("Confucius left the next day") from the thoughts and considerations of rulers in the coming centuries of war, is taken up by the Taoist philosopher Chuang-tzu, who lived in the fourth and third centuries B.C.E., right in the midst of the Warring States period. According to Chuang-tzu's enlargement on the theme, Yen Hui, the most enlightened disciple of Confucius, went to the teacher and asked about going to the state of Wei. Confucius said, "What are you going to do there?"

Yen Hui said, "I have heard that while the ruler of Wei is in the prime of life, his behavior is arbitrary—he exploits his country whimsically and does not see his own mistakes. He exploits his people frivolously, even unto death. Countless masses have died in that state, and the people have nowhere to turn. I have heard you say, 'Leave an orderly state, go to a disturbed state—at the physician's gate, many are the ailing.' I would like to use what I have learned to consider the guidance it offers, so that the state of Wei might be healed."

Confucius said, "You are bent on going, but you will only be punished."

Very few people of the time listened to the pacifistic humanism of Confucius and Mencius. Some say they did not listen because they could not implement the policies advocated by the original Confucians; others say they could not implement the policies because they did not listen, because they did not really want to be humane and just.

Those who listened to the pacifistic humanism of Lao-tzu and Chuang-tzu, on the other hand, generally concealed themselves and worked on the problem from different angles. Lao-tzu and Chuang-tzu show that the man of aggressive violence appears to be ruthless but is really an emotionalist; then they slay the emotionalist with real ruthlessness before revealing the spontaneous nature of free humanity.

The ancient Taoist masters show how real ruthlessness, the coldness of complete objectivity, always includes oneself in its cutting assessment of the real situation. The historical Buddha, a contemporary of Confucius who himself came from a clan of warriors in a time when the warrior caste was consolidating its political dominance, said that conflict would cease if we would be aware of our own death.

This is the ruthlessness of Lao-tzu when he says that the universe is inhumane and the sage sees people as being like the straw dogs used for ritual sacrifices. Chuang-tzu also gives numerous dramatic illustrations of ruthlessness toward oneself as an exercise in perspective designed to lead to cessation of internal and external conflict.

This "inhumanity" is not used by the original philosophers as a justification for quasi-ruthless possessive aggression, but as a meditation on the ultimate meaninglessness of the greed and possessiveness that underlie aggression.

In India, Buddhist aspirants used to visit burning grounds and watch the corpses of those whose families couldn't afford a cremation rot away. This they did to terrify the greed and possessiveness out of themselves. After that they turned their minds toward thoughts of ideal individuals and ideal societies.

Similarly, Master Sun has his readers dwell on the ravages of war, from its incipient phases of treachery and alienation to its extreme forms of incendiary attack and siege, viewed as a sort of mass cannibalism of human and natural resources. With this device he gives the reader an enhanced feeling for the significance of individual and social virtues espoused by the humanitarian pacifists.

From this point of view, it is natural to think of the Taoist thread in *The Art of War* not as a random cultural element, but as key to understanding the text at all of its levels. By the nature of its overt subject matter, *The Art of War* commanded the attention of people who were less likely to pay serious mind to the pacificistic teachings of the classical humanists.

Just as the *I Ching* preserved certain philosophical ideas through all sorts of political and social change through its popularity as an oracle and book of advice, so did *The Art of War* preserve a core of Taoist practical philosophy from destruction by its antithesis.

Paradox is often thought of as a standard device of Taoist psychology, used to cross imperceptible barriers of awareness. Perhaps the paradox of *The Art of War* is in its opposition to war. And as *The Art of War* wars against war, it does so by its own principles; it infiltrates the enemy's lines, uncovers the enemy's secrets, and changes the hearts of the enemy's troops.

The Commentators

The commentaries in this translation are selected from a standard collection of eleven interpreters.

CAO CAO (TS'AO TS'AO, 155–200 C.E.)

Cao Cao is one of the most distinguished military figures of Chinese history. Known for his keen intellect and his cunning, Cao received an honorary degree for social virtues and began his official career at the age of twenty. He held a number of important military posts and particularly distinguished himself in a campaign against rebels when he was about thirty years old.

After this he was given a local ministerial position, but was soon recalled to the region of the capital to take up a regional governorship. Citing health reasons, Cao Cao declined the governorship and returned to his homeland. When one of the most violent generals of the Han dynasty deposed the reigning emperor to set up his own puppet, however, Cao Cao came out of retirement, spending his family fortune to raise a private army in opposition to that general.

Subsequently promoted to high office by the emperor, Cao Cao overthrew would-be usurpers and became a general of the highest rank. He was eventually ennobled and was even encouraged to formally take over the throne of the crumbling Han dynasty, but Cao Cao would not do this, likening himself to King Wen of the ancient Chou dynasty, one of the authors of the *I Ching*, a civil and military leader whose personal qualities, social policies, and political accomplishments won a loyal following that formed the basis of the nascent Chou dynasty, but who never set himself up as supreme leader.

Cao Cao was known for his heroism, talent, and strategy, in which he mainly followed the teachings of Sun Tzu's classic, *The Art of War*. In the tradition of the ancient chivalric code, according to which Chinese knights were to be learned in both martial and cultural arts, in addition to his military accomplishments Cao Cao was fond of literature and is said to have made a habit of reading every day, even during military campaigns.

MENG SHI (LIANG DYNASTY, 502–556)

Meng Shi, or "Mr. Meng," is apparently known only for his commentary on *The Art of War*. His time was marked by civil war and massive suffering.

JIA LIN (TANG DYNASTY, 618–906)

Jia Lin seems to be known only for his commentary on *The Art of War*. During the Tang dynasty, China enlarged its empire, extending its cultural and political influence over other peoples, some of whom eventually used their experience under Chinese rule to take over large parts of China themselves. Tang-dynasty China also helped establish national governments in Japan, Tibet, and Yunnan.

LI QUAN (TANG DYNASTY, 618–906)

Li Quan was a devotee of Taoism as well as the martial arts. He lived on the Mountain of Few Abodes, where Bodhidharma, the semilegendary founder of Chan Buddhism, lived during his last years in China. Taoist tradition attributes Shaolin boxing, a popular school of martial arts, to this same Bodhidharma. Li Quan was a student of the *Yin Convergence Classic (Yinfu jing)*, a Taoist text attributed to antiquity and traditionally interpreted in both martial and cultural terms. He is said to have read this laconic text thousands of times without understanding its meaning. Later he went to Black Horse Mountain, the famous site of the tomb of the First Emperor of China, where he met an old woman who gave him a charm and explained the meaning of the classic to him. This woman is identified with the Old Woman of Black Horse Mountain of folklore, who was said to have been a ruler of ancient times, considered a Taoist immortal by the people of the Tang dynasty. Whatever the true identity of his mentor may have been, Li Quan is known for his military strategy and wrote a commentary on the *Yin Convergence Classic* from that point of view. Eventually he went into the mountains to study Taoism.

DU YOU (735–812)

Du You served as an official military advisor, war councillor, and military inspector in several regions. Later in life he also held distin-

guished posts in the central government, but he eventually gave up
office.

DU MU (803–852)

Du Mu was the grandson of the aforementioned Du You. Known as a
"knight of unflinching honesty and extraordinary honor," he earned
an advanced academic degree and served in several positions at the
imperial court. His fortunes declined in his later years, and he died at
the age of fifty. On his deathbed he composed his own epitaph and
burned all of his writings. He was known as an outstanding poet.

ZHANG YU (SUNG DYNASTY, 960–1278)

Zhang Yu is known only for his commentary on *The Art of War* and
a collection of biographies of military leaders. The Sung dynasty was
a time of more or less constantly increasing pressure from north Asia,
culminating in the loss of its ancient homeland and finally all of the
continental Chinese empire, to Mongolian invaders.

MEI YAOCHEN (1002–1060)

Mei Yaochen served in both local and central governments of the new
Sung dynasty that followed several generations of disunity after the
collapse of the Tang dynasty, and was chosen as one of the compilers
and editors of the documents of the Tang dynasty. Mei was a literary
correspondent of the famous poet Ou Yangxiu, and was himself a distinguished writer.

WANG XI (SUNG DYNASTY, EARLY
ELEVENTH CENTURY)

Wang Xi was a scholar in the Hanlin or Imperial Academy. He is the
author of two books on the *Spring and Autumn Annals (Qunqiu/
Ch'un-ch'iu)*, one of the Confucian classics of ancient illustrative history. While Sung dynasty China was beset with endless political, economic, and military problems, its culture was very lively, with
important new developments in Confucianism, Taoism, and Zen
Buddhism. These new forms of practical philosophy exerted a strong
influence not only on the Chinese people themselves but even on the
non-Chinese peoples who were taking over political control in China,

to say nothing of the Koreans, Vietnamese, and Japanese who were watching the continental mainland and were experimenting with these new forms of high culture from China.

CHEN HAO (SUNG DYNASTY, EARLY TWELFTH CENTURY)

Chen Hao was known for his extraordinary personal independence and his great aspirations. He became an officer of the state when he was only twenty years old. When the Jurchen people of north Asia invaded China in the mid 1120s, Chen assembled a patriotic army to defend the homeland. Later he also raised an army in secret to put down an attempted coup by a usurper.

HO YANXI (SUNG DYNASTY)

Nothing seems to be known of Ho Yanxi other than that he lived during the Sung dynasty and wrote this commentary on *The Art of War.*

The Translation

The language of the Chinese classics is different from that of even the earliest commentators, very different from that of the Tang and Sung writers, vastly different from modern Chinese. All Chinese classics, extensively studied as they are, contain words and passages interpreted differently among Chinese commentators themselves. These differences in reading and understanding are sometimes radical. It is only natural, therefore, that translations of ancient Chinese texts into modern Western languages, which differ so greatly from Chinese, should themselves exhibit a considerable range of variety.

This is especially true considering the pregnancy of the Chinese language and the abundant use of imagery and allusion in Chinese literature. There are many choices of techniques available to the translator for conveying the contents of classical Chinese writings to the reader in another language. In twenty years of translating, never have I seen or translated an Oriental classic that I did not find so rich as to be able to generate at least three possible translations.

There are, again, various options available for dealing with this situation. As in my other translations from Oriental classics, the technical aim of my approach to *The Art of War* has been to make the flesh transparent and the bones stand out, to reproduce an abstract form to be filled with the colors of the individual reader's own life situations. Therefore I have omitted some references to certain local content, such items as ancient Chinese weaponry, not as being without a certain interest, but as incidental to the question of present day application of relational structures presented in the strategy of the classic.

Translation of ideas nevertheless inevitably involves questions of broad cultural differences and how they are perceived. As far as it is relevant to a politically sensitive text like *The Art of War*, to Occidental eyes the distinguishing mark of traditional Chinese social thought in actual practice is authoritarianism, and there is much empirical evidence to support this view of Confucian society. While it is true that personal loyalty, such as would serve for a cement in an authoritarian structure, seems to be esteemed more highly in the social thought of China than in that of the West, nevertheless there is also a broader conception of loyalty to abstractions or ideals that surfaces even in Confucian thought.

In Confucian idealism, a man does not participate in an organization or cause that he does not believe is reasonable and just. Once he truly believes it is right, however, a man should not abandon a course of action even if it brings him hardship and peril. Confucius said that it is a disgrace to be rich and honored in an unjust state, and he himself nearly died for his independence. According to the classics, loyalty does not mean blind obedience to an individual or state, but includes the duty of conscientious protest. Loyalty to ideals above all may be rare in practice, but it always was a part of the Chinese worldview.

In the organizational science of *The Art of War*, loyalty is not so much a moral standard in itself but a product of social relations within the organization based on other professional and ethical standards. The quality of the relationship between the leaders and the troops is what cements loyalty, according to Master Sun, and this is reinforced by egalitarian adherence to established standards of behavior.

There are different ways of interpreting ideals in real life, of course, and there is not necessarily an unambiguous course of action dictated by the general concept of loyalty, when there are various levels of relevance to consider. One of the stories related in commentary on *The Art of War* concerns the whole question of loyalty addressed from different points of view, illustrating the interplay of these different views of an appropriate context for loyalty.

During a war a certain brigadier general had his entire contingent wiped out in battle; he himself fought until the end, then returned to headquarters to report. Now, since there had been some problems with discipline and morale, there was talk of making an example of this general, accusing him of deserting his troops—not dying with them—and putting him to death.

Finally it was objected, however, that he had in fact fought to the last man, after which there was no reason to continue, so he returned for reassignment; thus neither his loyalty to his troops nor his loyalty to his nation could be denied. Furthermore, if he were to be executed, it was argued in his defense, others would not necessarily be cowed into obedience but would more likely become alienated, seeing that there was no reason to return home.

On a level of understanding more sophisticated than that of broad generalizations, one of the most challenging and rewarding uses of classical literature is the exploration of the psychological nuances of basic concepts and their manifestations in practice. It is challenging because it demands immersion in the consciousness of the classics themselves; it is rewarding because it opens up realms of thought beyond predetermined subjective parameters. The key to this appreciation is a sensitivity to structure, traditionally awakened as much by allegory and imagery as by discourse and argument.

The use of imagery and suggestion in Chinese literature was practiced as a fine art in the Chan Buddhism of the Tang and Sung dynasties, which inherited the traditions of the Confucian and Taoist classics as well as those of the Buddhist sutras. Chan Buddhism influenced all the great scholars, artists, and poets of China then and thereafter, yet Chan was in its turn indebted to classical Taoism for support in the acceptance of its surprising literary devices. One of the linguistic techniques of this fine art that is of particular concern to the translator is the use of ambiguity.

Taoist and Buddhist literature have been described—both by Easterners writing for Westerners and by Westerners writing for other Westerners—as paradoxical, so frequently and to such a degree that paradox is commonly considered one of the major characteristics or devices of this literature. The orientation of *The Art of War* toward winning without fighting, for example, is typical of this sort of paradox, which is there to invite attention to its own logic. It may paradoxically be nonparadoxical, therefore, to find that the paradox of ambiguity is an exact science in the Taoist literature of higher psychology.

The first maneuver of this literature is to engage the participation of the reader in the work, just as the viewer is drawn into the pattern of suggestion spun by lines in space on seeing an expert Sung-dynasty ink line drawing. The result is partly from the writing and partly from the reading; used as a tool for the assessment of the mentality of the reader, each aphorism, each text, brings out a particular facet of human psychology. Chan Buddhists often used ambiguity primarily as a means of nondirective mirroring of personalities and mind sets; *The Art of War* similarly has the power to reveal a great deal about its readers through their reactions and interpretations.

As a translator, therefore, I have always considered the faithful reconstruction of a necessary or useful ambiguity to be among the most difficult subtleties of the craft. Commentators on Chinese classics have long shown how thoroughly different perspectives can be obtained by adopting the different sets of subject or object associations that certain sentences allow. In the later Chan schools, it was openly stated that classic texts were meant to be read by putting yourself in everyone's place to get a comprehensive view of subjective and objective relationships, and the Chan writers took this to breathtakingly distant lengths in an elaborate imagery of transformation and interpenetration of viewpoints.

In a classical aphorism on education frequently encountered in Chan literature, Confucius said, "If I bring up one corner, and those to whom I am speaking cannot come back with the other three, I don't talk to them anymore." Applied to a Chinese classic, this produces a fair description of the experience of reading such a book. Put in a positive way, Confucius said the classics give hints, suggestions that yield more only with time and thought given to applying these hints to present real situations. Similarly, in Taoist tradition they are used as visualization models, designed to awaken certain perceptions of human nature and the human condition.

It is the intention of this translation of *The Art of War*, therefore, to reproduce the classic as a study of relationships, or energy in potential and in motion, that could remain useful through changes in time, linked with the perennial Taoist tradition that marks the heart and soul of this classic text. Comments by the readers mentioned above, written over a period of nearly a thousand years, have been selected not only to elucidate the original text but also to illustrate the shifting of perspectives that the classic makes possible. The translation of the original has therefore been designed to provide conceptual space for different views in specific places.

The reason that classics remain classics over thousands of years, as *The Art of War* has remained along with the works of the original Confucian and Taoist sages, seems to be that they continue to have meaning. This continuing meaning, moreover, is not experienced only over generations. On a small scale, a classic yields significantly different meanings when read in different circumstances and moods; on a larger scale, a classic conveys wholly different worlds when read in different times of life, at different stages of experience, feeling, and understanding of life. Classics may be interesting and even entertaining, but people always find they are not like books used for diversion, which give up all of their content at once; the classics seem to grow wiser as we grow wiser, more useful the more we use them.

[1]

STRATEGIC ASSESSMENTS

Master Sun

Military action is important to the nation—it is the ground of death and life, the path of survival and destruction, so it is imperative to examine it.

LI QUAN

Military action is inauspicious—it is only considered important because it is a matter of life and death, and there is the possibility that it may be taken up lightly.

DU MU

The survival or destruction of a country and the life or death of its people may depend on military action, so it is necessary to examine it carefully.

JIA LIN

The ground means the location, the place of pitched battle—gain the advantage and you live, lose the advantage and you die. Therefore military action is called the ground of death and life. The path means the way to adjust to the situation and establish victory—find this and you survive, lose this and you perish. Therefore it is said to be imperative to examine it. An ancient document says, "There is a way of survival, which helps and strengthens you; there is a way of destruction, which pushes you into oblivion."

MEI YAOCHEN

Whether you live or die depends on the configuration of the battleground; whether you survive or perish depends on the way of battle.

Master Sun

Therefore measure in terms of five things, use these assessments to make comparisons, and thus find out what the conditions are. The five things are the way, the weather, the terrain, the leadership, and discipline.

DU MU

Five things are to be assessed—the way, the weather, the lay of the land, the leadership, and discipline. These are to be assessed at headquarters—first assess yourself and your opponent in terms of these five things, deciding who is superior. Then you can determine who is likely to prevail. Having determined this, only then should you mobilize your forces.

CAO CAO

Assessments of the following items are to be made at headquarters: the leadership, the opponent, the terrain, troop strength, distance, and relative danger.

WANG XI

Assess the leadership, the environmental conditions, discipline, troops, officers, and the system of rewards and punishments.

ZHANG YU

Master Guan said that assessments should be made at home before sending troops abroad. Assessments are the first order of business in military operations. Some say that military operations should be adjusted right on the spot, in confrontation with the opponent, but General Cao Cao says that assessments should be made at headquarters—this is because it is imperative first to assess the wisdom of the leaders, the strength of the opponent, the lay of the land, and the number of troops; then when the two armies confront one another, the adaptations to be made are determined by the leadership in a manner consistent with these calculations.

Discipline means that regulations are strict and clear. The reason that leadership and discipline come last in this list of five things is that whenever you mobilize to attack those who have done you wrong, it is necessary first to look into the matter of whether you are appreciated and trusted by your own people, then to assess the favorability or otherwise of weather conditions, and then examine the qualities of the terrain. Once these three things are fulfilled, then a leader is appointed to go forth on the expedition. Once the army has gone forth, all orders come from the general.

Wang Xi

Harmony among people is the basis of the Way of military operations; the right weather and an advantageous position help. When these three elements are present, then is the time to discuss mobilizing the army. Mobilizing the army requires ability on the part of the leadership. When the leadership is able, then there will be good discipline.

Master Sun

The Way means inducing the people to have the same aim as the leadership, so that they will share death and share life, without fear of danger.

Cao Cao

This means guiding them by instruction and direction. Danger means distrust.

Zhang Yu

If the people are treated with benevolence, faithfulness, and justice, then they will be of one mind, and will be glad to serve. The *I Ching* says, "Joyful in difficulty, the people forget about their death."

Du Mu

The Way means humaneness and justice. In ancient times a famous minister of state asked a political philosopher about military matters. The philosopher said, "Humaneness and justice are the means by which to govern properly. When government is carried out properly, people feel close to the leadership and think little of dying for it."

Jia Ling

If the leaders can be humane and just, sharing both the gains and the troubles of the people, then the troops will be loyal and naturally identify with the interests of the leadership.

Master Sun

The weather means the seasons.

Cao Cao

The rules of the ancient military state that operations should not be carried out in winter or summer, out of concern for the people.

Zhang Yu *(Quoting the founder of the Tang Dynasty)*

In ancient times many soldiers lost their fingers to frostbite on campaigns against the Huns, and many soldiers died of plague on campaigns against the southern tribes. This was because of carrying out operations in winter and summer.

Wang Xi *(Quoting Fan Li)*

This is the meaning of the saying, "Don't go into another's territory at an unfavorable time."

Master Sun

The terrain is to be assessed in terms of distance, difficulty or ease of travel, dimension, and safety.

ZHANG YU

In any military operation, it is important first to know the lay of the land. When you know the distance to be traveled, then you can plan whether to proceed directly or by a circuitous route. When you know the difficulty or ease of travel, then you can determine the advantages of infantry or mounted troops. When you know the dimensions of the area, then you can assess how many troops you need, many or few. When you know the relative safety of the terrain, then you can discern whether to do battle or disperse.

Master Sun

Leadership is a matter of intelligence, trustworthiness, humaneness, courage, and sternness.

CAO CAO

A general should have these five virtues.

DU MU

The Way of the ancient kings was to consider humaneness foremost, while the martial artists considered intelligence foremost. This is because intelligence involves ability to plan and to know when to change effectively. Trustworthiness means to make people sure of punishment or reward. Humaneness means love and compassion for people, being aware of their toils. Courage means to seize opportunities to make certain of victory, without vacillation. Sternness means to establish discipline in the ranks by strict punishments.

JIA LIN

Reliance on intelligence alone results in rebelliousness. Exercise of humaneness alone results in weakness. Fixation on trust results in folly. Dependence on the strength of courage results in violence. Excessive sternness of command results in cruelty. When one has all five virtues together, each appropriate to its function, then one can be a military leader.

Master Sun

Discipline means organization, chain of command, and logistics.

MEI YAOCHEN

Organization means that the troops must be grouped in a regulated manner. Chain of command means that there must be officers to keep the troops together and lead them. Logistics means overseeing supplies.

Master Sun

Every general has heard of these five things. Those who know them prevail, those who do not know them do not prevail.

ZHANG YU

Everyone has heard of these five things, but only those who deeply understand the principles of adaptation and impasse will win.

Master Sun

Therefore use these assessments for comparison, to find out what the conditions are. That is to say, which political leadership has the Way? Which general has ability? Who has the better climate and terrain? Whose discipline is effective? Whose troops are stronger? Whose officers and soldiers are the better trained? Whose system of rewards and punishment is clearer? This is how you can know who will win.

LI QUAN

A political leadership that has the Way will surely have a military leadership that has intelligence and ability.

DU MU

Ask yourself which political leadership—your own or that of your enemy—is able to reject flatterers and draw close to the wise.

Du You

The Way means virtue. It is first necessary to compare the political leadership of nations at war.

Mei Yaochen

The question regarding political leadership is, who is able to win the hearts of the people.

Ho Yanxi

The ancient classic of documents says, "The one who treats me well is my leader, the one who treats me cruelly is my enemy." The question is, which side has a humane government, and which side has a cruel government.

Zhang Yu

First compare the political leadership of the two nations at war, in terms of which one has the Way of benevolence and good faith. Then examine the military leadership—who has intelligence, trustworthiness, humaneness, bravery, and sternness. Now observe which side has the environmental advantages.

Cao Cao

Set up rules that are not to be broken, do not fail to punish any offenders.

Du Mu

When it comes to establishing rules and regulations, everyone, high and low, should be treated alike.

Du You

Compare whose orders are the more effective—whose subordinates do not dare to disobey.

Mei Yaochen

Make everyone equal under the law.

Wang Xi

See who is able to make rules clear and commands easy to follow, so that people listen and obey.

Du Mu *(On the matters of strength and training)*

When superior and subordinate are in harmony, equally brave in battle, that makes for strength.

Du You

Know whose armaments are more effective, and whose troops are carefully chosen and well trained. As it is said, "If soldiers do not practice day to day, on the front lines they will be fearful and hesitant. If generals do not practice day to day, on the front lines they will not know how to adapt."

Du Mu *(Turning to the subject of punishments and rewards)*

Rewards should not be out of proportion, punishments should not be arbitrary.

Du You

Know whose system of rewards for the good and punishments for the bad is clearly defined. As it is said, "If rewards are immoderate, there will be expenditure that does not result in gratitude; if punishments are immoderate, there will be slaughter that does not result in awe."

Mei Yaochen

When people deserve reward, this should be duly noted even if you personally detest them. When people deserve punishment, this should not be forgone even if they are close to you.

Cao Cao *(Summing up)*

By assessing these seven things you can know who will be victorious and who will be defeated.

MEI YAOCHEN

If you can find out the real conditions, then you will know who will prevail.

ZHANG YU

If you are superior in all of these seven things, you have won before you have even done battle. If you are inferior in all of these seven things, you have lost even before you go into battle. Therefore it is possible to know the victor beforehand.

Master Sun

Assess the advantages in taking advice, then structure your forces accordingly, to supplement extraordinary tactics. Forces are to be structured strategically, based on what is advantageous.

CAO CAO

Structure depends on strategy: strategy is determined according to events.

Master Sun

A military operation involves deception. Even though you are competent, appear to be incompetent. Though effective, appear to be ineffective.

CAO CAO

A military operation has no standard form—it goes by way of deception.

MEI YAOCHEN

Without deception you cannot carry out strategy, without strategy you cannot control the opponent.

WANG XI

Deception is for the purpose of seeking victory over an enemy; to command a group requires truthfulness.

ZHANG YU

While strong in reality, appear to be weak; while brave in reality, appear to be cowardly—this method was effective against the Huns.

LI QUAN

Li Quan told a story of how one of the generals of the Han dynasty rebelled and joined forces with the Huns. The emperor sent ten scouts to observe them, and all reported that they could be effectively attacked. The emperor then sent one Lou Jing, who reported that, on the contrary, the Huns could not be effectively attacked. When the emperor asked him why, he replied, "When two countries are at a standoff, they should be flaunting their strengths. When I went, all I saw were the feeble and the elderly—surely they are 'competent yet appearing to be incompetent,' so I consider it unfeasible to attack."

The emperor was wroth. He punished Lou Jing for getting in his way, and personally set out with a large contingent. They were hemmed in by the Huns, however, and cut off from supplies for seven days.

This, concluded Li, is the meaning of an army appearing to be weak.

DU MU

This is a matter of deceptively concealing your state. You should not let the opponent see what state you are in, for if the enemy sees your condition, he will surely have a response. An example of this is when the Huns let the emissaries of Han only see the feeble and the old.

DU YOU

This means that when you are really competent and effective you outwardly appear to be incompetent and ineffective, so as to cause the enemy to be unprepared.

Wang Xi

When strong, appear weak. Brave, appear fearful. Orderly, appear chaotic. Full, appear empty. Wise, appear foolish. Many, appear to be few. Advancing, appear to retreat. Moving quickly, appear to be slow. Taking, appear to leave. In one place, appear to be in another.

Zhang Yu

When you are going to do battle, make it seem as if you are retreating. When you are going to hasten, make it seem as if you are relaxing.

Master Sun

When you are going to attack nearby, make it look as if you are going to go a long way; when you are going to attack far away, make it look as if you are going just a short distance.

Li Quan

This is to cause the opponent to be unprepared.

Master Sun

Draw them in with the prospect of gain, take them by confusion.

Mei Yaochen

If they are greedy, lure them with goods.

Zhang Yu

Show them a little prospect of gain to lure them, then attack and overcome them.

Du Mu

When the enemy is confused, you can use this opportunity to take them.

JIA LIN

I would have crafty interlopers confuse them, then wait for them to fall into disarray in order to take them.

ZHANG YU

Use deception to throw them into confusion, lead them on in order to take them. When the states of Wu and Yue were at war with each other, Wu sent out three thousand criminals to give an appearance of disorder so as to lure Yue. Some of the criminals ran, some of them gave up; the Yue army fought with them, only to be defeated by the army of Wu.

Master Sun

When they are fulfilled, be prepared against them; when they are strong, avoid them.

DU MU

If the enemy's government is fulfilled—meaning that there is mutual love between the rulers and the ruled, there is clarity and trustworthiness in the system of rewards and punishments, and the soldiers are well trained—then you should be on guard against them. Do not wait for a clash to make your preparations. When the enemy's military is strong, you should avoid them for the time being, waiting until they slack off, watching for an opening to attack.

CHEN HAO

If the enemy does not stir, is complete and fulfilled, then you should prepare carefully. Fulfill yourself too, so as to be ready for them.

HO YANXI

If you only see fulfillment in the enemy, and do not see any gap, then you should build up your power to be prepared.

ZHANG YU

A classic says, "Struggling with them, you find out where they have plenty and where they are lacking." Having plenty is what is meant by being fulfilled, lacking is what is meant by having gaps. Once the military power of the adversary is full, you should treat them as if they were unbeatable, and not attack lightly. As a military guide says, "When you see a gap, then advance; when you see fullness, then stop."

JIA LIN

For the weak to control the strong, it is logically necessary to await a change.

DU YOU

When their storehouses are full and their soldiers are in top form, then you should withdraw in order to watch for an opening when they relax, observing any changes and responding to them.

Master Sun

Use anger to throw them into disarray.

CAO CAO

Wait for them to become decadent and lazy.

LI QUAN

When the military leadership is often angered, its strategy is easily thrown into confusion, for its nature is unstable.

DU MU

When their military leadership is obstreperous, you should irritate them to make them angry—then they will become impetuous and ignore their original strategy.

MEI YAOCHEN

If they are quick-tempered, then stir them up to excite them so that they go into battle carelessly.

ZHANG YU

If they are violent and easily angered, then use embarrassment to enrage them, so that their morale is upset—then they will proceed carelessly, without formulating a plan.

Master Sun

Use humility to make them haughty.

LI QUAN

If they ply you with expensive gifts and sweet talk, they are up to something.

DU YOU

When they are stirred up and about to make their move, then you should pretend to be cowed, so as to raise their spirits; wait for them to slack off, then regroup and attack.

MEI YAOCHEN

Give the appearance of inferiority and weakness, to make them proud.

WANG XI

Appear to be lowly and weak, so as to make them arrogant—then they will not worry about you, and you can attack them as they relax.

Master Sun

Tire them by flight.

Cao Cao

Use swiftness to wear them out.

Wang Xi

This means making a lot of surprise attacks. When they come out, you go home; when they go home, you go out. When they go to the aid of their left flank, you head to the right; when they go to the aid of their right flank, you go to the left. This way you can tire them out.

Zhang Yu

This way, your strength will remain intact, while they will be worn out.

Master Sun

Cause division among them.

Cao Cao

Send interlopers to cause rifts among them.

Li Quan

Break up their accords, cause division between the leadership and their ministers, and then attack.

Du Mu

This means that if there are good relations between the enemy leadership and its followers, then you should use bribes to cause division.

Chen Hao

If they are stingy, you be generous; if they are harsh, you be lenient. That way their leadership and followers will be suspicious of each other, and you can cause division between them.

Du You

Seduce them with the prospect of gain, send interlopers in among them, have rhetoricians use fast talk to ingratiate themselves with their leaders and followers, and divide up their organization and power.

Zhang Yu

You may cause rifts between the leadership and their followers, or between them and their allies—cause division, and then take aim at them.

Master Sun

Attack when they are unprepared, make your move when they do not expect it.

Cao Cao

Attack when they are slacking off, make your move when a gap opens up.

Meng Shi

Strike at their gaps, attack when they are lax, don't let the enemy figure out how to prepare. This is why it is said that in military operations formlessness is the most effective. One of the great warrior-leaders said, "The most efficient of movements is the one that is unexpected; the best of plans is the one that is unknown."

Master Sun

The formation and procedure used by the military should not be divulged beforehand.

Cao Cao

To divulge means to leak out. The military has no constant form, just as water has no constant shape—adapt as you face the enemy, with-

out letting them know beforehand what you are going to do. Therefore, assessment of the enemy is in the mind, observation of the
situation is in the eyes.

LI QUAN

Attack when they are unprepared and not expecting it, and you will
surely win. This is the essence of martial arts, to be kept secret and
not divulged.

DU MU

To divulge something means to speak of it. This means that all of the
aforementioned strategies for securing military victory can certainly
not be made uniform—first, see the enemy's formation, and only then
apply them. You cannot say what you will do before the event.

MEI YAOCHEN

Since you adapt and adjust appropriately in face of the enemy, how
could you say what you are going to do beforehand?

Master Sun

*The one who figures on victory at headquarters before even doing
battle is the one who has the most strategic factors on his side. The
one who figures on inability to prevail at headquarters before doing
battle is the one who has the least strategic factors on his side. The
one with many strategic factors in his favor wins, the one with few
strategic factors in his favor loses—how much the more so for one
with no strategic factors in his favor. Observing the matter in this
way, I can see who will win and who will lose.*

ZHANG YU

When your strategy is deep and far-reaching, then what you gain by
your calculations is much, so you can win before you even fight.
When your strategic thinking is shallow and nearsighted, then what

you gain by your calculations is little, so you lose before you do battle. Much strategy prevails over little strategy, so those with no strategy cannot but be defeated. Therefore it is said that victorious warriors win first and then go to war, while defeated warriors go to war first and then seek to win.

[2]

DOING BATTLE

LI QUAN

First establish your plans, then prepare your equipment. This is why the chapter on battle follows the chapter on strategic assessments.

Master Sun

When you do battle, even if you are winning, if you continue for a long time it will dull your forces and blunt your edge; if you besiege a citadel, your strength will be exhausted. If you keep your armies out in the field for a long time, your supplies will be insufficient.

JIA LIN

Even if you prevail over others in battle, if you go on too long there will be no profit. In military operations, total victory is important; if you dull your forces and blunt your edge, sustaining casualties and battle fatigue, then you will be exhausted.

ZHANG YU

When you are spending a great deal of money on a military operation, if the army is out in the field too long, your budget will not be enough to cover the expense.

LI QUAN

As the classic *Spring and Autumn Annals* says, "War is like a fire—if you do not put it out, it will burn itself out."

JIA LIN

If a military operation goes on for a long time without accomplishing anything, your rivals will begin to get ideas.

DU YOU

Arms are tools of ill omen—to employ them for an extended period of time will bring about calamity. As it is said, "Those who like to fight and so exhaust their military inevitably perish."

Master Sun

When your forces are dulled, your edge is blunted, your strength is exhausted, and your supplies are gone, then others will take advantage of your debility and rise up. Then even if you have wise advisers you cannot make things turn out well in the end.

LI QUAN

A large-scale operation involves enormous expense, which not only breaks you down in the field, but also exhausts you at home. Therefore a wise government does not keep its army in the field.

Master Sun

Therefore I have heard of military operations that were clumsy but swift, but I have never seen one that was skillful and lasted a long time. It is never beneficial to a nation to have a military operation continue for a long time.

CAO CAO

Some win through speed, even if they are clumsy.

DU MU

Some may be clumsy in attack, but they get the upper hand through extraordinary swiftness, because they are not subject to the problems of wearing out their forces and using up their resources.

CHEN HAO

As it is said, be swift as the thunder that peals before you have a chance to cover your ears, fast as the lightning that flashes before you can blink your eyes.

Master Sun

Therefore, those who are not thoroughly aware of the disadvantages in the use of arms cannot be thoroughly aware of the advantages in the use of arms.

LI QUAN

Advantages and disadvantages are interdependent—first know the disadvantages, then you know the advantages.

JIA LIN

When the generals are haughty and the soldiers are lazy, in their greed for gain they forget that there may be an unexpected turn of events—this is the greatest disadvantage.

DU YOU

This means that if you are planning to mobilize your forces and embark upon a campaign, if you do not first think about the calamities of danger and destruction, you will not be able to reap any advantage.

Master Sun

Those who use the military skillfully do not raise troops twice and do not provide food three times.

CAO CAO

This means you draft people into service once and then immediately seize victory—you do not go back to your country a second time to raise more troops. At first you provide food, after that you feed off the enemy; and then when your soldiers return to your country, you do not greet them with yet more free food.

Du Mu

Determine whether the enemy can be successfully attacked, determine whether you can do battle, and only afterward raise troops— then you can overcome the enemy and return home.

Li Quan

Do not raise troops twice, lest the citizenry become wearied and bitterness arise.

Master Sun

By taking equipment from your own country but feeding off the enemy you can be sufficient in both arms and provisions.

Cao Cao

When you are going to go to war, first you must calculate your expenses, and strive to feed off the opponent.

Li Quan

If you have your own arms and take food from the enemy, then even if the campaign takes you far afield you will not lack for anything.

Cao Cao

Armaments are taken from the homeland, provisions are taken from the enemy.

Master Sun

When a country is impoverished by military operations, it is because of transporting supplies to a distant place. Transport supplies to a distant place, and the populace will be impoverished.

Li Quan

Troops are raised repeatedly, and the levies are heavy.

Du Mu

Master Guan said, "When provisions go for three hundred miles, the country is out a year's supplies; when provisions go for four hundred miles, the country is out two years' supplies; when provisions go for five hundred miles, the people pale with hunger." This means that food should not be transported, for if it is, the producers will lose, so they cannot but be impoverished.

Jia Lin

Transporting supplies to distant places means that wealth is expended in travel and used up on transportation, so that the common people become poorer day by day.

Zhang Yu

When seven hundred thousand families have to support an army of one hundred thousand on a distant expedition, the common peoples cannot avoid impoverishment.

Master Sun

Those who are near the army sell at high prices. Because of high prices, the wealth of the common people is exhausted.

Cao Cao

When the army has gone forth, those who are near the troops, greedy for money, sell at high prices. Therefore the common people become destitute.

Li Quan

Near the army there is always trade; the common people use up their wealth to go along with it, and so become destitute.

JIA LIN

Wherever the troops gather, the prices of goods all soar. Since people are greedy for exceptional profits, they sell off all their goods. Though at first they make a great deal of profit, in the end they run out of goods. Also, since there are extraordinary levies, those with something to sell demand the highest prices they can get; the common people go broke trying to buy things, so the country naturally is impoverished.

WANG XI

When supplies are transported far away, the people are worn out by the expense. In the markets near the army, the prices of goods shoot up. Therefore long military campaigns are a plague to a nation.

Master Sun

When resources are exhausted, then levies are made under pressure. When power and resources are exhausted, then the homeland is drained. The common people are deprived of seventy percent of their budget, while the government's expenses for equipment amount to sixty percent of its budget.

DU MU

If the military situation is not resolved and the army is not demobilized, levies become increasingly oppressive, resulting in exhaustion of the resources of the people, so that they lose most of what they produce.

HO YANXI

The people are the basis of a country, food is the heaven of the people. Those who rule over others should respect this and be sparing.

MEI YAOCHEN

The common people provide goods, food, and labor for the use of the military, thus losing most of their own sustenance, while the government provides equipment for the use of the military, thus losing more than half of its budget. Therefore taxes are used up, the army is worn out, and the populace is exhausted. When levies are oppressive and the people are impoverished, the country is drained.

Master Sun

Therefore a wise general strives to feed off the enemy. Each pound of food taken from the enemy is equivalent to twenty pounds you provide by yourself.

Cao Cao

Transportation of provisions itself consumes twenty times the amount transported.

Zhang Yu

It takes twenty pounds of provisions to deliver one pound of provisions to a distant army. If the terrain is rugged, it takes even more than that. That is why an able general will always feed off the enemy.

Master Sun

So what kills the enemy is anger, what gets the enemy's goods is reward.

Zhang Yu

If you stir up your officers and troops so that they are all enraged, then they will kill the enemy. If you reward your men with spoils, that will make them fight on their own initiative, so the enemy's goods can be taken. That is why it is said that where there are big rewards there are valiant men.

Du You

If people know they will be richly rewarded if they overcome the opponent, then they will gladly go into battle.

WANG XI

This just means establishing rich rewards—if you let the troops plunder at will, they may get out of hand.

Master Sun

Therefore, in a chariot battle, reward the first to capture at least ten chariots.

MEI YAOCHEN

If you reward everyone, there will not be enough to go around, so you offer a reward to one in order to encourage everyone.

Master Sun

Change their colors, use them mixed in with your own. Treat the soldiers well, take care of them.

CAO CAO

You change their colors to make them the same as your own, you use them mixed in with your own so as not to leave them to their own devices.

JIA LIN

You change their colors so that they won't be recognizable to the enemy.

ZHANG YU

Captured soldiers should be well treated, to get them to work for you.

Master Sun

This is called overcoming the opponent and increasing your strength to boot.

DU MU

By capturing the opponent's soldiers and using the enemy's supplies, you increase your own strength.

MEI YAOCHEN

When you capture soldiers, give them responsibilities according to their strengths, take care of them kindly, and they will work for you.

HO YANXI

If you use the enemy to defeat the enemy, you will be strong wherever you go.

Master Sun

So the important thing in a military operation is victory, not persistence.

CAO CAO

Persistence is not profitable. An army is like fire—if you don't put it out, it will burn itself out.

MENG SHI

What is best is a quick victory and a speedy return.

MEI YAOCHEN

In all of the above-mentioned, it is important to be quick. If you are quick, then you can economize on expenditures and allow the people rest.

Master Sun

Hence, we know that the leader of the army is in charge of the lives of the people and the safety of the nation.

Cao Cao

If the military leadership is wise, the country is safe.

Mei Yaochen

This tells us how serious the matter of appointing military leaders is.

Wang Xi

The lives of the people and the order of the nation are in the charge of the generals. The difficulty of finding good leadership material is a perennial problem.

[3]
PLANNING A SIEGE

Master Sun

The general rule for use of the military is that it is better to keep a nation intact than to destroy it. It is better to keep an army intact than to destroy it, better to keep a division intact than to destroy it, better to keep a battalion intact than to destroy it, better to keep a unit intact than to destroy it.

CAO CAO

If you raise an army and penetrate deeply into your opponent's territory, keeping on the move, blocking the space between the inner stronghold and the outer city walls, cutting off communications between inside and outside, then if the opponent surrenders completely, that is best. If you attack destructively and take a nation by force, that is a lesser accomplishment.

JIA LIN

If you can keep the opponent's nation intact, then your own nation will also be intact. So this is best.

LI QUAN

This means that killing is not the important thing.

DU YOU

It is best if an enemy nation comes and surrenders of its own accord. To attack and defeat it is inferior to this.

HO YANXI

The best policy is to use strategy, influence, and the trend of events to cause the adversary to submit willingly.

ZHANG YU

Zhang Yu quoted a statement by Wei Liaozi: "Practicing martial arts, assess your opponents; cause them to lose spirit and direction so that even if the opposing army is intact it is useless—this is winning by the Tao. If you destroy the opposing army and kill the generals, mount the ramparts by shooting, gather a mob and usurp the land, this is winning by force."

Zhang Yu then explained, "So winning by the Tao and winning by force mean the same as keeping a nation intact and destroying a nation. Treating the people mercifully while punishing criminals, gaining complete victory with the country intact, is best."

WANG XI

Nation, army, division, battalion, unit—great or small, keep it intact and your dignity will be improved thereby; destroy it, and your dignity will suffer.

Master Sun

Therefore those who win every battle are not really skillful—those who render others' armies helpless without fighting are the best of all.

CAO CAO

The best victory is when the opponent surrenders of its own accord before there are any actual hostilities.

LI QUAN

Overcome your opponent by calculation.

CHEN HAO

When you do battle, it is necessary to kill people, so it is best to win without fighting.

JIA LIN

Best of all is when your troops are held in such awe that everyone comes to surrender. This is preferable to winning by trickery, violence, and slaughter.

MEI YAOCHEN

This is a matter of disliking to inflict injury.

ZHANG YU

If you can only prevail after doing battle, there will surely be many casualties, so this is not good. If you make it clear what is to be rewarded and what punished, make your directives reliable, keep your machines in good repair, train and exercise your officers and troops, and let their strengths be known so as to overcome the opponent psychologically, this is considered very good.

WANG XI

In military operations, what is valued is foiling the opponent's strategy, not pitched battle.

HO YANXI

Ho Yanxi related this story: When Wang Po of the latter Han dynasty struck Chu Chien and Su Mo, he returned to camp after battle. His enemies regrouped and tried to provoke another skirmish, but Wang Po refused to come out.

As Wang Po was having a dinner party with his officers, Su Mo's men showered the camp with a rain of arrows. One of them even struck the wine keg in front of Wang Po. Wang Po, however, sat there calmly, not stirring a bit.

At that point an officer remarked that Su Mo was already at the end of his rope and would be easy to strike. Wang Po refused, saying, "Su Mo's mercenaries are from far away, and they are short on supplies—that is why they are trying to pick a winner-take-all fight. If I close off my camp and keep my soldiers in, this is what is called 'best of all.' "

Master Sun

Therefore the superior militarist strikes while schemes are being laid.

CAO CAO

When the opponent is just beginning to plan its strategy, it is easy to strike.

DU YOU

Just when the opponent is setting up a plan to mobilize its forces, if your army strikes and suppresses them, that is best. Therefore one of the great warrior-emperors said, "Those who are good at getting rid of trouble are those who take care of it before it arises; those who are good at overcoming opponents are those who win before there is form."

MEI YAOCHEN

This means winning by intelligence.

WANG XI

It is best to thwart people by intelligent planning.

HO YANXI

When the enemy begins to plot an attack against you, you first attack them—this is easy. Figure out the direction of the enemy's plans and deploy your forces accordingly, attacking at the outset of their intentions.

ZHANG YU

Zhang Yu noted that some say that what Master Sun was saying here was that the best military operation is to attack strategically, meaning to use unusual tactics and secret calculations to seize victory without even battling.

Master Sun

The next best is to attack alliances.

LI QUAN

This means attacking when alliance are first established.

CHEN HAO

Some say this means that when the enemy has already mobilized and is negotiating, strike and overcome them—this is next best.

MENG SHI

If you carry on alliances with strong countries, your enemies won't dare to plot against you.

MEI YAOCHEN

This means winning by intimidation.

WANG XI

It means if you cannot completely thwart the schemes of the enemy, you should then work on his alliances, to try to make them fall apart.

HO YANXI

What Master Sun said was to attack when you come in contact with the enemy, meaning that when your forces are about to clash, you set up a dummy force to scare them and make them unable either to advance or retreat, and then take advantage of that opportunity to come up and conquer them. Since the neighbors have also been helped by this action of yours, the enemy cannot but be isolated and weak.

Master Sun

The next best is to attack the army.

CAO CAO

This means when the army is already formed.

JIA LIN

To be good at successful attack, deploying your forces without a hitch, is yet another notch down. Therefore a great warrior-emperor said, "One who fights for victory in front of bared blades is not a good general."

MEI YAOCHEN

This means winning by fighting.

Master Sun

The lowest is to attack a city. Siege of a city is only done as a last resort.

CAO CAO

When the enemy has called in its resources and is defending a city, to attack them in this condition is the lowest form of military operation.

LI QUAN

When you garrison an army in a walled city, the officers get stale and the soldiers get lazy.

DU YOU

This means that when you attack cities and butcher towns, this is the lowest form of attack, because there are many casualties.

WANG XI

Soldiers are killed and maimed without necessarily taking over the city.

ZHANG YU

The siege of cities and butchering of towns not only ages the army and wastes resources, it also has a lot of casualties, so it is the lowest form of attack. When you besiege a city, then your power will be used up in that, so you do it only if it is absolutely necessary, as a last resort.

Master Sun

Take three months to prepare your machines and three months to complete your siege engineering.

Du Mu

He means that it is necessary to take time to really prepare machines and constructions thoroughly, lest many people be injured. As one of the ancient strategists said, "Those who cannot deploy their machines effectively are in trouble."

Mei Yaochen

If neither intimidation nor intelligence are sufficient to overcome people, and you have no choice but to attack them where they live, then you must take adequate time to prepare.

Zhang Yu

Some say that Master Sun's point here is that you shouldn't get angry and rush to attack. This is why he says to take time, not because there is necessarily a specific time.

Master Sun

If the general cannot overcome his anger and has his army swarm over the citadel, killing a third of his soldiers, and yet the citadel is still not taken, this is a disastrous attack.

Cao Cao

If the general is so enraged that he cannot wait for the siege machines, and he sends his soldiers over the walls like a swarm of ants, this is killing and maiming the soldiers.

Jia Lin

Just ingratiate yourself with the people while causing inward rifts among the military, and the city will conquer itself.

Master Sun

Therefore one who is good at martial arts overcomes others' forces without battle, conquers others' cities without siege, destroys others' nations without taking a long time.

Li Quan

Use tactics to overcome opponents by dispiriting them rather than by battling with them; take their cities by strategy. Destroy their countries artfully, do not die in protracted warfare.

Mei Yaochen

Battle means hurting people, siege means destroying things.

Ho Yanxi

This means attacking at the planning and attacking the alliances, so as not to come to the point of actually doing battle. This is why classical martial arts say that the best of strategists does not fight. One who is good at laying siege does not lay siege with an army, but uses strategy to thwart the opponents, causing them to overcome themselves and destroy themselves, rather than taking them by a long and troublesome campaign.

Zhang Yu

A skillful martialist ruins plans, spoils relations, cuts off supplies, or blocks the way, and hence can overcome people without fighting. One way that a city can be taken is to attack a place they will be sure to want to save, so as to draw the enemy out of the city stronghold to come to the rescue, and then take the city by sneak attack.

Du Mu

When the enemy is in a condition that you can take advantage of, if you do not lose the opportunity to crush them as if they were dry rot, then it will not take long.

Master Sun

It is imperative to contest all factions for complete victory, so the army is not garrisoned and the profit can be total. This is the law of strategic siege.

Cao Cao

You do not fight with your enemy, but you do win completely, establishing victory everywhere, not garrisoning armies and bloodying blades.

Mei Yaochen

Complete victory is when the army does not fight, the city is not besieged, the destruction does not go on long, but in each case the enemy is overcome by strategy. This is called strategic siege. In this way you do not dull your army, and your profit is naturally complete.

Zhang Yu

If you do not fight, your soldiers will not be wounded, if you do not lay siege, your strength will not be exhausted, if you do not continue long, your resources will not be used up. This is how you establish yourself completely victorious over the world. Thereby there are none of the ills associated with garrisons and violence, and there are the benefits of a prosperous country and a strong army. This is the good general's art of strategic siege.

Master Sun

So the rule for use of the military is that if you outnumber the opponent ten to one, then surround them; five to one, attack; two to one, divide.

Cao Cao

When you outnumber the enemy ten to one, then surround them—that is, if the generals are equal in intelligence and bravery, and the soldiers are equal in competence. When you outnumber the enemy five to one, use three fifths of your forces for direct attacks, the other two fifths for surprise attacks. If you outnumber the enemy two to one, then divide your forces into two parts, one for direct assault and one for surprise attacks.

Du Mu

It takes ten times as many soldiers to surround an opponent, because you have to set your encirclement up at some distance from the enemy, so the area you are covering is large, and you have to be on strict guard, thus if you do not have a lot of soldiers there will be gaps and leaks.

Now if there is division among the ranks of the enemy, so that there is no coherent chain of command, then they will fall apart by themselves, even if you do not surround them. If you do surround them under such circumstances, needless to say they will be annihilated. When Master Sun says you need ten times their number to surround the enemy, this is when your leaders are equal in intelligence and courage and your soldiers are equal in competence, not when there is dissension in the enemy's own ranks.

Ho Yanxi

When you calculate and compare the strength of your forces and those of your opponent, take into account the talent, intelligence, and courage of the generals—if you are ten times stronger than the enemy, this is ten to one, and you can surround them, foiling any attempts to get away.

Du Mu

If you are five to one against your opponent, then you should take three fifths of your forces, divide them into three units to attack the enemy from one side, keeping back two fifths, watching for points of unpreparedness on the opponent's part, and taking advantage of them by surprise attacks.

CHEN HAO

When your forces are said to be five times those of the enemy, this just means you have extra power. Their forces are deployed here and there, so how could you attack them by only three routes? The specific numbers here only refer to attacking a citadel.

DU MU

If you are two to one against your opponent, you should take part of your forces and have them head for the opponent's critical points, or attack some point that the opponent will surely go to defend, so that the opponent will split off to go to the rescue, and you can use the other part of your forces to strike them. The principles of war are not a matter of numbers—in every engagement there are both surprise and frontal attacks, and you do not wait until you have a lot of soldiers to set up reserves for surprise attacks.

DU YOU

When you outnumber the opponent two to one, then one part of your attack force makes a direct assault, one part makes surprise attacks. As they are insufficient to adapt, this confuses the opponent's soldiers and separates them from their army. So a great warrior-emperor said, "If you cannot divide and move, you cannot talk about surprise maneuvers."

Master Sun

If you are equal, then fight if you are able. If you are fewer, then keep away if you are able. If you are not as good, then flee if you are able.

CAO CAO

If your forces are equal to those of the enemy, even if you are good you should still set up ambushes and surprise attacks to prevail over them. Otherwise, be defensive and do not engage in battle, or if outmatched, take your soldiers and run away.

WANG XI

To be able means to be able to motivate others to fight to the death. If you seize victory by raids and ambushes, this is called superiority in intelligence. It is not a matter of clash of armies.

LI QUAN

If you calculate your power to be less than that of the opponent, then strengthen your defense, do not go out and get your edge snapped. Wait until the mood of the enemy gets sluggish, and then go out and attack by surprise.

DU MU

If your forces are not equal to those of the enemy, avoid their edge for the time being, waiting for a gap; then make a determined bid for victory. To be able also means to be able to endure anger and humiliation, not going out to meet the opponent's challenges.

CHEN HAO

That is not so. It just means that if the enemy's soldiers are more than yours, then you should run away from them, thereby making them haughty and using this in your future plans. It does not mean enduring anger and humiliation.

JIA LIN

If they are more numerous than you, retreat and hide your troop formations so that the enemy does not know, then set out ambushers to lie in wait for them, set up ruses to confuse them. This, too, is a way of victory.

ZHANG YU

The advice to keep away and not do battle if the opponent is more numerous also applies to the case where all else is equal, the quality of the leadership and of the troops. If your forces are orderly while theirs are chaotic, if you are excited and they are sluggish, then even if they are more numerous you can do battle. If your soldiers, strength, strategy, and courage are all less than that of the opponent, then you should retreat and watch for an opening.

Master Sun

Therefore if the smaller side is stubborn, it becomes the captive of the larger side.

Li Quan

If the smaller side battles stubbornly without taking its strength into account, it will surely be captured by the larger side.

Meng Shi

The small cannot stand up to the large—this means that if a small country does not assess its power and dares to become the enemy of a large country, no matter how firm its defenses be, it will inevitably become a captive nation. The *Spring and Autumn Annals* say, "If you cannot be strong, and yet cannot be weak, this will result in your defeat."

Ho Yanxi

Ho Yanxi told the story of Right General Su Jian of the Han dynasty, a vice-general in the wars with the invading Huns of ancient times. Right General Su and Forward General Zhao of the Forward Army were leading a division of several thousand troops when he encountered a Hunnish force ten times as large.

They fought all day, until the Chinese army was decimated. Now Forward General Zhao, a foreigner who had earlier surrendered to the Chinese in exchange for rank and title, was invited by the Huns to join them, so he took the rest of his mounted troops, about eight hundred or so, and surrendered to the Shanyu, the Hunnish chieftain. Right General Su, now having lost his entire army, was at a loss to know where to go, being the sole survivor.

The great general asked several of his top advisers what to do about the case of Right General Su. One said, "We have not executed a single vice-general on this campaign. Now this Su Jian has deserted his army—we should execute him to show how serious we are."

But another said, "No, that is not right. The rule of martial arts says that it is the very stubbornness of the smaller side that makes it the captive of the larger side. Now this Su was alone with a few thousand troops when he ran into the Shanyu with a few tens of thousands; he fought hard for over a day, not daring to have any other thought as long as any of his soldiers were left. If we execute him now that he has come back by himself, this would be showing people there is no sense in returning!"

Master Sun

Generals are assistants of the nation. When their assistance is complete, the country is strong. When their assistance is defective, the country is weak.

Cao Cao

When the generals are completely thorough, their plans do not leak out. If they are defective, their formations are revealed outside.

Jia Lin

The strength or weakness of a country depends on its generals. If the generals help the leadership and are thoroughly capable, then the country will be strong. If the generals do not help the leadership, and harbor duplicity in their hearts, then the country will be weak. Therefore it is imperative to be careful in choosing people for positions of responsibility.

Ho Yanxi

Complete means having both ability and intelligence. When a country has generals that are thoroughly able and intelligent, then that country is safe and strong. This means that generals have to be completely capable and completely knowledgeable in all operations. Generals in the field must already be acquainted with all the sciences of warfare before they can command their own soldiers and assess battle formations.

Wang Xi

Complete means that when generals are good and wise, then they are both loyal and capable. To be lacking means to be missing something.

Zhang Yu

When the strategy of the generals is thoroughgoing, opponents cannot see into it, so the country is strong. If there is even a slight gap, then opponents can take aggressive advantage of this, so the country is weak.

Master Sun

So there are three ways in which a civil leadership causes the military trouble. When a civil leadership unaware of the facts tells its armies to advance when it should not, or tells its armies to retreat when it should not, this is called tying up the armies. When the civil leadership is ignorant of military affairs but shares equally in the government of the armies, the soldiers get confused. When the civil leadership is ignorant of military maneuvers but shares equally in the command of the armies, the soldiers hesitate. Once the armies are confused and hesitant, trouble comes from competitors. This is called taking away victory by deranging the military.

Wang Xi

To get rid of these problems, it is necessary to delegate unbridled authority, so it is imperative that officers who are to be generals be both loyal and talented.

Du Mu

If the military were to be governed in the same way as ordinary civilian society, then the soldiers would be confused, because there are already customs of military procedure and command in effect.

Mei Yaochen

Military and civil affairs are different, dealing with different matters. If you try to use the methods of civilian government to govern a military operation, the operation will become confused.

Zhang Yu

A nation can be governed by humanity and justice, but not an army. An army can be guided by maneuvering, but not a nation. When there are among civilian officials attached to military commands those who do not know about military strategy, if they are allowed to share in the responsibilities of the military leadership, then the chain of command will not be unified, and the soldiers will become hesitant.

Du Mu

Also, if a general lacks the planning ability to assess the officers and place them in positions where they can use the best of their abilities, instead assigning them automatically and thus not making full use of their talents, then the army will become hesitant.

Huang Shigong said, "Those who are good at delegating responsibility employ the intelligent, the brave, the greedy, and the foolish. The intelligent are glad to establish their merit, the brave like to act out their ambitions, the greedy welcome an opportunity to pursue profit, and the foolish do not care if they die."

If your own army is hesitant and confused, you bring trouble on yourself, as if you were to bring enemies in to overcome you.

Meng Shi

When the army troops are in doubt about their responsibilities and confused about what to do, then competitors will take advantage of this disorganized condition and cause trouble.

Master Sun

So there are five ways of knowing who will win. Those who know when to fight and when not to fight are victorious. Those who discern when to use many or few troops are victorious. Those whose upper and lower ranks have the same desire are victorious. Those who face the unprepared with preparation are victorious. Those whose generals are able and are not constrained by their governments are victorious. These five are the ways to know who will win.

Ho Yanxi

Assess yourselves and your opponents.

Du You

Sometimes a large group cannot effectively attack a small group, and then again sometimes weakness can be used to control the strong. Those who can adapt to the situation are victorious. This is why tradition in the *Spring and Autumn Annals* says, "Military conquest is a matter of coordination, not of masses."

Zhang Yu

Among the methods of deploying troops, there are ways by which a few can overcome many, and there are ways in which many can overcome a few. It is a matter of assessing their use and not misapplying them.

Also, when the generals are all of one mind, the armies coordinate their efforts, and everyone wants to fight, then no one can stand up to such a force.

Be invincible at all times, so as to be prepared for opponents. As Wu Qi said, "When you go out the door, be as if you were seeing an enemy." And Shi Li said, "Be prepared, and you will not be defeated."

When generals have intelligence and courage, they should be entrusted with the responsibility to accomplish their work, and not controlled by civilians.

Jia Lin

The movements of the armies must adapt to the situation on the spot—nothing causes more trouble than trying to run them from behind the lines.

Wang Xi

If the civilian leadership tries to control able generals, it will be unable to eliminate hesitation and avoidance. An enlightened leadership is one that knows its people and can delegate authority effectively. In the field it is necessary to take advantage of opportunities as they present themselves, without hesitation—how can this be controlled from far away?

HO YANXI

As a rule, in a military operation you need to change tactics a hundred times at every pace, proceeding when you see you can, falling back when you know there is an impasse. To talk about government orders for all this is like going to announce to your superiors that you want to put out a fire—by the time you get back with an order, there is nothing left but the ashes.

DU MU

Du Mu quoted Wei Liaozi, saying, "The general is not controlled by heaven above, is not controlled by earth below, is not controlled by humanity in between. This is why 'the military is an instrument of ill omen.' The general is an officer of death."

Master Sun

So it is said that if you know others and know yourself, you will not be imperiled in a hundred battles; if you do not know others but know yourself, you win one and lose one; if you do not know others and do not know yourself, you will be imperiled in every single battle.

LI QUAN

If you assess your strength and can fend off opponents, what danger is there? If because of your own strength you fail to measure opponents, then victory is uncertain.

DU MU

Compare your government to that of the enemy; compare your military leadership to that of the enemy; compare your logistics to that of your enemy; compare your ground to that of your enemy. Having established these comparisons, you will have a preview of superiorities and inferiorities, weaknesses and strengths; this will enable you to prevail every time in subsequent military operations.

ZHANG YU

When you know others, then you are able to attack them. When you know yourself, you are able to protect yourself. Attack is the time for defense, defense is a strategy of attack. If you know this, you will not be in danger even if you fight a hundred battles.

When you only know yourself, this means guarding your energy and waiting. This is why knowing defense but not offense means half victory and half defeat.

When you know neither the arts of defense nor the arts of attack, you will lose in battle.

[4]
FORMATION

Du Mu

You see the inner conditions of opponents by means of their external formations. The inner condition of the formless is inscrutable, whereas that of those who have adopted a specific form is obvious. The inscrutable win, the obvious lose.

Wang Xi

Those skilled in military operations are able to change their formations in such a way as to ensure victory based on the actions of opponents.

Zhang Yu

This means the offensive and defensive formations used by two armies. When they are hidden within, they cannot be known to others; when they are visible without, opponents can come in through the chinks. Formation is revealed by attack and defense, so discussion of formation follows the discussion of planning a siege.

Master Sun

In ancient times skillful warriors first made themselves invincible, and then watched for vulnerability in their opponents.

Zhang Yu

Making yourself invincible means knowing yourself; waiting for vulnerability in opponents means knowing others.

MEI YAOCHEN

Hide your form, be orderly within, and watch for gaps and slack.

Master Sun

Invincibility is in oneself, vulnerability is in the opponent.

DU MU

Keeping your own military in order, always being prepared for opposition, erase your tracks and hide your form, making yourself inscrutable to opponents. When you see that an opponent can be taken advantage of, then you emerge to attack.

WANG XI

Invincibility is a matter of self-defense; vulnerability is simply a matter of having gaps.

Master Sun

Therefore skillful warriors are able to be invincible, but they cannot cause opponents to be vulnerable.

DU MU

If opponents have no formation to find out, no gap or slack to take advantage of, how can you overcome them even if you are well equipped?

ZHANG YU

If you hide your form, conceal your tracks, and always remain strictly prepared, then you can be invulnerable yourself. If the forms of strength and weakness of opponents are not outwardly manifest, then how can you be assured of victory over them?

Master Sun

That is why it is said that victory can be discerned but not manu-factured.

Cao Cao

Victory can be discerned to the extent that you see a set formation; but to the extent that the enemy has preparations, it cannot be manu-factured.

Du Mu

You can only know if your own strength is sufficient to overcome an opponent; you cannot force the opponent to slack off to your ad-vantage.

Du You

When you have assessed the opponent and seen the opponent's for-mation, then you can tell who will win. If the opponent is inscrutable and formless, then you cannot presume victory.

Ho Yanxi

The victory that can be known is up to you, meaning that you are prepared. The victory that cannot be manufactured is up to the oppo-nent, meaning that the opponent has no form.

Master Sun

Invincibility is a matter of defense, vulnerability is a matter of at-tack.

Cao Cao

For an invincible defense, conceal your form. When opponents attack you, then they are vulnerable.

Du Mu

As long as you have not seen vulnerable formations in opponents, you hide your own form, preparing yourself in such a way as to be invincible, in order to preserve yourself. When opponents have vulnerable formations, then it is time to go out to attack them.

Zhang Yu

When you know you do not yet have the means to conquer, you guard your energy and wait. When you know that an opponent is vulnerable, then you attack the heart and take it.

Wang Xi

Those on the defensive are so because they do not have enough to win; those on the offense are so because they have more than enough to win.

Master Sun

Defense is for times of insufficiency, attack is for times of surplus.

Li Quan

Those whose strength is insufficient should defend, those whose strength is superabundant can attack.

Zhang Yu

When we are on the defensive, it is because there is some lack in terms of a way to seize victory. So we wait for what we need. When we are on the offensive, it is because we already have more than enough of what it takes to overcome an opponent. So we go forth and strike. This means that we will not do battle unless we are certain of complete victory, we will not fight unless we are sure it is safe. Some people think insufficiency means weakness and surplus means strength, but this impression is wrong.

Master Sun

*Those skilled in defense hide in the deepest depths of the earth,
those skilled in attack maneuver in the highest heights of the sky.
Therefore they can preserve themselves and achieve complete victory.*

Cao Cao

They hide in the depths of the earth by taking advantage of the fastness of the mountains, rivers, and hills. They maneuver in the heights
of the sky by taking advantage of the times of nature.

Du Mu

In defense, you hush your voices and obliterate your tracks, hidden
as ghosts and spirits beneath the earth, invisible to anyone. On the
attack, your movement is swift and your cry shattering, fast as thunder and lightning, as though coming from the sky, impossible to prepare for.

Wang Xi

Defense here means lying low when you do not see any effective way
to attack, sinking into stillness and recondite silence, not letting opponents find you out. Attack is for when you see an advantage to aim
for. On the attack you should be extremely swift, taking advantage of
unexpectedness, wary of letting opponents find you out and prepare
against you.

Master Sun

*To perceive victory when it is known to all is not really skillful.
Everyone calls victory in battle good, but it is not really good.*

Zhang Yu

What everyone knows is what has already happened or become obvious. What the aware individual knows is what has not yet taken
shape, what has not yet occurred. Everyone says victory in battle is

good, but if you see the subtle and notice the hidden so as to seize victory where there is no form, this is really good.

WANG XI

Ordinary people see the means of victory but do not know the forms by which to ensure victory.

LI QUAN

Everyone can easily see armed conflict—this takes no skill. Knowledge that does not go beyond what the generality knows is not really good.

JIA LIN

Firm in defense, victorious in offense, able to keep whole without ever losing, seeing victory before it happens, accurately recognizing defeat before it occurs—this is called truly subtle penetration of mysteries.

Master Sun

It does not take much strength to lift a hair, it does not take sharp eyes to see the sun and moon, it does not take sharp ears to hear a thunderclap.

WANG XI

What everyone knows is not called wisdom, victory over others by forced battle is not considered good.

LI QUAN

A military leader of wisdom and ability lays deep plans for what other people do not figure on. This is why Sun Tzu speaks of being unknowable as the dark.

Master Sun

In ancient times those known as good warriors prevailed when it was easy to prevail.

Cao Cao

Find out the subtle points over which it is easy to prevail, attack what can be overcome, do not attack what cannot be overcome.

Du Mu

When the strategy of opponents first makes an appearance, you operate secretly in such a way as to be able to attack it. Since the effort used is little, and your assurance of victory is done in a subtle way, it is said to be easy to prevail.

Zhang Yu

If you are only able to ensure victory after engaging an opponent in armed conflict, that victory is a hard one. If you see the subtle and notice the hidden, breaking through before formation, that victory is an easy one.

Master Sun

Therefore the victories of good warriors are not noted for cleverness or bravery. Therefore their victories in battle are not flukes. Their victories are not flukes because they position themselves where they will surely win, prevailing over those who have already lost.

Mei Yaochen

Great wisdom is not obvious, great merit is not advertised. When you see the subtle, it is easy to win—what has it to do with bravery or cleverness?

Ho Yanxi

When trouble is solved before it forms, who calls that clever? When there is victory without battle, who talks about bravery?

Zhang Yu

Secret plotting and covert operations seize victory in formlessness—no one hears of the knowledge that assesses opponents and en-sures victory, no one sees the success of those who take the flag and assassinate the generals. The way to be able to win without fail is to see when opponents are in vulnerable formations, and then disposition your forces to prevail over them.

Li Quan

When the army is old, the soldiers are lazy, and the discipline and command are not unified, this is an opponent that has already lost.

Master Sun

So it is that good warriors take their stand on ground where they cannot lose, and do not overlook conditions that make an opponent prone to defeat.

Li Quan

The army that finds its ground flourishes, the army that loses its ground perishes. Here the ground means a place of strategic importance.

Du Mu

Ground where one cannot lose means invincible strategy that makes it impossible for opponents to defeat you. Not overlooking conditions that make opponents prone to defeat means spying out the enemies' vulnerabilities, not missing any of them.

Master Sun

Therefore a victorious army first wins and then seeks battle; a defeated army first battles and then seeks victory.

Cao Cao

This is the difference between those with strategy and those without forethought.

Ho Yanxi

In a military operation, first determine a winning strategy, and only then send forth the troops. If you do not plan first, hoping to rely on your strength, your victory is uncertain.

Jia Lin

If you set forth your battle lines and lightly advance without knowing your own condition or that of your opponent, you may be seeking victory, but in the end you defeat yourself.

Master Sun

Those who use arms well cultivate the Way and keep the rules. Thus they can govern in such a way as to prevail over the corrupt.

Cao Cao

Skilled users of arms first cultivate the Way that makes them invincible, keep their rules, and do not miss defeatist confusion in opponents.

Li Quan

Using harmony to hunt down opposition, not attacking a blameless country, not taking captives or booty wherever the army goes, not razing the trees or polluting the wells, washing off and purifying the shrines of the towns and hills in the countryside you pass through, not repeating the mistakes of a moribund nation—all this is called the Way and its rules. When the army is strictly disciplined, to the point where soldiers would die rather than disobey, rewards and punishments that are trustworthy and just are established—when the military leadership is such that it can achieve this, it can prevail over an opponent's corrupt civil government.

Master Sun

The rules of the military are five: measurement, assessment, calculation, comparison, and victory. The ground gives rise to measure-

ments, *measurements give rise to assessments, assessments give rise to calculations, calculations give rise to comparisons, comparisons give rise to victories.*

Cao Cao

By the comparisons of measurements you know where victory and defeat lie.

Wang Xi

The heavy prevail over the light.

Master Sun

Therefore a victorious army is like a pound compared to a gram, a defeated army is like a gram compared to a pound.

When the victorious get their people to go to battle as if they were directing a massive flood of water into a deep canyon, this is a matter of formation.

Du Mu

When water accumulates in a deep canyon, no one can measure its amount, just as our defense shows no form. When the water is released it rushes down in a torrent, just as our attack is irresistible.

[5]
FORCE

WANG XI

Force means shifts in accumulated energy or momentum. Skillful warriors are able to allow the force of momentum to seize victory for them without exerting their strength.

Master Sun

Governing a large number as though governing a small number is a matter of division into groups. Battling a large number as though battling a small number is a matter of forms and calls.

CAO CAO

Forms and calls refer to the formations and signals used to dispose troops and coordinate movements.

Master Sun

Making the armies able to take on opponents without being defeated is a matter of unorthodox and orthodox methods.

JIA LIN

When you meet opponents head on, with coordinated surprise attacks all around, you can always win and never lose.

HO YANXI

A military body goes through myriad transformations, in which everything is blended. Nothing is not orthodox, nothing is not unorthodox. If the militia is raised for a just cause, that is orthodox. If it adapts to change in face of an enemy, that is unorthodox. What is orthodox for you, cause opponents to see as unorthodox; what is unorthodox for you, cause opponents to see as orthodox. The orthodox is also unorthodox, and the unorthodox is also orthodox. Generally in military operations there is always the orthodox and the unorthodox, or the straightforward and the surprise—victory without use of both orthodox and unorthodox methods is a lucky win in what amounts to a brawl.

ZHANG YU

Various people have different explanations of what is orthodox and what is unorthodox. Orthodoxy and unorthodoxy are not fixed, but are like a cycle. Emperor Taizong of the Tang dynasty, a famous warrior and administrator, spoke of manipulating opponents' perceptions of what is orthodox and what is unorthodox, then attacking unexpectedly, combining both into one, becoming inscrutable to opponents.

Master Sun

For the impact of armed forces to be like stones thrown on eggs is a matter of emptiness and fullness.

CAO CAO

Attack complete emptiness with complete fullness.

ZHANG YU

A later chapter says that good warriors make others come to them, and do not go to others. This is the principle of emptiness and fullness of others and self. When you induce opponents to come to you, then their force is always empty; as long as you do not go to them, your force is always full. Attacking emptiness with fullness is like throwing stones on eggs—the eggs are sure to break.

Master Sun

In battle, confrontation is done directly, victory is gained by surprise.

CAO CAO

Direct confrontation is facing opponents head on, surprise forces attack unexpectedly from the sides.

Master Sun

Therefore those skilled at the unorthodox are infinite as heaven and earth, inexhaustible as the great rivers. When they come to an end, they begin again, like the days and months; they die and are reborn, like the four seasons.

LI QUAN

Heaven and earth mean movement and stillness. Rivers represent a ceaseless flux. The changes of unorthodox surprise movements are like the ceaseless changes of the weather cycle.

ZHANG YU

Sun and moon travel through the sky, they set and rise again. The four seasons succeed one another, flourishing and then fading again. This is a metaphor for the interchange of surprise unorthodox movements and orthodox direct confrontation, mixing together into a whole, ending and beginning infinitely.

Master Sun

There are only five notes in the musical scale, but their variations are so many that they cannot all be heard. There are only five basic colors, but their variations are so many that they cannot all be seen. There are only five basic flavors, but their variations are so many that they cannot all be tasted. There are only two kinds of charge in battle, the unorthodox surprise attack and the orthodox direct attack, but variations of the unorthodox and the orthodox are endless. The unorthodox and the orthodox give rise to each other, like a beginningless circle—who could exhaust them?

Mei Yaochen

The comprehensiveness of adaptive movement is limitless.

Wang Xi

Opponents cannot exhaust you.

Master Sun

When the speed of rushing water reaches the point where it can move boulders, this is the force of momentum. When the speed of a hawk is such that it can strike and kill, this is precision. So it is with skillful warriors—their force is swift, their precision is close. Their force is like drawing a catapult, their precision is like releasing the trigger.

Du Mu

Their force is swift in the sense that the force of the momentum of battle kills when it is released—that is why it is likened to a drawn catapult.

Master Sun

Disorder arises from order, cowardice arises from courage, weakness arises from strength.

Li Quan

If you presume on the orderliness of government and fail to provide for the comfort of the governed, thus creating much resentment, disorder is certain to arise.

JIA LIN

If you presume an order, disorder will arise. If you presume on courage and strength, timidity and weakness will arise.

DU MU

What this means is that if you want to feign disorder so as to lead opponents on, first you must have complete order, for only then can you create artificial disorder. If you want to feign cowardice to spy on opponents, first you must be extremely brave, for only then can you act artificially timid. If you want to feign weakness to induce haughtiness in opponents, first you must be extremely strong, for only then can you pretend to be weak.

Master Sun

Order and disorder are a matter of organization, courage and cowardice are a matter of momentum, strength and weakness are a matter of formation.

WANG XI

Order and disorder are changes in organization. Organization means methodical regulation. Courage and cowardice are changes in momentum or force. Strength and weakness are changes in formation.

LI QUAN

When an army has the force of momentum, even the timid become brave; when it loses the force of momentum, even the brave become timid. Nothing is fixed in the laws of warfare—they develop based on momenta.

CHEN HAO

The brave act quickly, while the timid drag their feet. When opponents see you are not moving ahead, they will assume you are timid, and will take you lightly. You then take advantage of their laxity to use the force of momentum to attack them.

Master Sun

Therefore those who skillfully move opponents make formations that opponents are sure to follow, give what opponents are sure to take. They move opponents with the prospect of gain, waiting for them in ambush.

Cao Cao

Formations that opponents are sure to follow are formations that give the impression of exhaustion. Opponents are moved by the prospect of an advantage.

Du Mu

It does not only mean giving the impression of exhaustion and weakness. When you are stronger than your opponent, then you appear worn out to induce the opponent to come to you. When you are weaker than your opponent, then you appear strong to impel the opponent to go away. Thus the movements of opponents all follow your direction. When you move opponents with the prospect of an advantage, since opponents are following you, you wait for them in ambush with well-prepared forces.

Wang Xi

Whether you get opponents to follow you, or get them to take something, be sure you have crack troops ready for them first.

Master Sun

Therefore good warriors seek effectiveness in battle from the force of momentum, not from individual people. Therefore they are able to choose people and let the force of momentum do its work.

Li Quan

When you have the force of momentum in war, even the timid can be courageous. So it is impossible to choose them for their capabilities and give them the appropriate responsibilities. The brave can fight, the careful can guard, the intelligent can communicate. No one is useless.

MEI YAOCHEN

It is easy to get people to act by means of the force of momentum, whereas it is hard to demand power in individual people. The able have to choose the right people and also let the force of momentum do its work.

ZHANG YU

The rule for delegation of responsibility is to use greed, use folly, use intelligence, and use bravery, allowing for the natural force of each one, not blaming people for what they are incapable of, but choosing appropriate responsibilities for them according to their respective capacities.

Master Sun

Getting people to fight by letting the force of momentum work is like rolling logs and rocks. Logs and rocks are still when in a secure place, but roll on an incline; they remain stationary if square, they roll if round. Therefore, when people are skillfully led into battle, the momentum is like that of round rocks rolling down a high mountain—this is force.

DU MU

Roll rocks down a ten-thousand-foot mountain, and they cannot be stopped—this is because of the mountain, not the rocks. Get people to fight with the courage to win every time, and the strong and the weak unite—this is because of the momentum, not the individuals.

[6]

EMPTINESS AND FULLNESS

Du Mu

Militarists avoid the full and strike the empty, so they first have to recognize emptiness and fullness in others and themselves.

Master Sun

Those who are first on the battlefield and await the opponents are at ease; those who are last on the battlefield and head into battle get worn out.

Jia Lin

Those who first position themselves in an advantageous place and await opponents there are prepared, so the troops are relaxed. If the opponents are in an advantageous position, then you should not go to them, but withdraw your troops to another base, making it appear that you will not oppose their army. Opponents will then think that you have no strategy, and will come and attack you. Then you can turn things around and make opponents tired without wearing yourself out.

Master Sun

Therefore good warriors cause others to come to them, and do not go to others.

Du Mu

Causing opponents to come to you, you should conserve your strength and wait for them, not going to opponents for fear of wearing yourself out.

Zhang Yu

If you make opponents come to fight, then their force will always be empty. If you do not go to fight, then your force will always be full. This is the art of emptying others and filling yourself.

Master Sun

What causes opponents to come of their own accord is the prospect of gain. What discourages opponents from coming is the prospect of harm.

Ho Yanxi

Lure them with something to gain, and opponents will be tired while you are at ease.

Zhang Yu

The only way to get opponents to come to you is to lure them with gain. The only way to ensure that opponents will not get to you is to harm what they care about.

Cao Cao

To bring them to you, lure them with gain. To keep them from getting to you, attack where they will be sure to go to the rescue.

Du You

If you can cause them to run while you hold an essential pass, you can make it impossible for opponents to get to you. As it is said, "One cat at the hole, and ten thousand mice dare not come out; one tiger in the valley, and ten thousand deer cannot pass through."

Master Sun

So when opponents are at ease, it is possible to tire them. When they are well fed, it is possible to starve them. When they are at rest, it is possible to move them.

Cao Cao

You cause them trouble with some affair, you cut off their supply routes to starve them, you attack what they like and appear where they will go, thus causing opponents to have to go to the rescue.

Li Quan

You attack unexpectedly, causing opponents to become exhausted just running for their lives. You burn their supplies and raze their fields, cutting off their supply routes. You appear at critical places and strike when they least expect it, making them have to go to the rescue.

Du Mu

The arts of starving an opponent do not stop at cutting off supply lines. In the late sixth century, Yuwen Huaji led an armed force to attack Li Mi. Li Mi knew that Huaji was short on supplies, so he feigned conciliation in order to wear out his troops. Huaji was delighted, and fed his soldiers all they wanted, expecting that Li Mi was going to supply them. Subsequently the food ran out, and the generals from Li Mi's army who had pretended to join up with Huaji went back to Li Mi's camp with their troops. This finally led to Huaji's defeat.

Master Sun

Appear where they cannot go, head for where they least expect you. To travel hundreds of miles without fatigue, go over land where there are no people.

Cao Cao

Make it impossible for the enemy to get there to the rescue. Appear where there is an opening and strike at a gap; avoid where they are guarding, hit where they are not expecting it.

Chen Hao

Striking at an open gap does not only mean where the opponent has no defense. As long as the defense is not strict, the place is not tightly guarded, the generals are weak and the troops are disorderly, the supplies are scarce and the forces are isolated, if you face them with an orderly and prepared army, they will fall apart in front of you. This way you do not need to labor and suffer, for it is as if you were traveling over unpopulated territory.

Master Sun

To unfailingly take what you attack, attack where there is no defense. For unfailingly secure defense, defend where there is no attack.

Du Mu

If they are alert on their eastern flank, strike on their western flank. Lure them on from the front, strike them from behind.

Li Quan

It is easy to take over from those who have not thought ahead.

Chen Hao

Do not figure on opponents not attacking; worry about your own lack of preparation. When you can attack anywhere and defend everywhere, your military strategy is complete.

Wang Xi

Attack their gaps: incompetence on the part of the military leadership, lack of training among the troops, insubstantiality in fortifications, lack of strictness in preparations, inability to effect rescues, shortages of food, psychological disunity. Defend with fullness: competence in the military leaders, excellence in the soldiers, solidity in fortifications, strictness in preparation, ability to effect rescues, sufficiency of food, psychological unity.

ZHANG YU

Those who are good on the attack maneuver in the heights of the skies, making it impossible for opponents to prepare for them. If no one can prepare for you, then where you attack is unguarded. Those who are good on the defense hide in the depths of the earth, making it impossible for opponents to fathom them. If you are unfathomable, then what you guard is not attacked by opponents.

Master Sun

So in the case of those who are skilled in attack, their opponents do not know where to defend. In the case of those skilled in defense, their opponents do not know where to attack.

CAO CAO

This means true information is not leaked.

JIA LIN

When directives are carried out, people are sincerely loyal, preparations for defense are firmly secured, and yet you are so subtle and secretive that you reveal no form, opponents are unsure—their intelligence is of no avail.

MEI YAOCHEN

Those good at attack do not divulge their operational secrets; those good at defense prepare thoroughly, without gaps.

Master Sun

Be extremely subtle, even to the point of formlessness. Be extremely mysterious, even to the point of soundlessness. Thereby you can be the director of the opponent's fate.

Du Mu

The subtle is stillness, the mysterious is movement. Stillness is defense, movement is attack. Whether opponents live or die depends on you, so you are as though director of their fate.

Du You

This means being so subtle as to be imperceptible, and to be able to change suddenly like a mysterious spirit.

Mei Yaochen

Formlessness means being so subtle and secret that no one can spy on you. Soundlessness means being so mysteriously swift that no one notices you.

Master Sun

To advance irresistibly, push through their gaps. To retreat elusively, outspeed them.

Ho Yanxi

If your forces push through the opponent's gaps as they move forward and take advantage of speed when they retreat, then you can overcome the opponent while the opponent cannot overcome you.

Zhang Yu

At a standoff, if you rush in and strike when you see a gap, how can the enemy fend you off? Having gained the advantage, you retreat, hastening back to your stronghold for self-defense—then how can the enemy pursue you? Military conditions are based on speed—come like the wind, go like lightning, and opponents will be unable to overcome you.

Master Sun

Therefore when you want to do battle, even if the opponent is deeply entrenched in a defensive position, he will be unable to avoid fighting if you attack where he will surely go to the rescue.

CAO CAO AND LI QUAN

Cut off their supply routes, guard their return routes, and attack their civilian leadership.

DU MU

If you are on your home territory and the opponents are invaders, then cut off their supplies and guard their return routes. If you are on the opponent's home ground, then attack the civilian leadership.

Master Sun

When you do not want to do battle, even if you draw a line on the ground to hold, the opponent cannot fight with you because you set him off on the wrong track.

LI QUAN

Set opponents off on the wrong track by baffling them so that they cannot fight with you.

DU MU

This means that when opponents come to attack you, you do not fight with them but rather set up a strategic change to confuse them and make them uncertain, deflecting them from their original intention to attack, making them reluctant to fight with you.

ZHANG YU

When you are on your home ground and are well supplied compared to the number of soldiers you have, while opponents are on alien territory and have little food compared to their number, then it is to your advantage not to fight. If you want to be sure opponents will not dare come to do battle with you even though you are not heavily fortified, let them see a setup that confuses them and deflects their course. For example, when Sima Yi was going to attack Zhuge Liang, Zhuge took down his flags and put away his battle drums, opened the gates and swept the road. Yi suspected an ambush, so he withdrew his forces and fled.

Master Sun

Therefore when you induce others to construct a formation while you yourself are formless, then you are concentrated while the opponent is divided.

ZHANG YU

What is orthodox to you, make opponents see as unorthodox; what is unorthodox to you, make them see as orthodox. This is inducing others to construct a formation. To be able to use the unorthodox as orthodox and use the orthodox as unorthodox, changing in a whirl, making yourself unfathomable to opponents, is being formless. Once the opponent's formation is seen, you then mass your troops against it. Since your form is not revealed, the opponent will surely divide up his forces for security.

Master Sun

When you are concentrated into one while the opponent is divided into ten, you are attacking at a concentration of ten to one, so you outnumber the opponent.

ZHANG YU

Seeing where the enemy is solid and where the enemy is insubstantial, you do not go to the trouble of elaborate preparations and therefore are concentrated into one garrison. The enemy, on the other hand, not seeing your form, therefore divides up to cover numerous points—so you with your whole force strike individual fragments of the enemy. Thus you inevitably outnumber them.

Master Sun

If you can strike few with many, you will thus minimize the number of those with whom you do battle.

DU MU

While being deeply entrenched and highly barricaded, not allowing any information about yourself to become known, go out and in formlessly, attacking and taking unfathomably. Harry and confuse enemies so that they divide their troops in fear, trying to cover themselves on all sides. It is like climbing a high mountain to spy on a citadel—seeing out from behind a veil, you know all about the disposition of the enemy personnel, while the enemy cannot figure out your offense or defense. Therefore you can be unified while the enemy is divided. The power of those who are united is whole, while the power of those who are divided is reduced. By striking diminished power with whole power, it is possible always to win.

Master Sun

Your battleground is not to be known, for when it cannot be known, the enemy makes many guard outposts, and since multiple outposts are established, you only have to do battle with small squads.

CAO CAO

When your form is concealed, the enemy is in doubt, and so divides up his company to be on guard against you. This means that enemy groups are small and easy to hit.

WANG XI

Don't let the enemy know where you will clash, for if they know they will mass their strength to resist you.

Master Sun

So when the front is prepared, the rear is lacking, and when the rear is prepared the front is lacking. Preparedness on the left means lack on the right, preparedness on the right means lack on the left. Preparedness everywhere means lack everywhere.

DU YOU

This means that when troops are on guard in many places, they are perforce scattered into small bands.

Master Sun

The few are those on the defensive against others, the many are those who cause others to be on the defensive against themselves.

MEI YAOCHEN

The more defenses you induce your enemy to adopt, the more impoverished your enemy will be.

Master Sun

So if you know the place and time of battle, you can join the fight from a thousand miles away. If you do not know the place and time of battle, then your left flank cannot save your right, your right cannot save your left, your vanguard cannot save your rearguard, and your rearguard cannot save your vanguard, even in a short range of a few to a few dozen miles.

Du You

The ancient philosopher Master Guan said, "Go forth armed without determining strategy, and you will destroy yourself in battle."

Master Sun

According to my assessment, even if you have many more troops than others, how can that help you to victory?

Li Quan

If you do not know the place and time of battle, even though your troops outnumber others, how can you know whether you will win or lose?

Master Sun

So it is said that victory can be made.

Meng Shi

If you cause opponents to be unaware of the place and time of battle, you can always win.

Master Sun

Even if opponents are numerous, they can be made not to fight.

Jia Lin

Even though opponents be numerous, if they do not know the conditions of your troops and you constantly make them rush about trying to cover themselves, they will not have time to formulate battle plans.

Zhang Yu

Divide their forces, do not let them press forward at once with coordinated strength—then how could anyone fight with you?

Master Sun

So assess them to find out their plans, both the successful ones and the failures. Incite them to action in order to find out the patterns of their movement and rest.

MENG SHI

Assess opponents' conditions, observe what they do, and you can find out their plans and measures.

CHEN HO

Do something for or against them, making opponents turn their attention to it, so that you can find out their patterns of aggressive and defensive behavior.

DU MU

Stir opponents up, making them respond to you; then you can observe their forms of behavior, and whether they are orderly or confused. The military wizard Wu Qi devised this strategy for assessing generals: have brave young men lead crack troops on strikes and run away after skirmishing, without being punished for running away. Then observe the enemy's behavior—if there is orderly rule, and the enemy does not give chase to the fleeing troops and does not try to take advantage to grab what it can, this means the general has a strategy. On the other hand, if the enemy behaves like a mob, giving chase in total confusion and greedily trying to plunder, you can be sure that the directives of the generals are not carried out, so you can attack them without hesitation.

Master Sun

Induce them to adopt specific formations, in order to know the ground of death and life.

LI QUAN

When you break ranks and set up guerrilla squads, you may lay down your banners and drums, your signals and symbols of military organization, to use the appearance of weakness in order to induce them to adopt a specific form. Or you may set up false arrays of campfires and banners, to use the appearance of strength in order to induce them to adopt a specific form. If you die by going to them and live by getting them to come to you, this way death and life come about depending on the ground.

Du Mu

The ground of death and life is the battleground. If you go to the enemy on a ground of death you will live, while if you leave the enemy on a ground of life you will die. This means that you use many methods to confuse and disturb enemies to observe the forms of their response to you; after that you deal with them accordingly, so you can know what sort of situations mean life and what sort of situations mean death.

Master Sun

Test them to find out where they are sufficient and where they are lacking.

Du Mu

Compare where you are sufficient with where the enemy is sufficient, compare where you are lacking with where the enemy is lacking.

Wang Xi

Compare the strength of the enemy with your own, and you will know where there is sufficiency or lack. After that you can assess the advantages of attack or defense.

Master Sun

Therefore the consummation of forming an army is to arrive at formlessness. When you have no form, undercover espionage cannot find out anything, intelligence cannot form a strategy.

ZHANG YU

First you use emptiness and fullness to induce the enemy to adopt a specific formation while remaining unfathomable to the enemy, so that ultimately you reach formlessness. Once you have no perceptible form, you leave no traces to follow, so spies cannot find any chinks to see through and those in charge of intelligence cannot put any plans into operation.

Master Sun

Victory over multitudes by means of formation is unknowable to the multitudes. Everyone knows the form by which I am victorious, but no one knows the form by which I ensure victory.

MEI YAOCHEN

The multitudes know when you win, but they do not know that it is based on the formations of the enemy. They know the traces of attainment of victory, but do not know the abstract form that makes for victory.

LI QUAN

Victory in war is apparent to all, but the science of ensuring victory is a mysterious secret, generally unknown.

Master Sun

Therefore victory in war is not repetitious, but adapts its form endlessly.

LI QUAN

Determining changes as appropriate, do not repeat former strategies to gain victory.

DU MU

Whatever formations opponents may adopt, from the beginning I can adapt to them to attain victory.

Master Sun

Military formation is like water—the form of water is to avoid the high and go to the low, the form of a military force is to avoid the full and attack the empty; the flow of water is determined by the earth, the victory of a military force is determined by the opponent.

LI QUAN

How can you ensure victory if not on the basis of the enemy's own posture? A light brigade cannot hold out long, so if you keep it under siege it will inevitably lose; a heavy brigade will unfailingly respond to a provocation and expose itself. If the opposing army is angry, shame it; if the army is strong, get it to relax. If the opposing general is proud, humiliate him; if the general is greedy, bait him; if the general is suspicious, spy on him right back—therefore the manner of victory is determined according to the enemy.

Master Sun

So a military force has no constant formation, water has no constant shape: the ability to gain victory by changing and adapting according to the opponent is called genius.

[7]
ARMED STRUGGLE

LI QUAN

Struggle is pursuit of advantage; once emptiness and fullness are determined, one may then struggle with others for advantage.

WANG XI

Struggle means struggle for advantage; those who get the advantages are thereby victorious. One should first determine whether to use light or heavy arms, and assess whether to approach indirectly or directly, not allowing opponents to take advantage of one's toil.

Master Sun

The ordinary rule for use of military force is for the military command to receive the orders from the civilian authorities, then to gather and mass the troops, quartering them together. Nothing is harder than armed struggle.

ZHANG YU

To fight with people face to face over advantages is the hardest thing in the world.

Master Sun

The difficulty of armed struggle is to make long distances near and make problems into advantages.

CAO CAO

While giving the appearance of being far away, you step up your pace and get there before the opponent.

DU MU

Fool opponents into taking it easy, then make haste.

Master Sun

Therefore you make their route a long one, luring them on in hopes of gain. When you set out after others and arrive before them, you know the strategy of making the distant near.

JIA LIN

When the opponent really has but a short way to go, if you can lengthen his road by sending him on wild goose chases, you can mislead him so that he cannot come to you to fight.

HO YANXI

You use a special squad to lure the opponent on a wild goose chase, making it seem as though your main force is far away; then you send out a surprise attack force that gets there first, even though it sets out last.

Master Sun

Therefore armed struggle is considered profitable, and armed struggle is considered dangerous.

CAO CAO

For the skilled it is profitable, for the unskilled it is dangerous.

Master Sun

To mobilize the whole army to struggle for advantage would take too long, yet to struggle for advantage with a stripped-down army results in a lack of equipment.

So if you travel light, not stopping day or night, doubling your usual pace, struggling for an advantage a hundred miles away, your military leaders will be captured. Strong soldiers will get there first, the weary later on—as a rule, one in ten make it.

Jia Lin

When the road is long the people are weary; if their strength has been used up in travel, then they are worn out while their opponents are fresh, so they are sure to be attacked.

Master Sun

Struggling for an advantage fifty miles away will thwart the forward leadership, and as a rule only fifty percent of the soldiers make it.

Struggle for an advantage thirty miles away, and two out of three get there.

So an army perishes if it has no equipment, it perishes if it has no food, and it perishes if it has no money.

Mei Yaochen

These three things are necessary—you cannot fight to win with an unequipped army.

Master Sun

So if you do not know the plans of your competitors, you cannot make informed alliances.

Cao Cao

You cannot make alliances unless you know the conditions, feelings, and plans of opponents.

Du Mu

No, this means that you have to know competitors' plans before you can fight with them. If you don't know their strategy, you should certainly not do battle with them.

CHEN HAO

Both explanations make sense.

Master Sun

Unless you know the mountains and forests, the defiles and impasses, and the lay of the marshes and swamps, you cannot maneuver with an armed force. Unless you use local guides, you cannot get the advantages of the land.

LI QUAN

When you go into enemy territory, you need local people to guide you along the most convenient routes, lest you be hemmed in by mountains and rivers, get bogged down on swampy ground, or lack access to springs and wells. This is what the *I Ching* means when it says, "Chasing deer without a guide only takes you into the bush."

ZHANG YU

Only when you know every detail of the lay of the land can you maneuver and contend.

MEI YAOCHEN

Local guides can be captured or recruited, but it is best to have developed professional scouts, who need not be people of a specific area.

Master Sun

So a military force is established by deception, mobilized by gain, and adapted by division and combination.

DU MU

A military force is established by deception in the sense that you deceive enemies so that they do not know your real condition, and then can establish supremacy. It is mobilized by gain in the sense that it goes into action when it sees an advantage. Dividing and recombining is done to confuse opponents and observe how they react to you, so that then you can adapt in such a way as to seize victory.

Master Sun

Therefore when it moves swiftly it is like the wind, when it goes slowly it is like a forest; it is rapacious as fire, immovable as mountains.

LI QUAN

It is swift as the wind in that it comes without a trace and withdraws like lightning. It is like a forest in that it is orderly. It is rapacious as fire across a plain, not leaving a single blade of grass. It is immovable as a mountain when it garrisons.

WANG XI

It is swift as the wind in the speed with which it rushes into openings.

DU MU

It is so fiery and fierce that none can stand up to it.

JIA LIN

When it sees no advantage in action, it remains immovable as a mountain, even though opponents try to lure it out.

Master Sun

It is as hard to know as the dark; its movement is like pealing thunder.

MEI YAOCHEN

Hard to know as the dark means being unobtrusive and inscrutable. Moving like thunder means being so fast no one can get out of your way.

HO YANXI

You conceal your strategy in order to be able to exert this much energy all at once.

Master Sun

To plunder a locality, divide up your troops. To expand your territory, divide the spoils.

ZHANG YU

The rule for military operations is to feed off the enemy as much as possible. However, in localities where people do not have very much, it is necessary to divide up the troops into smaller groups to take what they need here and there, for only then will there be enough.

As for dividing the spoils, this means it is necessary to divide up the troops to guard what has been gained, not letting enemies get it. Some say it means that when you get land you divide it among those who helped you get it, but in this context I suspect this is not what is meant.

Master Sun

Act after having made assessments. The one who first knows the measures of far and near wins—this is the rule of armed struggle.

LI QUAN

The first to move is the guest, the last to move is the host. The guest has it hard, the host has it easy. Far and near means travel—fatigue, hunger, and cold arise from travel.

Master Sun

An ancient book of military order says, "Words are not heard, so cymbals and drums are made. Owing to lack of visibility, banners and flags are made." Cymbals, drums, banners, and flags are used to focus and unify people's ears and eyes. Once people are unified, the brave cannot proceed alone, the timid cannot retreat alone— this is the rule for employing a group.

Mei Yaochen

To unify people's ears and eyes means to make people look and listen in concert so that they do not become confused and disorderly. Signals are used to indicate directions and prevent individuals from going off by themselves.

Master Sun

So in night battles you use many fires and drums, in daytime battles you use many banners and flags, so as to manipulate people's ears and eyes.

Du Mu

Have your soldiers adapt their movements according to your signals.

Mei Yaochen

The reason you use many signals is to manipulate and confuse the perceptions of enemies.

Wang Xi

You use many signals to startle their perceptions and make them fear your awesome martial power.

Master Sun

So you should take away the energy of their armies, and take away the heart of their generals.

Zhang Yu

Energy is what battle depends on. Any living thing can be stirred to fight, but even those who fight without regard for death are the way they are because their energy compels them to be that way. Therefore the rule for military operations is that if you can stir up the soldiers of all ranks with a common anger, then no one can stand up to them. Therefore, when opponents first come and their energy is keen, you break this down by not fighting with them for the time being. Watch for when they slump into boredom, then strike, and their keen energy can be taken away.

As for taking away the heart of their generals, the heart is the ruler of the general—order and disorder, courage and timidity, all are based on the mind. So those killed in controlling opponents stir them into disorder, incite them to confusion, press them into fear—thus can the schemes in their hearts be taken away.

HO YANXI

First you must be capable of firmness in your own heart—only then can you take away the heart of opposing generals. This is why tradition says that people of former times had the heart to take away hearts, and the ancient law of charioteers says that when the basic mind is firm, fresh energy is victorious.

Master Sun

So morning energy is keen, midday energy slumps, evening energy recedes—therefore those skilled in use of arms avoid the keen energy and strike the slumping and receding. These are those who master energy.

MEI YAOCHEN

The morning means the beginning, midday means the middle, and the evening means the end. What this says is that soldiers are keen at first, but eventually they slump and think of going home, so at this point they are vulnerable.

HO YANXI

Everyone likes security and dislikes danger, everyone wants to live and fears death—so if you chase them to death's door for no reason, making them glad to go to battle, it must be because they have angry and contentious energy in their hearts that has temporarily been taken advantage of to stir them into such a state that they go into danger and imperil themselves without concern or trepidation. Invariably they will regret this and shrink back in fear. Now any weakling in the world will fight in a minute if he gets excited, but when it comes to actually taking up arms and seeking to do battle, this is being possessed by energy—when this energy wanes they will stop, get frightened, and feel regret. The reason that armies look upon strong enemies the way they look at virgin girls is that their aggressiveness is being taken advantage of, as they are stirred up over something.

Master Sun

Using order to deal with the disorderly, using calm to deal with the clamorous, is mastering the heart.

Du Mu

Once your basic mind is settled, you should just tune and order it, making it calm and stable, undisturbed by events, not deluded by prospects of gain. Watch for disorder and clamor among the enemy ranks, then attack.

Ho Yanxi

A general, with only one body and one heart, leads a million troops to face fierce enemies—gain and loss, victory and defeat, are intermixed; strategy and intelligence change ten thousand times—and this is placed in the general's chest. So unless your heart is wide open and your mind is orderly, you cannot be expected to be able to adapt responsively without limit, dealing with events unerringly, facing great and unexpected difficulties without upset, calmly handling everything without confusion.

Master Sun

Standing your ground awaiting those far away, awaiting the weary in comfort, awaiting the hungry with full stomachs, is mastering strength.

Li Quan

This refers to the forces of guest and host.

Du Mu

This is what is meant by getting others to come to you while avoiding being induced to go to others.

Master Sun

Avoiding confrontation with orderly ranks and not attacking great formations is mastering adaptation.

Ho Yanxi

This is what was earlier referred to as avoiding the strong.

Master Sun

So the rule for military operations is not to face a high hill and not to oppose those with their backs to a hill.

Du Mu

This means that when opponents are on high ground you shouldn't attack upward, and when they are charging downward you shouldn't oppose them.

Master Sun

Do not follow a feigned retreat. Do not attack crack troops.

Jia Lin

If opponents suddenly run away before their energy has faded, there are surely ambushes lying in wait to attack your forces, so you should carefully restrain your officers from pursuit.

LI QUAN

Avoid strong energy.
   Mei Yaochen added, "Watch for the energy to crumble."

Master Sun

Do not eat food for their soldiers.

DU MU

If the enemy suddenly abandon their food supplies, they should be tested first before eating, lest they be poisoned.

Master Sun

Do not stop an army on its way home.

LI QUAN

When soldiers want to go home, their will cannot be thwarted.

MEI YAOCHEN

Under these circumstances, an opponent will fight to the death.

Master Sun

A surrounded army must be given a way out.

CAO CAO

The ancient rule of the charioteers says, "Surround them on three sides, leaving one side open, to show them a way to life."

DU MU

Show them a way to life so that they will not be in the mood to fight to the death, and then you can take advantage of this to strike them.

Master Sun

Do not press a desperate enemy.

Mei Yaochen

An exhausted animal will still fight, as a matter of natural law.

Zhang Yu

If the opponents burn their boats, destroy their cooking pots, and come to fight it out once and for all, don't press them, for when animals are desperate they thrash about wildly.

Master Sun

These are rules of military operations.

[8]

ADAPTATIONS

ZHANG YU

Adaptation means not clinging to fixed methods, but changing appropriately according to events, acting as is suitable.

Master Sun

The general rule for military operations is that the military leadership receives the order from the civilian leadership to gather armies.

Let there be no encampment on difficult terrain. Let diplomatic relations be established at borders. Do not stay in barren or isolated territory.

When on surrounded ground, plot. When on deadly ground, fight.

JIA LIN

Being on surrounded ground means there is steep terrain on all sides, with you in the middle, so that the enemy can come and go freely but you have a hard time getting out and back. When you are on ground like this, you should set up special plans ahead of time to prevent the enemy from bothering you, thus balancing out the disadvantage of the ground.

LI QUAN

Place an army in a deadly situation and the soldiers will make it their own fight.

Master Sun

There are routes not to be followed, armies not to be attacked, cita-dels not to be besieged, territory not to be fought over, orders of civilian governments not to be obeyed.

LI QUAN

If there are narrow straits along the way and there may be ambush attacks, that road should not be taken.

DU MU

Don't attack crack troops, don't try to stop a returning army, don't press a desperate enemy, don't attack a ground of death. And if you are strong and the enemy is weak, don't strike their vanguard, lest you frighten the rest into retreating.

CAO CAO

It may be possible to strike an army, but not advisable, because the lay of the land makes it hard to persist, to stay there would mean loss of further gains, present gains would in any case be slight, and a desperate army will fight to the death.

When a citadel is small and secure, and has plenty of supplies, then do not besiege it. When a territory is of marginal benefit and is as easy to lose as it is to win, then don't fight over it. When it is a matter of expediting your work, don't be limited to the commands of the civil-ian leadership.

DU MU

Wei Liaozi said, "Weapons are instruments of ill omen, conflict is a negative quality, warrior-leaders are officers of death with no heaven above, no earth below, no opponent ahead, no ruler behind."

Master Sun

Therefore generals who know all possible adaptations to take ad-vantage of the ground know how to use military forces. If generals

*do not know how to adapt advantageously, even if they know the
lay of the land they cannot take advantage of it.*

*If they rule armies without knowing the arts of complete adaptivity, even if they know what there is to gain, they cannot get people
to work for them.*

JIA LIN

Even if you know the configuration of the land, if your mind is inflexible you will not only fail to take advantage of the ground but
may even be harmed by it. It is important for generals to adapt in
appropriate ways.

If you can change with the momentum of forces, then the advantage does not change, so the only ones who get hurt are others. Therefore there is no constant structure. If you can fully comprehend this
principle, you can get people to work.

Adaptation means things like avoiding a convenient route when it
is realized that it has features that lend themselves to ambush; not
attacking a vulnerable army when it is realized that the army is desperate and bound to fight to the death; not besieging an isolated and
vulnerable city when it is realized that it has abundant supplies, powerful weapons, smart generals, and loyal administrators, so there is
no telling what might happen; not fighting over territory that could
be contested when it is realized that even if it were won it would be
hard to keep, it would be of no use anyway, and it would cost people
life and limb; not following the directives of the civilian government,
which ordinarily should be followed, when it is realized that there
would be disadvantage and consequent harm in direction from behind
the lines.

These adaptations are made on the spot as appropriate, and cannot
be fixed in advance.

Greed for what can be gained means taking any shortcut, attacking
any isolated army, besieging any insecure city, contesting any territory that can be taken, taking command of any serviceable army. If
you are greedy for what you can get from these things and do not
know how to adapt to changes such as outlined above, not only will
you be unable to get people to work, you will destroy the army and
wound the soldiers.

Master Sun

Therefore the considerations of the intelligent always include both benefit and harm. As they consider benefit, their work can expand; as they consider harm, their troubles can be resolved.

Ho Yanxi

Benefit and harm are interdependent, so the enlightened always consider them.

Master Sun

Therefore what restrains competitors is harm, what keeps competitors busy is work, what motivates competitors is profit.

Zhang Yu

Put them in a vulnerable position and they will surrender on their own. Another strategy is to cause rifts in their ranks, causing harm by wearying them and putting the people out of work.

Du Mu

Wear enemies out by keeping them busy and not letting them rest. But you have to have done your own work before you can do this. This work means developing a strong militia, a rich nation, a harmonious society, and an orderly way of life.

Master Sun

So the rule of military operations is not to count on opponents not coming, but to rely on having ways of dealing with them; not to count on opponents not attacking, but to rely on having what cannot be attacked.

Ho Yanxi

If you can always remember danger when you are secure and remember chaos in times of order, watch out for danger and chaos while they are still formless and prevent them before they happen, this is best of all.

Master Sun

Therefore there are five traits that are dangerous in generals: Those who are ready to die can be killed; those who are intent on living can be captured; those who are quick to anger can be shamed; those who are puritanical can be disgraced; those who love people can be troubled.

CAO CAO

Those who are brave but thoughtless and insist on fighting to the death cannot be made to yield, but they can be struck by ambush.

MENG SHI

When the general is timid and weak and intent on getting back alive, his heart is not really in the battle and his soldiers are not really keen. Both officers and troops are hesitant, so they are vulnerable to attack and capture.

CAO CAO

Quick-tempered people can be lured into coming to you by anger and embarrassment, puritanical people can be lured into coming to you by slander and disgrace. And if you appear in a place they are sure to rush to defend, those who love the people there will invariably hasten there to rescue them, troubling and wearying themselves in the process.

Master Sun

These five things are faults in generals, disasters for military operations.

CHEN HAO

Good generals are otherwise: they are not committed to death yet do not expect to live; they act in accord with events, not quick to anger, not subject to embarrassment. When they see possibility, they are like tigers, otherwise they shut their doors. Their action and inaction are matters of strategy, and they cannot be pleased or angered.

[9]
MANEUVERING ARMIES

CAO CAO

This means choosing the most advantageous ways to go.

Master Sun

Whenever you station an army to observe an opponent, cut off the mountains and stay by the valleys.

LI QUAN

Cutting off the mountains means guarding the defiles, and staying by the valleys means being close to water and fodder.

Master Sun

Watch the light, stay on the heights. When fighting on a hill, do not climb. This applies to an army in the mountains.

DU MU

One version says, "Fight going down, not climbing up."

Master Sun

When cut off by water, always stay away from the water. Do not meet them in the water; it is advantageous to let half of them cross and then attack them.

CAO CAO AND LI QUAN

You induce the enemy to cross over.

Master Sun

When you want to fight, do not face an enemy near water. Watch the light, stay in high places, do not face the current of the water. This applies to an army on water.

JIA LIN

In a river basin your armies can be flooded out, and poison can be put in the streams. Facing the current means heading against the flow.

DU MU

It also means your boats should not be moored downstream, lest the enemy ride the current right over you.

Master Sun

Go right through salt marshes, just go quickly and do not tarry. If you run into an army in the middle of a salt marsh, stay by the waterplants, with your back to the trees. This applies to an army in a salt marsh.

WANG XI

Should you unexpectedly encounter an opponent in such a situation, here too you should take the most advantageous factors, with your backs toward the most secure direction.

Master Sun

On a level plateau, take up positions where it is easy to maneuver, keeping higher land to your right rear, with low ground in front and high ground behind. This applies to an army on a plateau.

Du Mu

The warrior emperor Taigong said, "An army must keep rivers and marshes to the left and hills to the right."

Mei Yaochen

Choose level ground, convenient for vehicles; keep hills to your right rear, and you will have a way of getting momentum. It is convenient for fighters if they are heading downhill.

Master Sun

It was by taking advantage of the situation in these four basic ways that the Yellow Emperor overcame four lords.

Zhang Yu

All martial arts began with the Yellow Emperor [a Taoist ruler of late prehistoric times, ca. 2400 B.C.E.], so he is mentioned here.

Master Sun

Ordinarily, an army likes high places and dislikes low ground, values light and despises darkness.

Mei Yaochen

High places are exhilarating, so people are comfortable, and they are also convenient for the force of momentum. Low ground is damp, which promotes illnesses, and makes it hard to fight.

Wang Xi

When people spend a long time in dark and wet places, they become depressed and ill.

Master Sun

Take care of physical health and stay where there are plenty of resources. When there is no sickness in the army, it is said to be invincible.

MEI YOACHEN

Those who know these things can be certain of victory by the force of their momentum.

Master Sun

Where there are hills or embankments keep on their sunny side, with them to your right rear. This is an advantage to a military force, the help of the land.

ZHANG YU

Advantage in a military operation is getting help from the land.

Master Sun

When it rains upstream and froth is coming down on the current, if you want to cross, wait until it settles.

CAO CAO

This is lest the river suddenly swell when you are half across.

Master Sun

Whenever the terrain has impassable ravines, natural enclosures, natural prisons, natural traps, natural pitfalls, and natural clefts, you should leave quickly and not get near them. For myself, I keep away from these, so that opponents are nearer to them; I keep my face to these so that opponents have their backs to them.

Cao Cao

In military operations, always keep away from these six kinds of dangerous ground formation, while maneuvering so that your enemy is near them, with his back to them. Then you have the advantage, and he is out of luck.

Master Sun

When an army is traveling, if there is hilly territory with many streams and ponds or depressions overgrown with reeds, or wild forests with a luxuriant growth of plants and trees, it is imperative to search them carefully and thoroughly. For these afford stations for bushwackers and spoilers.

Zhang Yu

It is imperative to dismount and search, lest there be ambush troops hiding in such places. Also, there is concern that spies might be lurking there watching you and listening to your directives.

Master Sun

When the enemy is near but still, he is resting on a natural stronghold. When he is far away but tries to provoke hostilities, he wants you to move forward. If his position is accessible, it is because that is advantageous to him.

Du Mu

What this means is that if an opponent does not keep a position on a natural stronghold but stations himself in a convenient place, it must be because there is some practical advantage in doing so.

Master Sun

When the trees move, the enemy is coming; when there are many blinds in the undergrowth, it is misdirection.

Du You

The idea of making many blinds in the underbush is to make you think there might be bushwhackers hidden behind them.

Master Sun

If birds start up, there are ambushers there. If the animals are frightened, there are attackers there. If dust rises high and sharp, vehicles are coming; if it is low and wide, footsoldiers are coming. Scattered wisps of smoke indicate woodcutters. Relatively small amounts of dust coming and going indicate setting up camp.

Mei Yaochen

Light troops set up camp, so the dust raised by their comings and goings is relatively little.

Master Sun

Those whose words are humble while they increase war preparations are going to advance. Those whose words are strong and who advance aggressively are going to retreat.

Cao Cao

If his emissaries come with humble words, send spies to observe him and you will find that the enemy is increasing his preparations.

Zhang Yu

When emissaries come with strong words, and their army also moves ahead, they want to threaten you, seeking to retreat.

Wang Xi

Their words are strong and their posture is aggressive, so you won't think they're going to go away.

Master Sun

When light vehicles come out first and stay to the sides, they are going to set up a battle line.

CAO CAO

They are arranging the troops to do battle.

DU MU

The light vehicles establish the boundaries of the battle line.

Master Sun

Those who come seeking peace without a treaty are plotting.

CHEN HAO

Seeking peace without a treaty is a general statement about cases where countries have been behaving aggressively toward each other, with neither giving in, then all of a sudden one of them comes seeking peace and friendship for no apparent reason. It must be that some internal crisis has arisen, and one side wants a temporary peace to take care of its own problems. Otherwise, it must be that they know you have power that can be used, and they want to make you unsuspecting, so they take the initiative in seeking peace and friendship, thereafter taking advantage of your lack of preparation to come and take over.

Master Sun

Those who busily set out arrays of armed vehicles are expecting reinforcements.

JIA LIN

They wouldn't rush around for an ordinary rendezvous—there must be a distant force expected at a certain time, when they will join forces to come and attack you. It is best to prepare for this right away.

Master Sun

If half their force advances and half retreats, they are trying to lure you.

Du Mu

They feign confusion and disorder to lure you into moving forward.

Master Sun

If they brace themselves as they stand, they are starving. When those sent to draw water first drink themselves, they are thirsty.

Zhang Yu

People lose their energy when they do not eat, so they brace themselves on their weapons to stand up. Since all the men in an army eat at the same time, if one is starving all are starving.

Wang Xi

By these you can see their ranks are pursued by hunger and thirst.

Master Sun

When they see an advantage but do not advance on it, they are weary.

Zhang Yu

When the officers and soldiers are tired out, they cannot be made to fight, so even if they see an advantage to be gained, the generals do not dare to proceed.

Master Sun

If birds are gathered there, the place has been vacated.

Li Quan

If there are birds on a citadel, the army has fled.

Master Sun

If there are calls in the night, they are afraid.

Cao Cao

When soldiers call in the night, it means the general is not brave.

Du Mu

They are fearful and uneasy, so they call to each other to strengthen themselves.

Chen Hao

If there is one person in ten with courage, even though the other nine are timid and cowardly, depending on the bravery of that one man they can still be secure. Now if the soldiers call out in the night, it is because the general has no courage, as Cao Cao says.

Master Sun

If the army is unsettled, it means the general is not taken seriously.

Li Quan

If the general lacks authority, the army is disorderly.

Master Sun

If signals move, that means they are in confusion.

Zhang Yu

Signals are used to unify the group, so if they move about unsteadily, it means the ranks are in disarray.

Master Sun

If their emissaries are irritable, it means they are tired.

JIA LIN

People are irritable when they are fatigued.

Master Sun

When they kill their horses for meat, it means that the soldiers have no food; when they have no pots and do not go back to their quarters, they are desperate adversaries.

MEI YAOCHEN

When they kill their horses for food, get rid of their cooking utensils, and stay out in the open, not returning to their quarters, they are desperadoes and will surely fight to the death for victory.

Master Sun

When there are murmurings, lapses in duties, and extended conversations, the loyalty of the group has been lost.

MEI YAOCHEN

Murmurings means people spitting out their true feelings, lapses in duties means negligence on the job; as for extended conversations, why would the strong fear the alienation of the group?

WANG XI

Murmurings describe talk of true feelings, lapses in duties indicate trouble with superiors. When the military leadership has lost the people's loyalty, they talk to each other frankly about the trouble with their superiors.

Master Sun

When they give out numerous rewards, it means they are at an impasse; when they give out numerous punishments, it means they are worn out.

Du Mu

When the force of their momentum is exhausted, they give repeated rewards to please their soldiers, lest they rebel en masse. When the people are worn out, they do not fear punishment, so they are punished repeatedly so as to terrorize them.

Mei Yaochen

When people are so worn out that they cannot carry out orders, they are punished again and again to establish authority.

Master Sun

To be violent at first and wind up fearing one's people is the epitome of ineptitude.

Li Quan

To act inconsiderately and later be afraid is bravery without firmness, which is extremely incompetent.

Master Sun

Those who come in a conciliatory manner want to rest.

Du You

If they come humbly in a conciliatory manner before they have been subdued in battle, it means they want to rest.

WANG XI

Their momentum cannot last long.

Master Sun

When forces angrily confront you but delay engagement, yet do not leave, it is imperative to watch them carefully.

CAO CAO

They are preparing a surprise attack.

Master Sun

In military matters it is not necessarily beneficial to have more strength, only to avoid acting aggressively; it is enough to consolidate your power, assess opponents, and get people, that is all.

CHEN HAO

When your military power is not greater than that of the enemy, and there is no advantage to move on, it is not necessary to ask for troops from other countries, just to consolidate your power and get people among the local workers—then you can still defeat the enemy.

JIA LIN

A large group striking a small group is not held in high esteem; what is held in high esteem is when a small group can strike a large group.

Master Sun

The individualist without strategy who takes opponents lightly will inevitably become the captive of others.

DU MU

If you have no ulterior scheme and no forethought, but just rely on your individual bravery, flippantly taking opponents lightly and giving no consideration to the situation, you will surely be taken prisoner.

Master Sun

If soldiers are punished before a personal attachment to the leadership is formed, they will not submit, and if they do not submit they are hard to employ.

WANG XI

If feelings of appreciation and trust are not established in people's minds from the beginning, they will not form this bond.

Master Sun

If punishments are not executed after personal attachment has been established with the soldiers, then they cannot be employed.

ZHANG YU

When there are underlying feelings of appreciation and trust, and the hearts of the soldiers are already bonded to the leadership, if punishments are relaxed the soldiers will become haughty and impossible to employ.

Master Sun

Therefore direct them through cultural arts, unify them through martial arts; this means certain victory.

CAO CAO

Cultural art means humaneness, martial art means law.

LI QUAN

Cultural art means benevolence and reward, martial art means sternness and punishment.

Mei Yaochen

Command them humanely and benevolently, unify them strictly and sternly. When benevolence and sternness are both evident, it is possible to be sure of victory.

Master Sun

When directives are consistently carried out to edify the populace, the populace accepts. When directives are not consistently carried out to edify the populace, the populace does not accept. When directives are consistently carried out, there is mutual satisfaction between the leadership and the group.

Du Mu

Consistent means all along: in ordinary times it is imperative that benevolence and trustworthiness along with dignity and order be manifest to people from the start, so that later, if they are faced with enemies it is possible to meet the situation in an orderly fashion, with the full trust and acceptance of the people.

[10]

TERRAIN

Master Sun

Some terrain is easily passable, in some you get hung up, some makes for a standoff, some is narrow, some is steep, some is wide open.

When both sides can come and go, the terrain is said to be easily passable. When the terrain is easily passable, take up your position first, choosing the high and sunny side, convenient to supply routes, for advantage in battle.

When you can go but have a hard time getting back, you are said to be hung up. On this type of terrain, if the opponent is unprepared, you will prevail if you go forth, but if the enemy is prepared, if you go forth and do not prevail you will have a hard time getting back, to your disadvantage.

When it is disadvantageous for either side to go forth, it is called standoff terrain. On standoff terrain, even though the opponent offers you an advantage, you do not go for it—you withdraw, inducing the enemy half out, and then you attack, to your advantage.

On narrow terrain, if you are there first, you should fill it up to await the opponent. If the opponent is there first, do not pursue if the opponent fills the narrows. Pursue if the opponent does not fill the narrows.

On steep terrain, if you are there first, you should occupy the high and sunny side to await the opponent. If the opponent is there first, withdraw from there and do not pursue.

On wide-open terrain, the force of momentum is equalized, and it is hard to make a challenge, disadvantageous to fight.

Understanding these six kinds of terrain is the highest responsibility of the general, and it is imperative to examine them.

Li Quan

These are the configurations of terrain; generals who do not know them lose.

Mei Yaochen

The form of the land is the basis on which the military is aided and victory is established, so it must be measured.

Master Sun

So among military forces there are those who rush, those who tarry, those who fall, those who crumble, those who riot, and those who get beaten. These are not natural disasters, but faults of the generals.

Those who have equal momentum but strike ten with one are in a rush. Those whose soldiers are strong but whose officers are weak tarry. Those whose officers are strong but whose soldiers are weak fall. When colonels are angry and obstreperous and fight on their own out of spite when they meet opponents, and the generals do not know their abilities, they crumble.

Zhang Yu

Generally speaking, the entire military leadership has to be of one mind, all of the military forces have to cooperate, in order to be able to defeat opponents.

Master Sun

When the generals are weak and lack authority, instructions are not clear, officers and soldiers lack consistency, and they form battle lines every which way, this is riot. When the generals cannot assess opponents, clash with much greater numbers or more powerful forces, and do not sort out the levels of skill among their own troops, these are the ones who get beaten.

Jia Lin

If you employ soldiers without sorting out the skilled and unskilled, the brave and the timid, you are bringing defeat on yourself.

Master Sun

These six are ways to defeat. Understanding this is the ultimate responsibility of the generals; they must be examined.

Chen Hao

First is not assessing numbers, second is lack of a clear system of punishments and rewards, third is failure in training, fourth is irrational overexcitement, fifth is ineffectiveness of law and order, and sixth is failure to choose the strong and resolute.

Zhang Yu

These are ways to certain defeat.

Master Sun

The contour of the land is an aid to an army; sizing up opponents to determine victory, assessing dangers and distances, is the proper course of action for military leaders. Those who do battle knowing these will win, those who do battle without knowing these will lose.

Zhang Yu

Once you know the opponent's conditions, and also know the advantages of the terrain, you can win in battle. If you know neither, you will lose in battle.

Master Sun

Therefore, when the laws of war indicate certain victory it is surely appropriate to do battle, even if the government says there is to be no battle. If the laws of war do not indicate victory, it is appropriate not to do battle, even if the government orders war. Thus one advances without seeking glory, retreats without avoiding blame, only protecting people, to the benefit of the government as well, thus rendering valuable service to the nation.

ZHANG YU

Advancing and retreating contrary to government orders is not done for personal interest, but only to safeguard the lives of the people and accord with the true benefit of the government. Such loyal employees are valuable to a nation.

Master Sun

Look upon your soldiers as you do infants, and they willingly go into deep valleys with you; look upon your soldiers as beloved children, and they willingly die with you.

LI QUAN

If you treat them well, you will get their utmost power.

Master Sun

If you are so nice to them that you cannot employ them, so kind to them that you cannot command them, so casual with them that you cannot establish order, they are like spoiled children, useless.

CAO CAO

Rewards should not be used alone, punishments should not be relied on in isolation. Otherwise, like spoiled children, people will become accustomed to either enjoying or resenting everything. This is harmful and renders them useless.

Master Sun

If you know your soldiers are capable of striking, but do not know whether the enemy is invulnerable to a strike, you have half a chance of winning. If you know the enemy is vulnerable to a strike, but do not know if your soldiers are incapable of making such a strike, you have half a chance of winning. If you know the enemy is vulnerable to a strike, and know your soldiers can make the strike, but do not know if the lay of the land makes it unsuitable for battle, you have half a chance of winning.

WANG XI

If you know yourself but not the other, or if you know the other but not yourself, in either case you cannot be sure of victory. And even if you know both yourself and your opponent and know you can fight, still you cannot overlook the question of the advantages of the terrain.

Master Sun

Therefore those who know martial arts do not wander when they move, and do not become exhausted when they rise up. So it is said that when you know yourself and others, victory is not in danger; when you know sky and earth, victory is inexhaustible.

DU MU

When victory and defeat are already determined before movement and uprising, you do not become confused in your actions and do not wear yourself out rising up.

MEI YAOCHEN

When you know what is to others' advantage and what is to your advantage, you are not in danger. When you know the season and the terrain, you do not come to an impasse.

[11]
NINE GROUNDS

Master Sun

According to the rule for military operations, there are nine kinds of ground. Where local interests fight among themselves on their own territory, this is called a ground of dissolution.

CAO CAO

When the soldiers are attached to the land and are near home, they fall apart easily.

Master Sun

When you enter others' land, but not deeply, this is called light ground.

CAO CAO

This means the soldiers can all get back easily.

DU MU

When an army goes forth and crosses a border, it should burn its boats and bridges to show the populace it has no intention of looking back.

Master Sun

Land that would be advantageous to you if you got it and to opponents if they got it is called ground of contention.

CAO CAO

Ground from which a few could overcome many, the weak could strike the powerful.

DU MU

A ground of inevitable contention is any natural barricade or strategic pass.

Master Sun

Land where you and others can come and go is called a trafficked ground.

ZHANG YU

If there are many roads in the area and there is free travel that cannot be cut off, this is what is called a trafficked ground.

Master Sun

Land that is surrounded on three sides by competitors and would give the first to get it access to all the people on the continent is called intersecting ground.

HO YANXI

Intersecting ground means the intersections of main arteries linking together numerous highway systems: first occupy this ground, and the people will have to go with you. So if you get it you are secure, if you lose it you are in peril.

Master Sun

When you enter deeply into others' land, past many cities and towns, this is called heavy ground.

CAO CAO

This is ground from which it is hard to return.

Master Sun

When you traverse mountain forests, steep defiles, marshes, or any route difficult to travel, this is called bad ground.

HO YANXI

Bad ground is land that lacks stability and is unsuitable for building fortifications and trenches. It is best to leave such terrain as quickly as possible.

Master Sun

When the way in is narrow and the way out is circuitous, so a small enemy force can strike you, even though your numbers are greater, this is called surrounded ground.

MEI YAOCHEN

If you are capable of extraordinary adaptation, you can travel this ground.

ZHANG YU

On ground that is hemmed in in front and walled off behind, a single defender can hold off a thousand men, so on such ground you win by ambush.

Master Sun

When you will survive if you fight quickly and perish if you do not, this is called dying ground.

CHEN HAO

People on dying ground are, as it were, sitting in a leaking boat, lying in a burning house.

MEI YAOCHEN

When you cannot press forward, cannot retreat backward, and cannot run to the sides, you have no choice but to fight right away.

Master Sun

So let there be no battle on a ground of dissolution, let there be no stopping on light ground, let there be no attack on a ground of contention, let there be no cutting off of trafficked ground. On intersecting ground form communications, on heavy ground plunder, on bad ground keep going, on surrounded ground make plans, on dying ground fight.

LI QUAN

On a ground of dissolution, the soldiers might run away.

MEI YAOCHEN

Light ground is where soldiers have first entered enemy territory and do not yet have their backs to the wall; hence the minds of the soldiers are not really concentrated, and they are not ready for battle. At this point it is imperative to avoid important cities and highways, and it is advantageous to move quickly onward.

CAO CAO

It is not advantageous to attack an enemy on a ground of contention; what is advantageous is to get there first.

WANG XI

Trafficked ground should not be cut off, so that the roads may be used advantageously as supply routes.

MENG SHI

On intersecting ground, if you establish alliances you are safe, if you lose alliances you are in peril.

CAO CAO

On heavy ground, plundering means building up supplies.

Li Quan added, "When you enter deeply into enemy territory you should not antagonize people by acting unjustly. When the founder of the great Han dynasty entered the homeland of the supplanted Qin dynasty, there was no rapine or pillage, and this is how he won the people's hearts."

LI QUAN

On bad ground, since you cannot entrench, you should make haste to leave there.

CAO CAO

On surrounded ground, bring surprise tactics into play.

CHEN HAO

If they fall into dying ground, then everyone in the army will spontaneously fight. This is why it is said, "Put them on dying ground, and then they will live."

Master Sun

Those who are called the good militarists of old could make opponents lose contact between front and back lines, lose reliability between large and small groups, lose mutual concern for the welfare of the different social classes among them, lose mutual accommodation between the rulers and the ruled, lose enlistments among the soldiers, lose coherence within the armies. They went into action when it was advantageous, stopped when it was not.

Li Quan

They set up changes to confuse their opponents, striking them here and there, terrorizing and disarraying them in such a way that they had no time to plan.

Master Sun

It may be asked, when a large, well-organized opponent is about to come to you, how do you deal with it? The answer is that you first take away what they like, and then they will listen to you.

Wang Xi

First occupy a position of advantage, and cut off their supply routes by special strike forces, and they will do as you plan.

Chen Hao

What they like does not only mean the advantages they rely on, it means that anything enemies care about is worth capturing.

Master Sun

The condition of a military force is that its essential factor is speed, taking advantage of others' failure to catch up, going by routes they do not expect, attacking where they are not on guard.

Chen Hao

This means that to take advantage of unpreparedness, lack of foresight, or lack of caution on the part of opponents, it is necessary to proceed quickly, it won't work if you hesitate.

Master Sun

In general, the pattern of invasion is that invaders become more intense the farther they enter alien territory, to the point where the native rulership cannot overcome them.

Du Mu

The pattern of invasive attack is that if they enter deeply into enemy territory, soldiers come to have the determination to fight to the death—they are singleminded, so the native rulers cannot beat them.

Master Sun

Glean from rich fields, and the armies will have enough to eat. Take care of your health and avoid stress, consolidate your energy and build up your strength. Maneuver your troops and assess strategies so as to be unfathomable.

Wang Xi

Consolidate your keenest energy, save up your extra strength, keep your form concealed and your plans secret, being unfathomable to enemies, waiting for a vulnerable gap to advance upon.

Master Sun

Put them in a spot where they have no place to go, and they will die before fleeing. If they are to die there, what can they not do? Warriors exert their full strength. When warriors are in great danger, then they have no fear. When there is nowhere to go they are firm, when they are deeply involved they stick to it. If they have no choice, they will fight.

Cao Cao

When people are desperate, they will fight to the death.

Master Sun

For this reason the soldiers are alert without being drilled, enlist without being drafted, are friendly without treaties, are trustworthy without commands.

Du Mu

This means that when warriors are in mortal danger everyone high and low has the same aim, so they are spontaneously on the alert without being drilled, are spontaneously sympathetic without being drafted, and are spontaneously trustworthy without treaties or commands.

Master Sun

Prohibit omens to get rid of doubt, and soldiers will never leave you. If your soldiers have no extra goods, it is not that they dislike material goods. If they have no more life, it is not that they do not want to live long. On the day the order to march goes out, the soldiers weep.

Cao Cao

They abandon their goods and go to their death because they have no choice. They weep because they all intend to go to their death.

Du Mu

If they have valuable possessions, soldiers may become attached to them and lack the spirit to fight to the death, and all are pledged to die.

Wang Xi

They weep because they are so stirred up.

Master Sun

So a skillful military operation should be like a swift snake that counters with its tail when someone strikes at its head, counters with its head when someone strikes at its tail, and counters with both head and tail when someone strikes at its middle.

ZHANG YU

This represents the method of a battle line, responding swiftly when struck. A manual of eight classical battle formations says, "Make the back the front, make the front the back, with four heads and eight tails. Make the head anywhere, and when the enemy lunges into the middle, head and tail both come to the rescue."

Master Sun

The question may be asked, can a military force be made to be like this swift snake? The answer is that it can. Even people who dislike each other, if in the same boat, will help each other out in trouble.

MEI YAOCHEN

It is the force of the situation that makes this happen.

Master Sun

Therefore tethered horses and buried wheels are not sufficiently reliable.

DU MU

Horses are tethered to make a stationary battle line, wheels are buried to make the vehicles immovable. Even so, this is not sufficiently secure and reliable. It is necessary to allow adaptation to changes, placing soldiers in deadly situations so that they will fight spontaneously, helping each other out like two hands—this is the way to security and certain victory.

Master Sun

To even out bravery and make it uniform is the Tao of organization. To be successful with both the hard and soft is based on the pattern of the ground.

CHEN HAO

If the orders are strict and clear, the brave cannot advance by themselves and the timid cannot shrink back by themselves, so the army is like one man.

ZHANG YU

If you get the advantage of the ground, you can overcome opponents even with soft, weak troops—how much the more with hard, strong troops? What makes it possible for both strong and weak to be useful is the configuration of the ground.

Master Sun

Therefore those skilled in military operations achieve cooperation in a group so that directing the group is like directing a single individual with no other choice.

DU MU

People having no other choice is a metaphor for the ease with which they can be directed.

Master Sun

The business of the general is quiet and secret, fair and orderly.

MEI YAOCHEN

If you are quiet and inconspicuous, others will not be able to figure you out. If you are accurate and orderly, others will not be able to disturb you.

ZHANG YU

His plans are calm and deeply hidden, so no one can figure them out. His regime is fair and orderly, so no one dares take him lightly.

Master Sun

He can keep the soldiers unaware, make them ignorant.

LI QUAN

This is because his plans are as yet unripe, and he does not want the soldiers to know them, because it is appropriate to enjoy the final accomplishment with them but not to plan the initial strategy with them.

DU MU AND ZHANG YU

This is to make them know nothing but to follow orders, unaware of anything else.

Master Sun

He changes his actions and revises his plans, so that people will not recognize them. He changes his abode and goes by a circuitous route, so that people cannot anticipate him.

ZHANG YU

When people never understand what your intention is, then you win. The Great White Mountain Man said, "The reason deception is valued in military operations is not just for deceiving enemies, but to begin with for deceiving one's own troops, to get them to follow unknowingly."

Master Sun

When a leader establishes a goal with the troops, he is like one who climbs up to a high place and then tosses away the ladder. When a leader enters deeply into enemy territory with the troops, he brings out their potential. He has them burn the boats and destroy the pots, drives them like sheep, none knowing where they are going.

CAO CAO

He unifies their minds.

LI QUAN

An army that comes back is one that has burned its boats and bridges to make fast its will; since the soldiers do not know the plans, they do not think of looking back either, so they are like herded sheep.

Master Sun

To assemble armies and put them into dangerous situations is the business of generals. Adaptations to different grounds, advantages of contraction and expansion, patterns of human feelings and conditions—these must be examined.

DU MU

When he talks about the advantages and disadvantages of contraction and expansion, he means that the ordinary patterns of human feelings all change according to the various types of ground.

Master Sun

Generally, the way it is with invaders is that they unite when deep in enemy territory but are prone to dissolve while on the fringes. When you leave your country and cross the border on a military operation, that is isolated ground. When it is accessible from all directions, it is trafficked ground. When penetration is deep, that is heavy ground. When penetration is shallow, that is light ground. When your back is to an impassable fastness and before you are narrow straits, that is surrounded ground. When there is nowhere to go, that is deadly ground.

So on a ground of dissolution, I would unify the minds of the troops. On light ground, I would have them keep in touch. On a ground of contention, I would have them follow up quickly. On an intersecting ground, I would be careful about defense. On a trafficked ground, I would make alliances firm. On heavy ground, I

would ensure continuous supplies. On bad ground, I would urge
them onward. On surrounded ground, I would close up the gaps.
On deadly ground, I would indicate to them there is no surviving.
So the psychology of soldiers is to resist when surrounded, fight
when it cannot be avoided, and obey in extremes.

Du Mu

Not until soldiers are surrounded do they each have the determination to resist the enemy and sustain victory. When they are desperate,
they put up a united defense.

Meng Shi

When they are fallen into dire straits, they obey completely.

Master Sun

Therefore those who do not know the plans of competitors cannot
prepare alliances. Those who do not know the lay of the land can-
not maneuver their forces. Those who do not use local guides can-
not take advantage of the ground. The military of an effective
rulership must know all these things.
When the military of an effective rulership attacks a large coun-
try, the people cannot unite. When its power overwhelms oppo-
nents, alliances cannot come together.

Wang Xi

If you are able to find out opponents' plans, take advantage of the
ground, and maneuver opponents so that they are helpless, then even
a large country cannot assemble enough people to stop you.

Zhang Yu

If you rely on the force of wealth and strength to hastily attack a large
country, your own people will resent the suffering this causes and
will not unite behind you. If you pose an overwhelming military

threat to rival nations, their leaders will fear you and not dare to form alliances.

Master Sun

Therefore if you do not compete for alliances anywhere, do not foster authority anywhere, but just extend your personal influence, threatening opponents, this makes town and country vulnerable.

ZHANG YU

If you do not compete for allies and helpers, then you will be isolated, with little help. If you do not foster your authority, then people will leave and the country will weaken. If you lash out in personal rage, threatening neighbors with violence, then in the end you bring destruction on yourself.

Another interpretation is that if an enemy country cannot unite its people and assemble its troops, and its alliances cannot come together, then you should cut off its relations and take away its authority, so that you can extend your desires and awe your enemies, so that their citadels can be taken and their countries overthrown.

Master Sun

Give out rewards that are not in the rules, give out directives that are not in the code.

MEI YAOCHEN

Consider the merit to give the reward, without rules set up beforehand; observe the opponent to make promises, without prior setup of codes.

JIA LIN

When you want to take a citadel and overthrow a nation, you establish punishments and rewards outside your country, and carry out directives outside your government, so you do not stick to your ordinary rules and codes.

Master Sun

Employ the entire armed forces like employing a single person. Employ them with actual tasks, do not talk to them. Motivate them with benefits, do not tell them about harm.

Mei Yaochen

Just employ them to fight, don't tell them your strategy. Let them know what benefit there is in it for them, don't tell them about the potential harm.

Wang Xi

If the truth leaks out, your strategy will be foiled. If the soldiers worry, they will be hesitant and fearful.

Zhang Yu

Human psychology is to go for perceived benefits and try to avoid prospective harm.

Master Sun

Confront them with annihilation, and they will then survive; plunge them into a deadly situation, and they will then live. When people fall into danger, they are then able to strive for victory.

Mei Yaochen

Until they are trapped on difficult ground, soldiers are not fully concentrated in mind; once they have fallen into danger and difficulty, then the question of winning or losing depends on what people do.

Master Sun

So the task of a military operation is to accord deceptively with the intentions of the enemy. If you concentrate totally on the enemy, you can kill its military leadership a thousand miles away. This is skillful accomplishment of the task.

DU MU

If you want to attack an enemy but do not see an opening, then conceal your form and erase your tracks, going along with what the enemy does, not causing any surprises. If the enemy is strong and despises you, you appear to be timid and submissive, going along for the moment with his strength to make him haughty, waiting for him to become complacent and thus vulnerable to attack. If the enemy wants to retreat and go home, you open up a way to let him out, going along with his retreat so that he will not have any desire to fight, ultimately to take advantage of this to attack. Both of these are techniques of according with the enemy.

ZHANG YU

First you go along with their intentions, subsequently you kill their generals—this is skill in accomplishing the task.

Master Sun

So on the day war is declared, borders are closed, passports are torn up, and emissaries are not let through.

ZHANG YU

Once top-level assessments have been made and military strategy has been developed, then the borders are sealed and passports are revoked, not letting messengers through, lest there be information leaks.

Master Sun

Matters are dealt with strictly at headquarters.

MEI YAOCHEN

Strictness at headquarters in the planning stage refers to secrecy.

Master Sun

When opponents present openings, you should penetrate them immediately. Get to what they want first, subtly anticipate them. Maintain discipline and adapt to the enemy in order to determine the outcome of the war. Thus, at first you are like a maiden, so the enemy opens his door; then you are like a rabbit on the loose, so the enemy cannot keep you out.

12

FIRE ATTACK

Master Sun

There are five kinds of fire attack: burning people, burning supplies, burning equipment, burning storehouses, and burning weapons.

The use of fire must have a basis, and requires certain tools. There are appropriate times for setting fires, namely when the weather is dry and windy.

Generally, in fire attacks it is imperative to follow up on the crises caused by the fires. When fire is set inside an enemy camp, then respond quickly from outside. If the soldiers are calm when fire breaks out, wait—do not attack. When the fire reaches the height of its power, follow up if possible, hold back if not.

DU MU

In general, fire is used to throw enemies into confusion so that you can attack them. It is not simply to destroy enemies with fire. When you hear fire has erupted, you should then attack; once the fire has been brought under control and the people have settled down, it is no use to attack, so Master Sun says you should respond quickly.

Master Sun

When fire can be set out in the open, do not wait until it can be set inside a camp—set it when the time is right.

ZHANG YU

Fire can also be set outside, in the field; it is not necessary to wait until fire can be set inside an enemy camp. As long as there is an opportunity, fire can be set at an appropriate time.

Master Sun

When fire is set upwind, do not attack downwind.

MEI YAOCHEN

It is not effective to go against the momentum of the fire, because the enemy will surely fight to the death.

Master Sun

If it is windy during the day, the wind will stop at night.

MEI YAOCHEN

A daytime wind will stop at night, a night wind will stop at daylight.

Master Sun

Armies must know there are adaptations of the five kinds of fire attack, and adhere to them scientifically.

ZHANG YU

It will not do just to know how to attack others with fire, it is imperative to know how to prevent others from attacking you. You should figure out the weather patterns and adhere strictly to the principle of setting fire attacks only on suitably windy days.

Master Sun

So the use of fire to help an attack means clarity, use of water to help at attack means strength. Water can cut off, but cannot plunder.

ZHANG YU

When you use fire to help an attack, clearly you can win thereby. Water can be used to divide up an opposing army, so that their force is divided and yours is strong.

Master Sun

To win in battle or make a successful siege without rewarding the meritorious is unlucky and earns the name of stinginess. Therefore it is said that an enlightened government considers this, and good military leadership rewards merit. They do not mobilize when there is no advantage, do not act when there is nothing to gain, do not fight when there is no danger.

ZHANG YU

Armaments are instruments of ill omen, war is a dangerous affair. It is imperative to prevent disastrous defeat, so it will not do to mobilize an army for petty reasons—arms are only to be used when there is no choice but to do so.

Master Sun

A government should not mobilize an army out of anger, military leaders should not provoke war out of wrath. Act when it is beneficial, desist if it is not. Anger can revert to joy, wrath can revert to delight, but a nation destroyed cannot be restored to existence, and the dead cannot be restored to life. Therefore an enlightened government is careful about this, a good military leadership is alert to this. This is the way to secure a nation and keep the armed forces whole.

CAO CAO

Do not use arms because of your own emotions.

WANG XI

If you are inconsistent in your feelings, you will lose dignity and trust.

ZHANG YU

If the government is always prudent about the use of arms, it can thereby make the nation secure. If the military leadership is always wary of taking war lightly, it can therefore keep the armed forces whole.

13

ON THE USE OF SPIES

Master Sun

A major military operation is a severe drain on the nation, and may be kept up for years in the struggle for one day's victory. So to fail to know the conditions of opponents because of reluctance to give rewards for intelligence is extremely inhumane, uncharacteristic of a true military leader, uncharacteristic of an assistant of the government, uncharacteristic of a victorious chief. So what enables an intelligent government and a wise military leadership to overcome others and achieve extraordinary accomplishments is foreknowledge.

Foreknowledge cannot be gotten from ghosts and spirits, cannot be had by analogy, cannot be found out by calculation. It must be obtained from people, people who know the conditions of the enemy.

There are five kinds of spy: The local spy, the inside spy, the reverse spy, the dead spy, and the living spy. When the five kinds of spies are all active, no one knows their routes—this is called organizational genius, and is valuable to the leadership.

Local spies are hired from among the people of a locality. Inside spies are hired from among enemy officials. Reverse spies are hired from among enemy spies. Dead spies transmit false intelligence to enemy spies. Living spies come back to report.

ZHANG YU

Inside spies are drawn from among disaffected officials of the opposing regime, or from among relatives of officials who have been executed.

Du Mu

Among officials of the opposing regime, there are intelligent ones who lose their jobs, there are those who are punished for excesses, there are also greedy favorites. There are those confined to the lower ranks, there are those who fail to get appointments, there are those who seek to take advantage of a collapse to extend their own wealth and power, and there are those who always act with deceit and duplicity. Any of them can be secretly approached and bribed so as to find out conditions in their country and discover any plans against you; they can also be used to create rifts and disharmony.

Li Quan

When enemy agents come to spy on you, bribe them generously to make them spy for you instead. They are then reverse spies, renegades, or double agents.

Wang Xi

Reverse spies are enemy spies who are detained and induced to give information, or who are sent back with false information. Dead spies are those who are fooled by their own leaders into passing on false information to the enemy; when the facts are determined, they are inevitably killed.

Du You

When your spies are given false information that they hand on to the enemy when they are captured, the enemy makes preparations according to this information. When things turn out differently, the spies then die. Therefore they are called dead spies.

Du Mu

Living spies are those that come and go with information. For living spies, it is imperative to choose those who are inwardly bright but outwardly appear to be stupid, who are inconspicuous in appearance but strong of heart, who are fast, powerful, and brave, who are immune to seduction, who can endure hunger, cold, and dishonor.

Master Sun

Therefore no one in the armed forces is treated as familiarly as are spies, no one is given rewards as rich as those given to spies, and no matter is more secret than espionage.

DU YOU

If spies are not treated well, they may become renegades and work for the enemy, leaking out information about you. They are given rich rewards and relied upon to do their work. If they do not keep their espionage secret, this is suicidal.

Master Sun

One cannot use spies without sagacity and knowledge, one cannot use spies without humanity and justice, one cannot get the truth from spies without subtlety. This is a very delicate matter indeed. Spies are useful everywhere.

DU MU

Every matter requires prior knowledge.

Master Sun

If an item of intelligence is heard before a spy reports it, then both the spy and the one who told about it die.

MEI YAOCHEN

The spy is killed for leaking information, the one who told about it is killed to stop him from talking.

Master Sun

Whenever you want to attack an army, besiege a city, or kill a person, first you must know the identities of their defending generals,

their associates, their visitors, their gatekeepers, and their cham-
berlains, so have your spies find out.

DU MU

Whenever you are going to attack and fight, first you have to know
the talents of the people employed by the opponent, so you can deal
with them according to their abilities.

Master Sun

You must seek out enemy agents who have come to spy on you,
bribe them and induce them to stay with you, so you can use them
as reverse spies. By intelligence thus obtained, you can find local
spies and inside spies to employ. By intelligence thus obtained, you
can cause the misinformation of dead spies to be conveyed to the
enemy. By intelligence thus obtained, you can get living spies to
work as planned.

ZHANG YU

By means of these reverse spies, you find out greedy locals and vulnerable officials who can be induced to work for you. By means of these
reverse spies, you can find out how the enemy can be deceived, and
send dead spies to misinform them. By means of these reverse spies
you can find out the conditions of the enemy, so that living spies can
go and return as planned.

Master Sun

It is essential for a leader to know about the five kinds of espionage,
and this knowledge depends on reverse spies, so reverse spies must
be treated well.

DU MU

It is by finding out the conditions of the enemy through the agency
of reverse spies that all the other kinds of espionage can be used, so

reverse spies, renegades or double agents, are most important and must be treated well.

Master Sun

So only a brilliant ruler or a wise general who can use the highly intelligent for espionage is sure of great success. This is essential for military operations, and the armies depend on this in their actions.

Du Mu

It will not do for the army to act without knowing the opponent's condition, and to know the opponent's condition is impossible without espionage.

MASTERING THE ART OF WAR

Zhuge Liang and Liu Ji

NOTE ON PRONUNCIATION

The Chinese proper names in this book are transliterated in Pinyin, the most widely accepted method of romanization for Chinese. In actual usage, Chinese phonetics are so complex that a detailed treatment of Chinese pronunciation is outside the scope of this book. For the comfort and ease of the reader, however, it is useful to note a few letters that are commonly used in Pinyin spelling but are relatively uncommon in English and are given different values.

There are five consonants that are typically found to cause problems because of their special usage: *c, q, x, z* and *zh*. The following chart represent rough equivalents to these consonants in English:

c resembles *ts*
q resembles *ch*
x resembles *sh*
z resembles *dz*
zh resembles *j*

Translator's Introduction

Skilled warriors of old were subtle,
Mysteriously powerful,
So deep they were unknowable.

Tao Te Ching

Be extremely subtle
Even to the point of formlessness
Be extremely mysterious
Even to the point of soundlessness
Thereby you can be the director
Of an opponent's fate

The Art of War

Change and movement have their times; safety and danger
are in oneself. Calamity and fortune, gain and loss, all start
from oneself. Therefore those who master change are those
who address themselves to the time. For those who address
themselves to the time, even danger is safe; for those who
master change, even disturbance is orderly.

The Book of Balance and Harmony

The study and practice of strategic living in the midst of all situations
and events have been a central concern of practical philosophers of
all the great cultures since ancient times. In China, one of the oldest
living civilizations on earth, the classical philosophers concerned
themselves with humanity's struggle to survive and find security in
the midst of endless change and movement. Many of the ancient
teachers of wisdom were also artisans and scientists, seeking new
strategies for living in their study of human nature and destiny; oth-

ers were political and even military leaders, studying the most complex and difficult problems of society.

According to the philosophers of ancient China, when the pristine sociability of humanity had become distorted by personal ambitions, it fell into a state of perpetual inner war. This war manifested itself in social unrest, class conflict, and eventually armed aggression. From this time on the philosophers made it their particular concern to study mechanisms of human conflict and develop their understanding into practical sciences of crisis management.

For this reason, very early classical Chinese literature is already examining war deliberately, not only from the point of view of when and how to prosecute war, but also from the point of view of its impact on society and the resulting ethical implications. The *Yin Convergence Classic*, for example, is considered a most ancient Taoist text, believed to antedate even the *Tao Te Ching* ("The Way and Its Power"), having such consequent prestige that it is avidly studied by both social strategists and mystics: in a typically laconic manner this short work already summarizes the attitudes to war later adopted by various schools of thought, including the perennial Taoist and Confucian philosophies: "Cut off one wellspring, that of profiteering," the classic says, "and that is ten times better than mobilizing the army."

Later the *Tao Te Ching*, undoubtedly the most famous pure Taoist classic, elaborated on the theme of greed as the motive force underlying aggression:

> When the world has the Way,
> Running horses are retired to till the fields.
> When the world lacks the Way,
> War-horses are bred in the countryside.
> No crime is greater than approving of greed,
> No calamity is greater than discontent,
> No fault is greater than possessiveness.

The same fundamental theme is carefully elaborated in the *I Ching* ("Book of Changes"), another early Chinese classic, one that is devoted, as the title suggests, to a science of mastering change, the basic fact of life. The same passage of the *Yin Convergence Classic* goes on to explain that cutting off the wellspring of greed begins at home: "Introspect three times day and night, and that is ten thousand times better than mobilizing the army." This is also one meaning of the now proverbial line of the *Tao Te Ching:* "The journey of a thousand miles begins with the first step," which from the original may also be translated, "The journey of a thousand miles begins at your feet."

Later classics also follow this theory that social reform must begin within the individual, and the implication that inward renewal of conscience is ultimately more effective than external imposition of law. For this reason Chinese philosophers concluded that education was of ever-increasing importance to society as a whole. They often had radically different ideas about the kind of education they considered necessary, but all of them agreed to include the study of conflict. And as it turned out, in spite of the variety of their ideas on other subjects, the ancient Chinese philosophers often came to the same conclusions on conflict. Thus the classics on strategy in conflict, such as the famous handbook known as *The Art of War* by Sun Tzu, generally contain an amalgam of the major philosophies of ancient China, particularly those derived from the *I Ching.*

The history of warfare in China reaches back into ancient myths representing great warriors as mystics and magicians whose legendary struggles came to typify the philosophers' ideals of justice and social service in the early emergence of civilization. The realities of war in historical times were never quite as clear and simple as the paradigms of legend, but certain fundamental images and concepts were tenaciously held by politicians, philosophers, and warriors throughout the centuries in their thinking about contention and conflict.

China is a heterogeneous civilization with vast territories encompassing and bordering on an even greater variety of peoples. Its history is marked by centuries of warfare both civil and foreign. The persistence of certain causes and patterns of conflict over nearly three thousand years makes the study of warfare and the philosophy of the warriors potentially instructive and even enlightening, bringing out the essence of conflict.

Reduced to simple formulae, the power struggles that underlie three thousand years of warfare in China represent elaborations of a few basic antagonisms. The early warfare of Chinese folklore was tribal war among the peoples who lived or moved along the Yellow River. Certain tribes came to dominate others, until relatively large and quite powerful confederations developed along the Yellow River during the third and second millennia B.C.E. During the extended lives of these confederations, warfare broke out among regional interests in the control of the clans who organized and dominated them. This gradually intensified in frequency and violence, culminating in a prolonged period of virtually continuous warfare appropriately known as the era of the Warring States, which lasted from the fifth through the third centuries B.C.E.

A relentless campaign of the late third century finally ended these interstate wars and created a united China for the first time in history. This was followed by wars of expansion, which are analogous to the ancient tribal wars through which the proto-Chinese people originally established dominance over the Yellow River basin. Under the united Chinese regime, warfare between the ruled and the rulers became a typical pattern of conflict, in which regionalism continued to play a part.

Struggles between local interests and central control, and between overclasses and underclasses, played themselves out in various combinations and elaborations of these elements through countless civil and foreign intrigues and wars in the centuries to come. Added to this were clan and family rivalries, as well as political conflicts among the intelligentsia, palace eunuchs, and imperial in-laws. On greater and smaller scales, the race for power and possessions became a distinct facet of human events, to which practical philosophers responded with a science of security and strategic action.

Some of the most poignant statements on war and warriorhood originate in the classic *Tao Te Ching*, generally thought to have been compiled during the early to middle Warring States era. In the characteristic fashion of Taoism, this popular text seeks out the confluence of ethical and practical wisdom:

> Weapons, being instruments of ill omen,
> Are not the tools of the cultured,
> Who use them only when unavoidable,
> And consider it best to be aloof.
> They win without beautifying it:
> Those who beautify it
> Enjoy killing people.
> Those who enjoy killing people
> Cannot get their will of the world.
> When you are in ascendancy of power,

> You handle it as you would a mourning:
> When you have killed many people,
> You weep for them in sorrow.
> When you win a war,
> You celebrate by mourning.

The same classic also describes the skilled warrior in similar terms, as the antithesis of bravado and violence:

> Skilled warriors of old were subtle,
> Mysteriously powerful,
> So deep they were unknowable.
> Just because they are unknowable,
> I will try to describe them:
> Their wariness was as that of one
> Crossing a river in winter;
> Their caution was as that of one
> In fear of all around.
> They were serious as guests,
> Relaxed as ice at the melting point.
> Simple as uncarved wood,
> Open as the valleys,
> They were inscrutable as murky water.

This Taoist stream of thought had a distinct influence on the strategic outlook of *The Art of War,* and elements of its penetrating criticism of tyranny in all forms also appear in the ideas of the later Warring States philosophers Mozi and Mencius. Both of these thinkers, especially Mozi, were activists, noted for their strong views on warfare.

Teaching that social well-being derives from universal love, Mozi described warfare as mass murder and ridiculed the states of his time for punishing individual thefts and murders while rewarding pillage and massacre. Mozi himself designed war machinery and organized a highly mobile brigade of ascetic religious warriors to go to the rescue of small states victimized by larger ones. After his passing, Mozi's followers continued this tradition until about the end of the Warring States era.

Mencius, who lived somewhat after the time of Mozi, is famous for his elaboration of the teachings of the great educator Confucius.

Whereas Mozi had focused his attention on interstate conflicts, Mencius was more concerned with class conflicts. His work strongly upholds the principle and practice of identity of interests as essential to social and political health. Accordingly, Mencius repudiated the last vestiges of ancient beliefs in the divine right of kings, and articulated the moral basis of rebellion by oppressed peoples.

Both Mozi and Mencius came to be regarded by Taoists as of their number in some sense, as were Confucius and other early philosophers who wrote the *I Ching* and *The Art of War*. In the second century B.C.E., all of these schools of thought were incorporated in some way into one book, the distinguished Taoist classic known as *The Masters of Huainan*. The subject matter of this extraordinary book covers a wide range of inquiry including politics, sociology, ecology, biology, and psychology, weaving them into a unified science of life. *The Masters of Huainan* combines the teachings of the *I Ching*, the *Tao Te Ching*, and the higher teachings of *The Art of War*, as typified in a story on a way to practice the dictum of the last-mentioned classic of strategy, that "to win without fighting is best."

> When the state of Jin marched on the state of Chu, the grandees of Chu asked the king to attack, but the king said, "Jin did not attack us during the reign of our former king; now that Jin is attacking us during my reign, it must be my fault. What can be done for this disgrace?"
>
> The grandees said, "Jin did not attack us in the time of previous ministries; now that Jin is attacking us during our administration, it must be our fault."
>
> The king of Chu bowed his head and wept. Then he rose and bowed to his ministers.
>
> When the people of Jin heard about this, they said, "The king of Chu and his ministers are competing to take the blame on themselves; and how easily the king humbles himself to his subordinates. They cannot be attacked."
>
> So that night the Jin army turned around to go home.
>
> This is why the *Tao Te Ching* says, "Who can accept the disgrace of a nation is called ruler of the land."

The Masters of Huainan relates another anecdote to illustrate a corollary principle of *The Art of War*, to the effect that when contention escalates to conflict there is already loss even in victory, and this can lead to even greater loss even after it has ended:

> The Martial Lord of Wei asked one of his ministers what had caused the destruction of a certain nation-state. The minister said, "Repeated victories in repeated wars."
>
> The Martial Lord said, "A nation is fortunate to win repeated victories in repeated wars. Why would that cause its destruction?"
>
> The minister said, "Where there are repeated wars, the people are weakened; when they score repeated victories, rulers become haughty. Let haughty rulers command weakened people, and rare is the nation that will not perish as a result."

Eventually the whole range of Chinese thought on the practicalities of life was inherited by the Chan Buddhists, who subjected the understanding of every school of ideas to the most rigorous examination in order to cull the essence and sense of each one. Thus one of the most excellent presentations of the hierarchy of Chinese philosophies of war can be found in the writings of the illustrious eleventh-century Buddhist Mingjiao, who was a scholar and historian as well as a master of Chan Buddhist mysticism:

> The use of arms is for dealing with criminal acts; it comes from humanitarianism and is based on justice. It comes from humanitarianism in the sense of sympathy for those whose lives are being disrupted, and is based on justice in the sense of stopping violence.
>
> When violence is stopped justly, there is mutual realignment, not mutual disturbance. When those whose lives are disrupted are pitied for humanitarian reasons, plans are made to foster life, not to kill.
>
> Therefore the armed actions of the idealized leaders of ancient times are called corrective punishments and campaigns for justice.
>
> When social cohesion waned and the Warring States era set in, the course of military science changed: humanitarianism and justice faded out; instead military affairs came from violence and went to treachery. Strong states became unrestrained through militarism, large states grew arrogant because of their

armies, angry states used their weapons to incite disturbance, and greedy states used their armed forces to invade others.

"Military action is a perverse affair, used by the civilized only when unavoidable." Therefore sages value moral power, not military power. This is why those who understand military science should not run the world alone.

"Putting on armor is not the way to promote a country's welfare; it is for eliminating violence."

"A lost country wars with weapons; a dictatorship wars with cunning; a kingdom wars with humanitarian justice; an empire wars with virtue; a utopia wars with nondoing."

A later Chan Buddhist, also an enlightened scholar and poet, added other points of view to his predecessor's account of the classical philosophies of war. He recorded his observations in hauntingly beautiful poetry while hiding in the mountains after falling victim to an intrigue. A strong Taoist element, part of the ancient heritage of Chan Buddhism, is evident in the poet's incisive vision of history and impartial understanding of the beauty and tragedy of contending interests in the course of human life.

IMPRESSIONS ON READING HISTORY

The enlightened and the good get things done only from time to
    time
While petty bureaucrats always support one another.
Once slanderers and flatterers get their wishes
Sages and philosophers are deterred.
The Great Process makes myriad beings
Of countless different types.
Fragrant and foul are not put together
The humane and the violent apply different norms.
If you put them together
How can they get along?

LAMENT OF A SOLDIER'S WIFE

You're better off grass by the roadside
Than wife to a soldier at war.

The wedding bed not even warm
Her man's now on the northern front.
She remembers the day they parted
How the snow flew o'er the landscape
Bow and arrows heavy at his side
Ice splitting his horse's hooves
He is so far from home
How can they hope to meet?
It saddens her even to see sun and moon
That shine on both her and her man
Pining and pining she longs
When will it ever end?
Every night in labored dreams
Her spirit crosses the northern front so far.
But there is a rule in the army
To be careful all of the time
They cannot think of home and family
But work mindlessly for defense
Since ancient times men loyal to duty
All have learned to die.

THE ART OF WAR AND THE
I CHING: STRATEGY AND CHANGE

The Art of War and the *I Ching* are two perennial Chinese classics, ancient books that have been studied by civil and military strategists throughout the ages in China and neighboring Asian countries. *The Art of War* includes the cultural within the martial; the *I Ching* includes the martial within the cultural. In classical Chinese political ideology, military strategy was a subordinate branch of social strategy. Accordingly, the first line of national defense against disruption of order by external or internal forces was believed to lie in the moral strength of a united people. It was further maintained that people could be united by policies that fostered the general welfare. Since unity was distinguished from uniformity in the *I Ching*, purist ideology maintained that these policies had to be adapted to the time, place, and people they were supposed to serve.

The following studies of *The Art of War* survey both ideas and events in the philosophy and application of conflict management according to this tradition. The connection between the philosophy and organizational science of *The Art of War* and the even more ancient *I Ching* is cited in the introduction to my translation of *The Art of War*. In order to put this classic of strategy in its philosophical perspective, it is logical to begin with the teachings on contention and military action outlined in the *I Ching* itself.

To many readers both East and West, the *I Ching* may be familiar as an ancient book of omens, used for millennia as a fortune-telling handbook. It is still undoubtedly used for prognostication, but this practice has not been endorsed by leading philosophers or political scientists. Divination has been explicitly prohibited by military scientists at least as far back in history as *The Art of War* itself.

For the social scientist, the *I Ching* is a book of strategic assessments, whose design is supposed to help the individual lead a more rational and effective life. Its structure is based on a quadrangle of four fundamental sets of ideas, on which revolves a cycle of three hundred and sixty states of opportunity. The number three hundred and sixty corresponds to the days of the lunar year, which in turn is emblematic of totality and completeness. These states are grouped into sixty major configurations, represented by symbolic signs, or hexagrams, consisting of six elements each.

Every hexagram is given a name and a theme, which stands for some aspect of life and development in the midst of change. This is accompanied by observations and images of possibility and change that can take place within human relationships under such conditions, when analogous opportunities develop in the course of events. The six elements within each hexagram are also accompanied by observations and images that further analyze the theme from different points of view, according to the various relative positions in which people may find themselves under given conditions.

The two themes in the *I Ching* that are most prominently relevant to a study of *I Ching* influence in *The Art of War* would be those of the sixth and seventh hexagrams, "Contention" and "The Army." Considered in succession according to the traditional order of study used for temporal events, the observations of these two *I Ching* themes form an outline of classical thinking on the structure of conflict response.

The statement of the *I Ching* on the hexagram for "Contention" reads, "In contention there is sincerity." Cheng Yi, one of the best *I Ching* readers in history, an idealist interpreter under the influence of Taoism and Chan Buddhism, explains this idea simply by saying that "Contention arises because of need." With customary ambiguity, this remark applies to both predatory and defensive warfare.

In its overall symbolism, the hexagram for "Contention" shows internal desire and outward strength. This combination is taken to represent the greedy and aggressive possibilities in human psychology and behavior that lead to contention. Thus the "need" Cheng Yi calls the source from which contention arises may be understood to refer to the internal forces compelling an aggressor as well as the external forces necessitating defense against aggression.

In the code of ethics outlined in the *I Ching*, contention is considered justifiable when it is in resistance to oppression, or in opposition to suffering caused by greed and aggression. This principle is confirmed in all three of the major Ways of Chinese thought, in Confucianism and Taoism as well as in Buddhism. Therefore "contention that is just" also arises because of need. This is the "sincerity in contention" of which the *I Ching* speaks. Cheng Yi says, "Without sincerity and truthfulness, contention is merely intrigue and leads to misfortune."

This code is also reflected in the practical teachings of *The Art of War*. In the chapter on "Maneuvering Armies," Master Sun says, "To be violent at first and wind up fearing one's people is the epitome of ineptitude." In the chapter on "Fire Attack," he says, "A government should not mobilize an army out of anger, leaders should not provoke war out of wrath. Act when it is beneficial, desist if it is not."

The *I Ching*'s statement on "Contention" continues, "[When] obstructed, be careful to be balanced, for that will lead to good results. Finality leads to bad results." Cheng Yi says:

> People who contend match their reasoning with others in anticipation of a decision. Though they may be sincere and truthful, [if there is contention, that means] they are necessarily obstructed; something must be unresolved, for if that were not the case, the matter would already be clear and there would be no dispute.
>
> Since the matter is not yet settled, one cannot necessarily say whether it will turn out well or badly. Therefore there is great concern that an auspicious balance be achieved and maintained. If you achieve balance, that bodes well. "Finality leads to bad results" means that if you conclude affairs with unmitigated finality, that bodes ill.

On the same principle, in the chapter on "Fire Attack" *The Art of War* says, "Anger can revert to joy, wrath can revert to delight, but a nation destroyed cannot be restored to existence, and the dead cannot be restored to life. Therefore an enlightened government is careful about this, a good military leadership is alert to this."

In its technical sense in *I Ching* philosophy, a state of balance or centeredness means an attitude that is not affected by emotion. According to the traditional formula as cited in *The Book of Balance and Harmony*, a neo-Taoist classic based on the *I Ching*, "Before emotions arise is called balance; when emotions arise yet are moderate, this is called harmony." Traditional Taoist teaching understands *bal-*

ance to mean being objective and impartial. In the classical formula of "balance and harmony," this objective impartiality is always placed first, because it is held to be the practical means whereby harmony can subsequently be attained.

Because of the serious consequences of decisions made in contention, the *I Ching* adds to its statement, "It is beneficial to see a great person." This is a stock phrase, traditionally understood to mean that real wisdom and knowledge are essential and cannot be replaced by emotional opinion. Cheng Yi describes great people, or people of wisdom, as those who "can settle disputes with firm understanding that is balanced and true."

The Art of War also places great emphasis on the importance of mature guidance, which becomes increasingly critical in times of conflict and crisis: "Leadership is a matter of intelligence, trustworthiness, humaneness, courage, and sternness" ("Strategic Assessments"). According to classical philosophers, impartial wisdom is valuable to all parties in a dispute, insofar as loss already starts with contention and is maximized when contention becomes conflict. Furthermore, for those already involved in struggle, effective deployment of energies depends on guidance or leadership to concentrate them.

In both classical and modern terms, the *I Ching*'s statement that "it is beneficial to see great people" is also taken to refer to the importance of education, exposing the population to the thoughts of great minds; this too is a form of leadership, one which philosophers believed should also inform the exercise of personal leadership.

The final word of the *I Ching*'s observation on the general theme of "Contention" says, "It is not beneficial to cross great rivers." According to Cheng Yi, this means that one should take safety precautions and not become reckless in contention. According to the tradition of strategists, knowledge of conditions is the basis of caution and preparedness: in its chapter on "Planning a Siege," *The Art of War* says, "If you do not know others and do not know yourself, you will be imperiled in every single battle." In actual conflict, this naturally extends to matters of logistics: in the chapter on "Doing Battle," *The Art of War* also says, "When a country is impoverished by military operations, it is because of transporting supplies to a distant place. Transport supplies to a distant place, and the populace will be impoverished."

The remark that "it is not beneficial to cross great rivers" in contention can also be read as a restatement of the basic principle of ethical contention that distinguishes it from invasive and aggressive action. In the chapter on "Terrain," *The Art of War* says, "One advances without seeking glory, retreats without avoiding blame, only protecting people." Similarly, the Taoist classic *The Masters of Huainan* says of adventurism, "Covetous people with many desires are lulled to sleep by power and profit, seduced into longing for fame and status. They wish to rise in the world through exceptional cunning, so their vitality and spirit are daily depleted and become further and further away."

The theme of "Contention" is further analyzed in the *I Ching*'s statements on each individual element of the hexagram. The first element shows lowliness and weakness. The statement of the text says, "When you do not persist forever in an affair, there is a little criticism, but the end is auspicious." Cheng Yi explains, "This is because contention in general is not something that should be prolonged; and weak people in low positions in particular hardly ever have any luck in contention."

The Art of War also reflects this principle of minimalism in its strategy; in the chapter on "Doing Battle," it says, "When you do battle, even if you are winning, if you continue for a long time it will dull your forces and blunt your edge; if you besiege a citadel, your strength will be exhausted. If you keep your armies out in the field for a long time, your supplies will be insufficient."

Cheng Yi's observation that powerless people in positions of weakness rarely have luck in contention also illustrates one reason why peasant uprisings throughout Chinese history have generally had among their leaders people from the intellectual, religious, military, or aristocratic classes. Cheng Yi says, "It is because there is corresponding assistance from a higher level that people in this position are able to refrain from persisting in an affair," since collaboration reduces conflict.

According to interpretation based on ethical idealism, the second element of the hexagram represents ambitious strength contending against a just order. Because this is contention motivated by personal desire and not by moral necessity, it is countermanded in the *I Ching*'s statement: "Not pressing your contention, go back to escape in your hometown; then you will be free from fault." Cheng Yi explains, "If you know that what is right and just is not to be opposed, and you go back home to live modestly, minding your own business, then you will be free from fault."

The third element of the "Contention" hexagram represents people who are pliable and weak in positions of relative strength. In the construction of a hexagram, the third position is strong insofar as it represents the highest place among the lower echelons. This corresponds to positions of subordinate authority, on more local and diffuse dimensions than the authority and power represented by the upper strata of the hexagram, which represent the higher and more concentrated levels of influence and leadership.

In "Contention," weakness at the top of the lower echelons is represented as characteristic of situations in which contention arises. The *I Ching*'s statement reads, "Living on past virtues, be steadfast." What the text means by "past virtues" may be the labor of one, two, three, or more generations, generations of work forming the basis for the status of the present generation. From this point of view, to be steadfast (a stock *I Ching* term also meaning "chaste" and "true") can mean being careful not to lose what progress has been made, even over generations. In the context of the theme of this sign, to be steadfast or chaste would imply that losing or despoiling "past virtues" by contending for what is as yet unearned is something to be positively avoided.

In his interpretation, the idealist Cheng Yi gives a very specific understanding of what this line means to him in the context of one generation: "Living on past virtues," he says, "means living on what one has earned according to one's means." "Being steadfast," he continues, "means being firmly in control of oneself." Again, this line of the *I Ching* contains parallel social and strategic teachings. When *The Art of War* says, in its chapter on "Formation," that "good warriors take their stand on ground where they cannot lose," this also means that warriors are living on past accomplishments when they stand on secure ground in war.

Conversely, when *The Art of War* is reinterpreted sociologically, the meaning of this passage is identical to the understanding of the social idealist Cheng Yi—when warriors for good want to take their stand on ground where they cannot lose, they can do so only by living on what they have earned according to their means and by being in control of themselves.

This sort of parallelism of principle in different realms is characteristic of literature derived from or influenced by Taoist and Buddhist schools; and it is no doubt a factor in the perennial popularity of works such as the *I Ching* and *The Art of War* beyond their original contexts.

The *I Ching's* reading for the third element of "Contention" also says, "Danger ends up all right." Cheng Yi explains, "Though you be in danger, if you know how to be wary, you will have good luck in the end." The word for *danger,* another standard *I Ching* term, also means "strict," "intense," and "diligent," encompassing reference to both problem and solution in one symbol, in accord with the *I Ching* principle of "using unfortunate events for good purposes," such as using stressful situations to arouse the willpower to overcome obstacles. *The Art of War,* in "Nine Grounds," says, "If they are to die there, what can they not do? Warriors exert their full strength. When warriors are in great danger, then they have no fear."

The final saying of the *I Ching* statement on the third element of "Contention" is, "If you work for the king, you will not accomplish anything." Cheng Yi interprets this to mean that people like those represented by this component should not arrogate to themselves the accomplishments that take place through participation in an existing system or a public forum. In this sense they need to recognize that they are "living on the past virtues" of many other people, and therefore not contend for special prominence or distinction simply on account of having done their work.

Echoing this principle of unobtrusive action and unassuming service, in the chapter on "Formation" *The Art of War* says, "In ancient times those known as good warriors prevailed when it was easy to prevail. Therefore the victories of good warriors are not noted for cleverness or bravery." This is also characteristic of Taoist philosophy; while undramatic, the indicated approach is held forth as a way to success: the *Tao Te Ching* says, "Plan for difficulty when it is still easy, do the great when it is still small."

The Art of War continues its description of the unassuming warriors of old by saying, "Therefore their victories in battle are not flukes. Their victories are not flukes because they position themselves where they will surely win, prevailing over those who have already lost." They take advantage of the structure and momentum in situations, so they do not seem to be doing anything themselves; this is one aspect of the Taoist "nondoing that does everything."

The fourth element of the "Contention" hexagram represents people with personal power at the bottom of the upper echelons. These are people within the established power structure who are forceful and contentious, people whose strength is not in balance. The *I Ching* addresses such situations in these terms: "Not pressing your contention, you return to order and change. Remain steadfast for good fortune." In a strategic reconstruction of this principle, the chapter on "Doing Battle" in *The Art of War* says, "It is never beneficial to a nation to have a military operation continue for a long time. Therefore those who are not thoroughly aware of the disadvantages in the use of arms cannot be thoroughly aware in the advantages in the use of arms."

Again using an idealistic ethical framework of interpretation, Cheng Yi explains that the contentious person within a duly established power structure has no one to contend with justly, therefore not pressing contention is a social duty. Returning to order, according to Cheng, means overcoming the emotions that feed contentiousness, so as to change the mentality to an even-minded, objective view of true facts. When this more positive attitude is stabilized, there is normally better luck in social relations and consequent conflict resolution and avoidance.

Cheng Yi goes on to say, "Order means real truth; if you lose real truth, that is to go against order. So coming back to order is returning to truth. Ancient classics speak of the more obvious manifestations and consequences of going against order in terms of the brutalization and destruction of peoples." *The Art of War* says, "A nation destroyed cannot be restored to existence, the dead cannot be restored to life," merging utilitarian strategy and humanitarian ethics to conclude that in cases of contention "to win without fighting is best."

Cheng Yi continues: "The point is that when strength is not balanced correctly it behaves impulsively; it does not stay peacefully in place. Because it is not balanced correctly it is not steady; and it is precisely this insecurity that makes it contentious. If you do not press any contention that you should not press, and go back to find out the real truth, you will change insecurity into security, which is fortunate."

The fifth element of the "Contention" hexagram represents a strong and balanced leadership able to settle contention. The statement reads, "The contention is very auspicious." Cheng Yi interprets thusly: "Settling contention in a way that is balanced accurately is the way to results that are very auspicious and completely good." He also warns that the object of contention is not victory by any means, or at any cost: "Remember," he writes, "that there are cases where people are very lucky but the results are not entirely good."

Projecting the concept of "auspicious contention" into the domain of crisis management, in the chapter on "Planning a Siege" *The Art of War* says, "Those who win every battle are not really skillful—those who render others' armies helpless without fighting are the best of all." In terms that can be seen as ethical, yet even when purely utilitarian still translate into humanitarian practicalities on the battlefield, *The Art of War* also says, "Act when it is beneficial, desist if it is not," and "do not fight when there is no danger" ("Fire Attack").

The sixth and topmost element of the "Contention" hexagram represents aggressive people in high positions, "at the peak of power and also at the end of contention," Cheng Yi says, "characteristic of those who bring contention to its ultimate conclusion." Here this means people who adamantly pursue contention to its final limit; Cheng Yi says, "When they indulge in their strength, and when they get desperate, people resort to contention, thus causing themselves trouble and even destroying themselves, a logical conclusion."

Liu Ji, the scholar-warrior whose recitals of history and military science are presented in Part Two of this book, applies this principle to the monumental Sui dynasty. The Sui dynasty briefly united China in the late sixth century, after hundreds of years of civil and colonial warfare. Speaking of the second emperor, who inherited the empire his father had labored to consolidate, Liu Ji said, "It is not that his country was not large, nor that his people were not many. But he made a hobby of martial arts, and he liked to fight; so he practiced with his weapons every day, and went on endless expeditions to attack neighboring peoples. Then things took a turn, and his army was beaten while his cabinet opposed him. Is he not ridiculous to people of later generations? Had human rulers not better be careful?"

Aggressive and contentious people in high positions, used to getting their way, do not suffer only when they happen to fail; even in success they are in danger, for this success itself becomes an object of contention that continues to animate the aggressive tendencies of all people on this level. The *I Ching*'s statement on this point says,

"Honor given you will be taken away from you three times before the day is out."

According to Cheng Yi, in a military, governmental, or other institutional context, "even if people contend successfully to the end, until they are rewarded for service to the regime, this reward is still an object of contention—how can it be kept secure?" Liu Ji gives an excellent version of the traditional formulation of the answer among the rules of war related in his history stories: "When you have won, be as if you had not."

When contention is taken to its limit, it becomes conflict, and conflict taken to extremes leads to armament and war. Therefore the hexagram following "Contention" in the conventional order of the *I Ching* is the hexagram for "The Army." The word used for this sign has a whole family of meanings, including "a military force," "a military expedition," and "a military leader." From the last sense is derived another common usage of the same Chinese character, the meaning of "teacher, director, or master of an art or science."

The idea of the teacher fits in with the needs of military command or general crisis management; and the image of war is also used in both Taoism and Buddhism as a general metaphor for contending with any sort of difficulty, hardship, or problem, whether or not it involves interpersonal conflict. This concept also passed into the vocabulary of folklore and proverb.

The statement on the hexagram of "The Army" says, "For the army to be right, mature people are good. Then there is no fault." The implication is that there is a right way to use arms, and this leads back to the basic principle of ethical warfare according to the Taoist, Confucian, and Buddhist ways of thought: that war should be undertaken only as a last resort, and only in a just cause. This generally means defensive war, but it can also mean punitive war to stop the strong from bullying the weak. In either case, leadership has both a moral and a technical basis. The essays of Zhuge Liang translated in Part One of this book are particularly concerned with the characteristics and capacities of "mature people" capable of maintaining justice and order in military matters.

According to the classical traditions of China, war should be minimized even when it is justified. In ethical terms, this principle could be extended to mean war that is not minimized is for that very reason not just; in the strategic science of *The Art of War*, prolonging or expanding hostilities unnecessarily is regarded as one of the major causes of self-destruction, which is considered neither ethical nor practical. This means in principle that the right way to carry out war, in the event of its necessity, is normally the right way from both humanitarian and utilitarian points of view.

History demonstrates clearly enough that in the absence of education from model moral leadership, war can easily turn into rapine and bloodlust, an outlet of frustration and oppression. On the other hand, without education from model technical leadership, armed forces can become clumsy and ineffective even if they are large in numbers. Therefore the *I Ching* says, "mature people are good," and adds, "then there is no fault." This parallel moral and technical leadership is constantly emphasized by Zhuge Liang and other noted strategists.

Cheng Yi explains this statement on "The Army" in these terms: "The course pursued by the army should be correct: if you raise an army and mobilize troops in a cause that is not right and only creates trouble, the people do not really obey, they are merely coerced. Therefore the guiding principle of the army should be uprightness."

Furthermore, not only does solidarity require that the cause be just in the eyes of those expected to fight for it, but competent leadership is also essential to direct and focus the process of struggle. Cheng Yi says, "Even if the army acts in the right way, the leaders must be mature to obtain good results. After all, there are those who are lucky but also faulty, and there are those who are faultless but still not lucky. To be lucky and also faultless is as mature as people can get. Mature people are stern and worthy of respect. If those who are to lead a group are not respected, trusted, and obeyed by the group, how can they get the people to follow willingly?"

Master Sun the Martialist makes the same point in the opening chapter of *The Art of War:* "The Way means inducing the people to have the same aim as the leadership, so that they will share death and share life, without fear of danger" ("Strategic Assessments"). Zhuge Liang's essays on generalship in the present volume stress the theme of harmonization among the different echelons of an organization as well as society in general. Liu Ji's war stories, in turn, include several cases of deliberate use of sternness and kindness in specific proportion to unify the minds of a military force.

The first element of the hexagram for "The Army" represents the beginning of mobilization. The statement of the original text says, "The army is to go forth in an orderly manner. Otherwise, doing well turns out badly." This theme of order permeates *The Art of War*, which views the functions and malfunctions of order from various angles. The great statesman and warrior Zhuge Liang is particularly famous for his insistence upon order in times of crisis. As a commander, he is said to have been strict yet impartial, with the result that his people regarded him with simultaneous awe and admiration, so that he was both honored and obeyed.

Two traditional Chinese concepts of the role or mode of human leadership in maintaining order were explained by a distinguished Chan Buddhist in these terms: "There are those who move people by enlightened virtue and those who make people obedient by the power of authority. It is like the phoenix in flight, which all the animals admire, or tigers and wolves stalking, which all the animals fear." In the martial tradition, authority means not only rank, but also personal power, awesome, charismatic, or both. Classical Chinese thought refers to this as a combination of the cultural and the martial, and this is considered standard for civilization after the prehistoric fall of humanity from pristine simplicity.

Even in the pacifist schools of Buddhism and Taoism, the martial image is retained for various practices, including critical analysis, intuitive penetration, and psychological purification, as well as hygienic and therapeutic exercises. It is well known, furthermore, that certain exercise movements are also used to train strength for combat, and other movements can be speeded up to produce martial effects.

One famous example of this is that of the Shaolin Boxers, a school recognized by Taoists but associated by them with Chan Buddhism. The appearance of fighting monks in China was in the defense of the country against invaders; followers of offshoots of these practices also kept theories of classical chivalry in their own codes, thus scattering the original principles of the *I Ching* throughout Chinese chivalric lore in the middle ages.

Cheng Yi also takes a characteristically moral view of the *I Ching*'s statement, "The army is to go forth in an orderly manner; otherwise doing well turns out badly." To the idealist Cheng, this reaffirms the importance of ethical human values in conflict. He says, "An 'orderly manner' means a combination of justice and reason. This means that the mission of the army is to stop disorder and get rid of violence. If the army acts unjustly, then even if it does well the affair turns out badly. In this sense, 'doing well' means winning victories; 'turning out badly' means killing people unjustly."

The second element of "The Army" hexagram represents the military leadership. It is placed in a subordinate position with respect to the civil leadership, representing the principle that the military exists to serve the nation and people, not the other way around. Cheng Yi says, "That means the leader of the army should be the leader only in the army." Zhuge Liang, who was both a civil and military director, also said, "Culture takes precedence over the martial."

The *I Ching*'s statement on the second element reads, "In the army, balanced, one is fortunate and blameless," meaning, "the leadership of a militia is lucky and blameless if it is balanced." Cheng Yi says, "Those who assume sole charge (of a militia) yet who manage to steer a balanced middle course are fortunate because of this, and are blameless."

In respect to the nature of military authority in the total context of society as symbolized by this hexagram, Cheng Yi defines one meaning of *balance* in these terms: "The point seems to be that if one presumes upon authority one strays from the right path of subordination; yet if one does not exercise authority there is no way to accomplish anything. Therefore it is best to find a balanced middle way." In abstract terms, a general stands for someone who has been entrusted with the responsibility for a task and, while exercising leadership and organizational skills to carry it through, does so with the awareness that field command, while completely in the hands of the general, is based on delegated authority. Although the qualities of leadership are essential in the leader of a delegation, it is the purpose and not the person that is of paramount importance in the whole event.

The statement of the *I Ching* on this element also says, "The king thrice bestows a mandate." This restates the constitutional imperative of *I Ching* culture, that the authorization for militia and military action comes from civil government. It is also taken to mean that if a militia or other special task force does its job well, then it is deemed trustworthy and therefore gives peace of mind to the populace. The practice of employing standing armies for public works projects originally grew out of this principle.

When this practice was employed in China, it brought armies

closer to the general populace, often providing unique opportunities for contact between people from radically different areas of China, all the while giving the military—and by extension the government—a chance to establish public rapport by model behavior. Zhuge Liang was one of those known for his genius at winning popular support and was highly acclaimed as a civil administrator. His method of success seems to have been based to a large extent on his consistent practical application of Taoist and Confucian ethical principles.

This is something that distinguishes Zhuge Liang from many other intellectuals and administrators in Chinese history. Most such people did at least read or hear about these principles, but many used them only when it suited their immediate personal ambitions to do so. The epic *Tales of the Three Kingdoms*, a neoclassical historical novel strongly flavored with Taoist psychology, immortalizes the spiritual brilliance of Zhuge Liang as it satirizes and ridicules the warmongers who had a classical principle handy to rationalize every act of greed, treachery, and violence.

Cheng Yi explains the *I Ching*'s statement on bestowing mandates in these terms: "If it is employed in the best possible way, the army can accomplish works and make the world peaceful. It is for this reason that rulers entrust generals with important mandates time and again." In *The Art of War*, Master Sun also says, "Thus one advances without seeking glory, retreats without avoiding blame, only protecting people, to the benefit of the government as well, thus rendering valuable service to the nation" ("Terrain"). Zhuge Liang says, "A good general does not rely or presume on strength or power. He is not pleased by favor and does not fear vilification. He does not crave whatever material goods he sees, and he does not rape whatever women he can. His only intention is to pursue the best interests of the country" ("Loyalty in Generals").

In civilian terms, any delegated authority puts people in a similar position to that of the army in *I Ching* sociology; from the point of view of *I Ching* ethics, it is natural reason to carry out the duties of this delegated authority in an orderly and therefore efficient manner, without arrogating arbitrary authority to oneself. Cheng Yi says, "Even though it is in charge of itself, whatever the power of the army can bring about is all due to what is given to it by the leadership, and any accomplishment is all in the line of duty." The *I Ching* and derivative works on planning all stress the danger of the military leaving its subservient position and usurping the position of the civil authority. Any specialization can threaten society in the same way when it becomes self-serving instead of subservient to the whole body of society.

The Biblical saying that "the sabbath was made for man, and not man for the sabbath" is similar in this sense: reason says that institutions are created to provide service for humanity, not to advance the personal interests of those mandated to serve. In the same vein, Zhuge Liang writes, "When offices are chosen for persons, there is disorder; when persons are chosen for offices, there is order."

The proliferation of titles, offices, and emoluments to satisfy members of powerful and well-connected clans and interest groups was always one of the banes of Chinese government and religion, increasing the burdens on the taxpayers while hastening sclerosis in practical administration. Taoist philosophers said that this can happen in any domain of organized activity, of which national government is a highly visible and consequential example. Zhuge Liang emphatically stressed the idea that government should be streamlined, in accord with Taoist political theory, much of which is particularly designed for use in times of conflict and duress.

The third element of the hexagram for "The Army" symbolizes the secondary leaders within the army. The reading emphasizes the special importance of mutual understanding and order in the relationships on this level, as well as in relationships between this level of the chain of command and the central military leadership. This is also on the analogy of the subordination of the whole martial entity to the whole cultural entity.

The *I Ching*'s statement on the third element says, "It bodes ill for the army to have many bosses." Discord and competition in the lower ranks of command naturally weaken the whole body, especially by damaging and distorting the connection between the leadership and the common soldiery. Cheng Yi interprets, "The responsibility for a military expedition should be unified; one in a position of authority should concentrate on this." This also applies, like other *I Ching* metaphors, to other domains; in this case to the negative effects of extreme division and disunity on analogous levels of organization, from the organization of an individual life to the organization of a collective enterprise.

The Art of War also makes a point of the vulnerability inherent in disunity and directs its strategy at this weakness: in the chapter "Nine Grounds," Master Sun the Martialist says, "Those who are called the good militarists of old could make opponents lose contact between front and back lines, lose reliability between large and small groups, lose mutual concern for the welfare of the different social classes among them, lose mutual accommodation between the rulers and the ruled, lose enlistments among the soldiers, lose coherence within the armies." This is the familiar rule of "divide and conquer," amplifying the *I Ching* rule and carrying it into each dimension of an organization.

The fourth element of the hexagram for "The Army" represents being in a weak position and at a disadvantage in times of conflict. The statement says, "The army camps; no blame," meaning that it is normal to hold back or withdraw from an impossible position. Identical strategic principles are emphasized several times in *The Art of War*, as in the chapter on "Armed Struggle," which says, "Avoiding confrontation with orderly ranks and not attacking great formations is mastering adaptation." In the chapter on "Nine Grounds," it also says that good militarists of yore "went into action when it was advantageous, stopped when it was not."

The fifth element represents the civil leadership, whose authority is the source of the military's mandate. Since this serves as a general representation of delegation of authority for special purposes, the civil leadership is behind the scenes in "The Army." The *I Ching*'s statement, which simply summarizes the logic and ethic of warfare, begins, "When there are vermin in the fields, it is advantageous to denounce them; then there will be no fault." Cheng Yi understands this to mean eradicating active menaces to society, distinguishing this from acts of tyrannical aggression and paranoia: "The army should be mustered only when aggressors are hurting the people. . . . If it is a case like when vermin get into the fields and damage the crops, and it is justly appropriate to hunt them down, then hunt them down; act in this way and there will be no fault. Act at whim, thus harming the world, and the fault is great indeed. To 'denounce' means to make clear what has been done wrong, in order to stop it. Some martial tyrants have scoured the very mountains and forests for those whom they considered 'vermin,' but it was not that there were vermin in their own fields."

The *I Ching*'s statement concludes, "A mature person leads the army; there will be bad luck if there are many immature bosses, even if they are dedicated." This is a recapitulation of the general doctrine of the *I Ching* on the importance of wisdom in leadership and unity in organization. Cheng Yi says, "The way to mandate a general to direct an army calls for having a mature person lead the force. . . . If a group of immature people boss the army, then even if what they do is right, it will turn out badly."

The need for certain qualities in military leadership and unity in organization is among the first premises of *The Art of War,* and is a central theme of Zhuge Liang's writings on generalship. In his essay "Capacities of Commanders," Zhuge describes the greatest of military leaders in grandiose terms thoroughly consistent with *I Ching* idealism: "One whose humanitarian care extends to all under his command, whose trustworthiness and justice win the allegiance of neighboring nations, who understands the signs of the sky above, the patterns of the earth below, and the affairs of humanity in between, and who regards all people as his family, is a world-class leader, one who cannot be opposed."

The sixth and final element of the hexagram for "The Army" represents the end of the mission of the armed forces and the reintegration of warriors into civilian society. This can stand symbolically for the absorption of the results of any specialization into the whole body of society. In the context of civil or international warfare, here the *I Ching* reaffirms both the parallel and the contrast between martial and civil matters, as defined throughout its treatment of this theme.

Here, at the end of "The Army," the *I Ching* says, "The great leader has a command to start nations and receive social standing." Originally cast in a feudal setting, this statement illustrates a principle more generally understood here and now in bureaucratic or corporate contexts, for bureaucracies and conglomerates are the heirs of feudalism, though they rendered and consumed their parents some time ago.

Because many of the qualities needed for crisis management were also qualities needed for ordinary management, and because a complete education in China was believed to encompass both cultural and martial arts, a person might be both a military and a civilian leader, simultaneously or at different times. Zhuge Liange and Liu Ji are outstanding examples of individuals who were called upon to fulfill both military and civilian duties.

The *I Ching* implies that warriors rejoin civilization when war is over, thus avoiding the pitfalls of a socially isolated warrior caste and also contributing the knowledge, character, and experience gained in war to the society for which the war was waged. According to the *I Ching*'s statement, the ideal government contributes to this reintegration by entitling warriors according to their achievements. Cheng Yi says, "The great leader rewards the successful with entitlement, making them overseers of groups, and gives them social distinction for their capability." This is an example of the more general principle of meritocracy, a cornerstone of *I Ching* ideology written into the fundamentals of Confucian philosophy.

The underlying implication in the case of "The Army" and its end is the corollary doctrine, embraced by strategists like Zhuge Liang, that military personnel, and especially military leaders, should have a good general education as well as special technical and military training. In Chinese this is called the combination of *wen* and *wu*. *Wen*, or culture, deals with the cultivation of constructive social skills and values. *Wu*, or the martial, deals with both practical and theoretical sciences of crisis management. According to Chinese military science in the *I Ching*–Taoist tradition as represented by *The Art of War* and certain later adepts, balance in *wen* and *wu* is believed to be better for warriors even on campaigns and in combat, as well as when they are eventually reinstated into civilian society.

Therefore the *I Ching*'s statement concludes with the warning, "Petty people are not to be employed." In this context, the statement means that when it comes to integrating warriors into society, achievement in war should not be viewed in isolation as the only criterion of advancement, in disregard of the moral integrity and total person of the individual concerned. Cheng Yi says, "As for petty people, even if they have achieved, they are not to be employed. There is more than one way to raise an army, go on an expedition, and achieve success; those who do so are not necessarily good people."

Zhuge Liang is a model example of a leader in both realms, a beloved civil administrator as well as a distinguished strategist and general. His writings show a particularly deep savor of serious *I Ching* learning, combining Confucian and Taoist thought into an ethical yet pragmatic program for acute crisis management. Because of his fidelity to the classic traditions of humanitarian warrior-statesmen, the original roots and broad outlines of Zhuge Liang's thought can be traced in the fecund abstractions of the *I Ching* itself. This is also true of the work of Liu Ji, who goes even further than Zhuge Liang into the derivative traditions, especially the practical strategy and warrior ethos of *The Art of War.*

Notes on Sources

Taoist Works Cited

The Yin Convergence Classic (Yinfujing). Included in *Vitality, Energy, Spirit: A Taoist Sourcebook*, translated and edited by Thomas Cleary, from Shambhala Publications.
Tao Te Ching
The Masters of Huainan (Huainanzi). A condensed translation of this text appears in *The Book of Leadership and Strategy: Lessons of the Chinese Masters* translated by Thomas Cleary, from Shambhala Publications.
The Book of Balance and Harmony (Zhonghoji), translated by Thomas Cleary, from North Point Press.

I Ching Studies

Material from and about the *I Ching* is excerpted from two translations by Thomas Cleary: *I Ching: The Tao of Organization* and *I Ching Mandalas* (both from Shambhala Publications).

Historical Material

For background on Liu Ji I used the Ming dynastic history and other standard reference works. For background on the Buddhist rebellions in which the Ming dynasty had its early roots, I am indebted to the extensive historical introduction of J. C. Cleary's *Zibo: China's Last Great Zen Master*. For corroboration of Liu Ji's recitals and other historical documentation, I am also indebted to Li Zhi's *Hidden Documents (Zang shu)* and *Hidden Documents Continued (Xu zang shu)*. The stories with Liu Ji's introductions that are translated in the present volume are drawn from *Extraordinary Strategies in a Hundred Battles (Baizhan qilue)*, evidently the most popular of Liu's many literary works. The excerpt from his work *The Cultured One* is from Liu's *Youlizi*. Liu's poems are translated from *Chengyibo wenshu*. For background on Zhuge Liang I used *Records of the Three Kingdoms (Sanguo zhi)*, a court history of that era; *Tales of the Three Kingdoms (Sanguo yanyi)*, a much later historical novel about the civil wars of the time, written from a very different point of view than the court history on which it is based; and *Works by and about the Loyal Lord at Arms (Zhongwuhou ji)*, a study of Zhuge Liang found in the Taoist canon. The translations from Zhuge's writings contained in this volume are taken from collections of his essays, letters, and poetry included verbatim in the aforementioned study of his life and work in the Taoist canon.

Besides Sun Tzu's *The Art of War*, Liu Ji also quotes the following sources for his rules of battle:

"Book of the Latter Han Dynasty" *(Houhan shu)*
"Dialogues of Li, Lord of Wei" *(Li Weigong wenda)*
"Sima's Rules" or "Sima's Art of War" *(Sima bingfa)*
"Six Secrets" *(Liutao)*
"Three Strategies" *(Sanlue)*
"Zuo Family Tradition on the Spring and Autumn Annals" *(Zuo-chuan)*

Part One

The Way of the General

Essays on Leadership and Crisis Management

Zhuge Liang

Translator's Introduction

Zhuge Liang, commonly known by his style, Kongming, was born around the year 180, the son of a provincial official in the latter days of the Han dynasty. At that time, the dynasty was thoroughly decrepit, nearly four hundred years old and on the verge of collapse. For most of his adult life, Zhuge was to play a major role in the power struggles and civil wars that followed the demise of the ancient Han.

Orphaned at an early age, he and his younger brother were taken in by an uncle, a local governor in southern China. When this uncle was replaced with another officer, he and his charges went to join an old family friend, a member of the powerful Liu clan who was currently a governor in central China. The imperial house of Han was a branch of the greater Liu clan, which as a whole retained considerable wealth, prestige, and influence even after the passing of the Han dynasty itself.

Zhuge Liang's uncle died during his sojourn in central China. Then in his twenties, Zhuge stayed there, supporting himself by farming. According to *Records of the Three Kingdoms*, at this early age Zhuge was aware of his own genius, but few took him seriously; he was, after all, an orphan and subsistence farmer. His fortunes took a turn, however, when the great warrior Liu Bei, founder of the kingdom of Shu in western China, garrisoned in the area where Zhuge Liang was living.

Zhuge was recommended to the warrior chief by a member of the influential Xu clan, which produced many outstanding Taoists of the early churches. According to *Records of the Three Kingdoms*, Zhuge's friend said to Liu Bei, "Zhuge Kongming is a dragon in repose—would you want to meet him?"

Liu Bei said, "You come with him."

The friend said, "It is possible to go see this man, but you cannot make him come to you. You, General, should go out of your way to look in on him."

The record states that Liu Bei finally went to see Zhuge Liang, adding that he had to go no fewer than three times before the young genius agreed to meet the warrior chieftain. When at length they were together, the record continues, Liu Bei dismissed everyone else so that he could be alone with Zhuge Liang. Then he said, "The house of Han is collapsing; treacherous officials are usurping authority; the emperor is blinded by the dust." The warlord went on to solicit Zhuge's advice, and Zhuge became one of his top strategists. The story of this famous meeting is related in the first of Liu Ji's war tales.

The intrigues of the era of the Three Kingdoms are too complex to detail here; indeed, they fill the one hundred chapters of the massive neoclassic historical novel *Tales of the Three Kingdoms*. Suffice it to say here that the time was one of constant turmoil, tension, and strife. In the midst of unending warfare among the three kingdoms, Zhuge Liang was appointed to positions of highest responsibility in both civil and military leadership.

When Liu Bei died, his heir was still young, so Zhuge Liang also served as the de facto regent for the new king as well as a top general and strategist. He never fell in battle, but he did die on a campaign, garrisoned in the field. Carrying burdens enough to kill two men, Zhuge Liang succumbed to illness at the age of fifty-four. Immortalized in literature for his intelligence and humanity, he was greatly admired as a warrior and administrator. His last will and testament, addressed to the young ruler of Shu, illustrates the thought and character of this remarkable individual:

> It seems to me that I am a simpleton by nature. Having run into the troubles of the times, I mobilized an army on an expedition north. Before being able to achieve complete success, I unexpectedly became mortally ill, and now I am on the brink of death.
>
> I humbly pray that the ruler will purify his heart, minimize his desires, restrain himself and love the common people, convey respect to the former ruler, spread humaneness through the land, promote conscientious individualists in order to get wise and good people into positions of responsibility, and throw out traitors and calumniators in order to make the manners of the people more substantial.

I have eight hundred mulberry trees and eight acres of thin fields, so my children and grandchildren are self-sufficient in food and clothing. I am abroad, without any particular accoutrements; I wear government-issue clothing and eat government-issue food, and do not have any other source of income for my personal use. When I die, do not let there be any extra cotton on the corpse, or any special burial objects, for which I would be indebted to the nation.

As this testament shows, there is a strong undercurrent of Taoist thought in Zhuge Liang's attitudes toward life and work. This undercurrent is even more evident in his letters of advice to his nephew and his son. To his nephew he wrote:

Aspirations should remain lofty and far-sighted. Look to the precedents of the wise. Detach from emotions and desires; get rid of any fixations. Elevate subtle feelings to presence of mind and sympathetic sense. Be patient in tight situations as well as easy ones; eliminate all pettiness.

Seek knowledge by questioning widely; set aside aversion and reluctance. What loss is there in dignity, what worry is there of failure?

If your will is not strong, if your thought does not oppose injustice, you will fritter away your life stuck in the commonplace, silently submitting to the bonds of emotion, forever cowering before mediocrities, never escaping the downward flow.

To his son, he gave this advice:

The practice of a cultivated man is to refine himself by quietude and develop virtue by frugality. Without detachment, there is no way to clarify the will; without serenity, there is no way to get far.

Study requires calm, talent requires study. Without study there is no way to expand talent; without calm there is no way to accomplish study.

If you are lazy, you cannot do thorough research; if you are impulsive, you cannot govern your nature.

The years run off with the hours, aspirations flee with the years. Eventually one ages and collapses. What good will it do to lament over poverty?

Finally, Zhuge's own motto illustrates a central quality for which he is especially honored, the quality of sincerity. Zhuge's honesty and integrity in public and private life are legendary, and his writings on social and political organization show that he considered sincerity fundamental to success in these domains. He formulated the rule of his life in this motto:

> Opportunistic relationships can hardly be kept constant. The acquaintance of honorable people, even at a distance, does not add flowers in times of warmth and does not change its leaves in times of cold: it continues unfading through the four seasons, becomes increasingly stable as it passes through ease and danger.

The following essays on leadership and organization are taken from a collection of works by and about Zhuge Liang, *Records of the Loyal Lord of Warriors*, as preserved in the Taoist canon.

THE WAY OF THE GENERAL

The Authority of the Military Leadership

Military authority, directing the armed forces, is a matter of the authoritative power of the leading general.

If the general can hold the authority of the military and operate its power, he oversees his subordinates like a fierce tiger with wings, flying over the four seas, going into action whenever there is an encounter.

If the general loses his authority and cannot control the power, he is like a dragon cast into a lake; he may seek the freedom of the high seas, but how can he get there?

Chasing Evils

There are five types of harm in decadence among national armed forces.

First is the formation of factions that band together for character assassination, criticizing and vilifying the wise and the good.

Second is luxury in uniforms.

Third is wild tales and confabulations about the supernatural.

Fourth is judgment based on private views, mobilizing groups for personal reasons.

Fifth is making secret alliances with enemies, watching for where the advantage may lie.

All people like this are treacherous and immoral. You should distance yourself from them and not associate with them.

Knowing People

Nothing is harder to see into than people's natures. Though good and bad are different, their conditions and appearances are not always uniform. There are some people who are nice enough but steal. Some people are outwardly respectful while inwardly making fools of everyone. Some people are brave on the outside yet cowardly on the inside. Some people do their best but are not loyal.

Hard though it be to know people, there are ways.

First is to question them concerning right and wrong, to observe their ideas.

Second is to exhaust all their arguments, to see how they change.

Third is to consult with them about strategy, to see how perceptive they are.

Fourth is to announce that there is trouble, to see how brave they are.

Fifth is to get them drunk, to observe their nature.

Sixth is to present them with the prospect of gain, to see how modest they are.

Seventh is to give them a task to do within a specific time, to see how trustworthy they are.

Types of Generals

There are nine types of generals.

Those who guide with virtue, who treat all equally with courtesy, who know when the troops are cold and hungry, and who notice when they are weary and pained, are called humanistic generals.

Those who do not try to avoid any task, who are not influenced by profit, who would die with honor before living in disgrace, are called dutiful generals.

Those who are not arrogant because of their high status, who do not make much of their victories, who are wise but can humble themselves, who are strong but can be tolerant, are called courteous generals.

Those whose extraordinary shifts are unfathomable, whose movements and responses are multifaceted, who turn disaster into fortune and seize victory from the jaws of danger, are called clever generals.

Those who give rich rewards for going ahead and have strict penalties for retreating, whose rewards are given right away and whose penalties are the same for all ranks, even the highest, are called trustworthy generals.

Those who go on foot or on a war-horse, with the mettle to take on a hundred men, who are skilled in the use of close-range weapons, swords, and spears, are called infantry generals.

Those who face the dizzying heights and cross the dangerous defiles, who can shoot at a gallop as if in flight, who are in the vanguard when advancing and in the rear guard when withdrawing, are called cavalry generals.

Those whose mettle makes the armies tremble and whose determination makes light of powerful enemies, who are hesitant to engage in petty fights while courageous in the midst of major battles, are called fierce generals.

Those who consider themselves lacking when they see the wise, who go along with good advice like following a current, who are magnanimous yet able to be firm, who are uncomplicated yet have many strategies, are called great generals.

Capacities of Commanders

The capacities of commanders are not the same; some are greater, some are lesser.

One who spies out treachery and disaster, who wins the allegiance of others, is the leader of ten men.

One who rises early in the morning and retires late at night, and whose words are discreet yet perceptive, is the leader of a hundred men.

One who is direct yet circumspect, who is brave and can fight, is the leader of a thousand men.

One of martial bearing and fierceness of heart, who knows the hardships of others and spares people from hunger and cold, is the leader of ten thousand men.

One who associates with the wise and promotes the able, who is careful of how he spends each day, who is sincere, trustworthy, and magnanimous, and who is guarded in times of order as well as times of disturbance, is the leader of a hundred thousand men.

One whose humanitarian care extends to all under his command, whose trustworthiness and justice win the allegiance of neighboring nations, who understands the signs of the sky above, the patterns of the earth below, and the affairs of humanity in between, and who regards all people as his family, is a world-class leader, one who cannot be opposed.

Decadence in Generals

There are eight kinds of decadence in generalship.

First is to be insatiably greedy.
Second is to be jealous and envious of the wise and able.
Third is to believe slanderers and make friends with the treacherous.
Fourth is to assess others without assessing oneself.
Fifth is to be hesitant and indecisive.
Sixth is to be heavily addicted to wine and sex.
Seventh is to be a malicious liar with a cowardly heart.
Eighth is to talk wildly, without courtesy.

Loyalty in Generals

"Weapons are instruments of ill omen"; generalship is a dangerous job. Therefore if one is inflexible there will be breakdowns, and when the job is important there will be danger.

This is why a good general does not rely or presume on strength or power. He is not pleased by favor and does not fear vilification. He does not crave whatever material goods he sees, and he does not rape whatever women he can. His only intention is to pursue the best interests of the country.

Skills of Generals

There are five skills and four desires involved in generalship.

The five skills are: skill in knowing the disposition and power of enemies, skill in knowing the ways to advance and withdraw, skill in knowing how empty or how full countries are, skill in knowing nature's timing and human affairs, and skill in knowing the features of terrain.

The four desires are: desire for the extraordinary and unexpected in strategy, desire for thoroughness in security, desire for calm among the masses, and desire for unity of hearts and minds.

Arrogance in Generals

Generals should not be arrogant, for if they are arrogant they will become discourteous, and if they are discourteous people will become alienated from them. When people are alienated, they become rebellious.

Generals should not be stingy, for if they are stingy they will not reward the trustworthy, and if they do not reward the trustworthy, the soldiers will not be dedicated. If the soldiers are not dedicated, the armed forces are ineffective, and if the armed forces are ineffective, the nation is empty. When a nation is empty, its opponents are full.

Confucius said, "People may have the finest talents, but if they are arrogant and stingy, their other qualities are not worthy of consideration."

Military Preparedness

Military preparedness is the greatest task of the nation. A small mistake can make a huge difference. When the force of momentum by which soldiers are killed and generals are captured can move with sudden rapidity, should we not be wary?

Therefore when a nation is in trouble, the ruler and ministers urgently work on strategy, selecting the wise and assessing the able to delegate responsibilities to them.

If you count on safety and do not think of danger, if you do not know enough to be wary when enemies arrive, this is called a sparrow nesting on a tent, a fish swimming in a cauldron—they won't last the day.

Traditions say, "Without preparation, military operations are unfeasible."

"Preparedness against the unexpected is a way of good government."

"Even bees have venom—how much the more do nations. If you are unprepared, even if there are many of you, mere numbers cannot be counted on."

A classic document says, "Only when we do our tasks are we prepared; when we are prepared, there is no trouble."

Therefore the action of the military forces must have preparation.

Training

Soldiers without training cannot stand up to one out of a hundred
opponents, yet they are sent out against a hundred each. This is why
Confucius said, "To send people to war without teaching them is
called abandoning them." It is also said, "Teach the people for seven
years, and they too can go to war."

Therefore soldiers must be taught without fail. First train them in
conduct and duty, teach them to be loyal and trustworthy, instruct
them in rules and penalties, awe them with rewards and punishments. When people know enough to follow along, then train them
in maneuvers.

One person can teach ten, ten people can teach a hundred, a hundred people can teach a thousand, a thousand can teach ten thousand,
thus developing the armed forces. Train like this, and opponents will
surely lose.

Corruption in the Armed Forces

In military operations it may happen that scouts are not careful of
their signal fires; or there may be mistakes in calculation and consequent delays, infractions of rules, failure to respond to the time and
situation, disorder in the ranks, callous and unreasonable demands
made by superiors on their subordinates, pursuit of self-interest, lack
of concern for the hungry and cold, tall tales and fortune telling, rab-
ble rousing, confusing the officers, refusal of the mettlesome to submit to authority, contempt of superiors, or using supplies for personal
enjoyment. These things corrupt the armed forces. When they are
present, there is certain to be defeat.

Loyal Hearts

Those who would be military leaders must have loyal hearts, eyes
and ears, claws and fangs. Without people loyal to them, they are like
someone walking at night, not knowing where to step. Without eyes

and ears, they are as though in the dark, not knowing how to proceed. Without claws and fangs, they are like hungry men eating poisoned food, inevitably to die.

Therefore good generals always have intelligent and learned associates for their advisors, thoughtful and careful associates for their eyes and ears, brave and formidable associates for their claws and fangs.

Careful Watching

The loss of an army is always caused by underestimating an opponent and thus bringing on disaster. Therefore an army goes out in an orderly manner. If order is lost, that bodes ill.

There are fifteen avenues of order:

1. Thoughtfulness, using secret agents for intelligence
2. Organization, gathering news and watching carefully
3. Courage, not being disturbed by the number of the enemy
4. Modesty, thinking of justice and duty when seeing the opportunity for gain
5. Impartiality, being egalitarian in matters of rewards and punishments
6. Forbearance, being able to bear humiliation
7. Magnanimity, being able to accept the masses
8. Trustworthiness, so that there can be serious cooperation
9. Respect, honoring the wise and able
10. Clarity of mind, not listening to slander
11. Reason, not forgetting past experience
12. Human kindness, taking care of the soldiers
13. Loyalty, devoting oneself to the nation
14. Moderation, knowing to stop when you have enough of anything
15. Planning, assessing yourself first, and then assessing others

Formation of Opportunity

To overcome the intelligent by folly is contrary to the natural order of things; to overcome the foolish by intelligence is in accord with the natural order. To overcome the intelligent by intelligence, however, is a matter of opportunity.

There are three avenues of opportunity: events, trends, and conditions. When opportunities occur through events but you are unable to respond, you are not smart. When opportunities become active through a trend and yet you cannot make plans, you are not wise. When opportunities emerge through conditions but you cannot act on them, you are not bold.

Those skilled in generalship always achieve their victories by taking advantage of opportunities.

Good Generalship

Good generals of ancient times had some overall principles:

1. Show people when to proceed and when to withdraw, and people will learn regulation.
2. Array them on the lines rightly and justly, and people will be orderly.
3. Show respect for them by your judgments, and people will be enthusiastic.
4. Motivate them with rewards and penalties, and people will be trusting.

Regulation, order, enthusiasm, and trust are the overall principles of generals, by which they are able to ensure victory in battle.

The mediocre are not like this: they cannot stop their troops when they retreat, they cannot control their troops when they advance, they mix up good and bad, the soldiers are not given instruction and encouragement, rewards and punishments are not fair. Because people are not trusting, the wise and the good withdraw, while flatterers are promoted. Such an army will therefore inevitably be defeated in war.

Discerning Bases

If you attack evils based on social trends, no one can rival you in dignity. If you settle victory based on the power of the people, no one can rival you in achievement.

If you can accurately discern these bases of action, and add dignity and faith to them, you can take on the most formidable opponent and prevail over the most valiant adversary.

Victory and Defeat

When the wise and talented are in the higher positions and undesirables are in low positions, the armed forces are happy. When the soldiers are scared, if they talk to each other of valiant combat, look to each other for martial dignity, and urge each other on by rewards and penalties, these are signs of certain victory.

When the armies have been shaken up several times, if the soldiers become lazy, insubordinate, untrustworthy, and unruly, if they scare each other with talk about the enemy, if they talk to each other about booty, make hints to each other of disaster and fortune, or confuse each other with weird talk, these are signs of certain defeat.

Using Authority

People's lives depend on generals, as do success and failure, calamity and fortune; so if the rulership does not give them the power to reward and punish, this is like tying up a monkey and trying to make it cavort around, or like gluing someone's eyes shut and asking him to distinguish colors.

If rewards are up to powerful civilians and punishments do not come from the generals, people will seek personal profit—then who will have any interest in fighting? Even with superlative strategy and performance, self-defense would be impossible under these circumstances.

Therefore Sun Tzu the Martialist said, "When a general is in the field, there are some orders he doesn't accept from the civilian ruler." It is also said, "In the army, you hear the orders of the generals, you don't hear about commands from the emperor."

Grieving for the Dead

Good generals of ancient times took care of their people as one might take care of a beloved child. When there was difficulty they would face it first themselves, and when something was achieved they would defer to others. They would tearfully console the wounded and sorrowfully mourn the dead. They would sacrifice themselves to feed the hungry and remove their own garments to clothe the cold. They honored the wise and provided for their living; they rewarded and encouraged the brave. If generals can be like this, they can take over anywhere they go.

Allies

To operate, the armed forces need allies as consultants and assistants to the leadership.

Everyone looks up to those who are thoughtful and have unusual strategies beyond the ordinary ken, who are widely learned and have broad vision, and who have many skills and great talents. Such people can be made top allies.

Those who are fierce, swift, firm, and sharp are heroes of an age. Such people can be made second-ranked allies.

Those who talk a lot but not always to the point, who are slight in ability, with little that is extraordinary, are people with ordinary capabilities. They can be brought along as the lower class of allies.

Responsiveness

When you plan for difficulty in times of ease, when you do the great while it is still small, when you use rewards first and penalties later, this is refinement in use of the military.

When the troops are already on the battlefield, the cavalries are charging each other, the catapults have been set in position, and the infantries meet at close range, if you can use awesome authoritativeness to convey a sense of trust such that opponents surrender, this is ability in use of the military.

If you plunge into a hail of arrows and rocks, facing off in a contest for victory, with winning and losing distinct, if your adversary is wounded but you die, this is inferiority in use of the military.

Taking Opportunities

The art of certain victory, the mode of harmonizing with changes, is a matter of opportunity. Who but the perspicacious can deal with it? And of all avenues of seeing opportunity, none is greater than the unexpected.

Assessing Abilities

Those who employed warriors skillfully in ancient times assessed their abilities in order to calculate the prospects of victory or defeat:

Who has the wiser ruler?
Who has the more intelligent generals?
Who has the more able officers?
Whose food supplies are most abundant?
Whose soldiers are better trained?
Whose legions are more orderly?
Whose war-horses are swifter?
Whose formations and situation are more dangerous?
Whose clients and allies are smarter?
Whose neighbors are more frightened?
Who has more goods and money?
Whose citizenry is calmer?

When you consider matters along these lines, structural strengths and weaknesses can be determined.

Facilitating Battle

A scorpion will sting because it has poison; a soldier can be brave when he can rely on his equipment. Therefore when their weapons are sharp and their armor is strong, people will readily do battle. If armor is not strong, it is the same as baring one's shoulders. If a bow cannot shoot far, it is the same as a close-range weapon. If a shot cannot hit the mark, it is the same as having no weapon. If a scout is not careful, it is the same as having no eyes. If a general is not brave in battle, it is the same as having no military leadership.

Striking Power

Skilled warriors of ancient times first found out the condition of their enemies, and then made plans to deal with them. There is no doubt of success when you strike enemies under the following conditions:

Their fighting forces are stale.
Their supplies are exhausted.

Their populace is full of sorrow and bitterness.
Many people are physically ill.
They do not plan ahead.
Their equipment is in disrepair.
Their soldiers are not trained.
Reinforcements do not show up.
Night falls when they still have a long way to go.
Their soldiers are worn out.
Their generals are contemptuous and their officers inconsiderate.
They neglect to make preparations.
They do not form battle lines as they advance.
When they do form battle lines, they are not stable.
They are disorderly when they travel over rough terrain.
There is discord between commanders and soldiers.
They become arrogant when they win a battle.
There is disorder in the ranks when they move their battle lines.
The soldiers are tired and prone to upset.
The army is supplied, but the people do not eat.
Each man moves on his own—some go ahead, some lag behind.

When opponents have the following qualities, however, withdraw and avoid them:

Superiors are considerate and subordinates are obedient.
Rewards are sure and punishments certain.
The forces are set out in an orderly fashion.
They give responsibility to the wise and employ the able.
The army is courteous and mannerly.
Their armor is strong and their weapons keen.
They have plenty of supplies and equipment.
Their government and education are substantial.
They are on good terms with all of their neighbors.
They are backed by great nations.

Psychological Configurations

Some generals are brave and think lightly of death. Some are hasty and impulsive. Some are greedy and materialistic. Some are humane but lack endurance. Some are intelligent but timid. Some are intelligent but easygoing at heart.

Those who are brave and think lightly of death are vulnerable to assault. Those who are hasty and impulsive are vulnerable to delay. Those who are greedy and materialistic are vulnerable to loss. Those who are humane but lack endurance are vulnerable to fatigue. Those who are intelligent but timid are vulnerable to pressure. Those who are intelligent but easygoing are vulnerable to sudden attack.

Orderly Troops

In military operations, order leads to victory. If rewards and penalties are unclear, if rules and regulations are unreliable, and if signals are not followed, even if you have an army of a million strong it is of no practical benefit.

An orderly army is one that is mannerly and dignified, one that cannot be withstood when it advances and cannot be pursued when it withdraws. Its movements are regulated and directed; this gives it security and presents no danger. The troops can be massed but not scattered, can be deployed but not worn out.

Inspiring Soldiers

Honor them with titles, present them with goods, and soldiers willingly come join you. Treat them courteously, inspire them with speeches, and soldiers willingly die. Give them nourishment and rest so that they do not become weary, make the code of rules uniform, and soldiers willingly obey. Lead them into battle personally, and soldiers will be brave. Record even a little good, reward even a little merit, and soldiers will be encouraged.

Self-Exertion

Sages follow the rules of heaven; the wise obey the laws of earth; the intelligent follow precedent. Harm comes to the arrogant; calamity visits the proud. Few people trust those who talk too much; few people feel indebted to the self-serving. Rewarding the unworthy causes alienation; punishing the innocent causes resentment. Those whose appreciation or anger are unpredictable perish.

Harmonizing People

Harmonizing people is essential in miliary operations. When people are in harmony, they will fight on their own initiative, without exhortation. If the officers and the soldiers are suspicious of one another, then warriors will not join up. If no heed is paid to the strategies of the loyal, then small-minded people will backbite. When the sprouts of hypocrisy arise, even if you have the wisdom of the great warrior-kings of old, you will not be able to prevail over an ordinary man, much less a whole group of them. Therefore tradition says, "A military operation is like fire; if it is not stopped, it burns itself out."

The Condition of a General

According to the code of generalship, generals do not say they are thirsty before the soldiers have drawn from the well; generals do not say they are hungry before the soldiers' food is cooked; generals do not say they are cold before the soldiers' fires are kindled; generals do not say they are hot before the soldiers' canopies are drawn. Generals do not use fans in summer, do not wear leather in winter, do not use umbrellas in the rain. They do as everyone does.

Order and Disorder

When a nation is perilous and disorderly, and the people are not secure in their homes, this is because the ruler has made the mistake of neglecting to find wise people.

When the wise are disaffected, a nation is in peril; when the wise are employed, a nation is secure. When offices are chosen for persons, there is disorder; when persons are chosen for offices, there is order.

Observant Government

An observant and perceptive government is one that looks at subtle phenomena and listens to small voices. When phenomena are subtle they are not seen, and when voices are small they are not heard; therefore an enlightened leader looks closely at the subtle and listens for the importance of the small voice.

This harmonizes the outside with the inside, and harmonizes the inside with the outside; so the Way of government involves the effort to see and hear much.

Thus when you are alert to what the people in the lower echelons have to say, and take it into consideration, so that your plans include the rank and file, then all people are your eyes and a multitude of voices helps your ears. This is the reason for the classic saying, "A sage has no constant mind—the people are the sage's mind."

Rulers and Ministers

For rulers, generosity to subordinates is benevolence; for ministers, service of the government is duty. No one should serve the government with duplicity; ministers should not be given dubious policies.

When both superiors and subordinates are given to courtesy, then the people are easy to employ. When superiors and subordinates are in harmony, then the Way of rulers and ministers is fulfilled: rulers employ their ministers courteously, while ministers work for the rulers loyally; rulers plan the government policies, while ministers plan their implementation.

Knowledgeable Rule

Rulers are considered knowledgeable according to how much they have seen, and are considered capable according to how much they have heard.

Everyone knows the saying that an intelligent ruler is constant through the day and night, discharging the affairs of office by day and attending to personal matters at night. Yet there may be grievances that do not get a hearing, and there may be loyal people promoting good who are not trusted.

If grievances are not heard, the bent cannot be straightened. If promotion of good is not accepted, the loyal are not trusted and the treacherous enter with their schemes.

This is the meaning of the proverb in the ancient "Classic of Documents": "Heaven sees through the seeing of my people, heaven hears through the hearing of my people."

Not Knowing

Confucius said that an enlightened ruler does not worry about people not knowing him, he worries about not knowing people. He worries not about outsiders not knowing insiders, but about insiders not knowing outsiders. He worries not about subordinates not knowing superiors, but about superiors not knowing subordinates. He worries not about the lower classes not knowing the upper classes, but about the upper classes not knowing the lower classes.

Adjudication

When rulers adjudicate criminal cases and execute punishments, they worry that they may be unclear. The innocent may be punished while the guilty may be released. The powerful may arrogate to themselves alone the right to speak, while the powerless may have their rights infringed upon by those who bear grudges against them. Honesty may be distorted; those who are wronged may not get a chance to express themselves. The trustworthy may be suspected; the loyal may be attacked. These are all perversions, problems causing disaster and violence, aberrations causing calamity and chaos.

Disturbance and Security

It is said that when officials are severe in everything, no one knows where it will end. If they feed off the people so severely that people are hungry and impoverished, this produces disturbance and rebellion.

Encourage people in productive work, don't deprive them of their time. Lighten their taxes, don't exhaust their resources. In this way the country is made wealthy and families secure.

Appointments

The official policy of making appointments should be to promote the upright and place them over the crooked. Governing a country is like governing the body. The way to govern the body is to nurture the spirit; the way to govern a country is to promote the wise. Life is sought by nurturing the spirit; stability is sought by promoting the wise.

So public servants are to a nation as pillars are to a house: the pillars should not be slender; public servants should not be weak. When pillars are slender the house collapses; when public servants are weak the nation crumbles. Therefore the way to govern a nation is to promote the upright over the crooked; then the nation is secure.

Pillars of State

For strong pillars you need straight trees; for wise public servants you need upright people. Straight trees are found in remote forests; upright people come from the humble masses. Therefore when rulers are going to make appointments they need to look in obscure places.

Sometimes there are disenfranchised people with something of value in them; sometimes there are people with extraordinary talent who go unrecognized. Sometimes there are paragons of virtue who are not promoted by their hometowns; sometimes there are people who live in obscurity on purposes.

Sometimes there are people who are dutiful and righteous for purely philosophical or religious reasons. Sometimes there are loyal people who are straightforward with rulers but are slandered by cliques. Ancient kings are known to have hired unknowns and nobodies, finding in them the human qualities whereby they were able to bring peace.

Evaluation and Dismissal

The official policy of evaluation and dismissal should be to promote the good and dismiss the bad. An enlightened leadership is aware of good and bad throughout the realm, not daring to overlook even minor officials and commoners, employing the wise and good, and dismissing the greedy and weak-minded.

With enlightened leadership and good citizens, projects get accomplished, the nation is orderly, and the wise gather like rain; this is the way to promote the good and dismiss the bad, setting forth what is acceptable and what is blameworthy. Therefore a policy of evaluation and dismissal means effort to know what hurts the people.

What Hurts the People

There are five things that hurt the people:

1. There are local officials who use public office for personal benefit, taking improper advantage of their authority, holding weapons in one hand and people's livelihood in the other, corrupting their offices, and bleeding the people.

2. There are cases where serious offenses are given light penalties; there is inequality before the law, and the innocent are subjected to punishment, even execution. Sometimes serious crimes are pardoned, the strong are supported, and the weak are oppressed. Harsh penalties are applied, unjustly torturing people to get at facts.

3. Sometimes there are officials who condone crime and vice, punishing those who protest against this, cutting off the avenues of appeal and hiding the truth, plundering and ruining lives, unjust and arbitrary.

4. Sometimes there are senior officials who repeatedly change department heads so as to monopolize the government administration, favoring their friends and relatives while treating those they dislike with unjust harshness, oppressive in their actions, prejudiced and unruly. They also use taxation to reap profit, enriching themselves and their families by exactions and fraud.

5. Sometimes local officials extensively tailor awards and fines, welfare projects, and general expenditures, arbitrarily determining prices and measures, with the result that people lose their jobs.

These five things are harmful to the people, and anyone who does any of these should be dismissed from office.

Military Action

"Weapons are instruments of ill omen, to be used only when it is unavoidable." The proper course of military action is to establish strategy first, and then carry it out. Monitor the environment, observe the minds of the masses, practice the use of military equipment, clarify the principles of reward and punishment, watch the schemes of enemies, note the perils of the roads, distinguish safe and dangerous places, find out the conditions of the parties involved, and recognize when to proceed and when to withdraw. Follow the timing of opportunities, set up preparations for defense, strengthen your striking power, improve the abilities of your soldiers, map out decisive strategies, and consider life and death issues. Only after doing all this should you send out armed forces, appointing military leaders and extending the power to capture enemies. This is the overall scheme of things in military matters.

Rewards and Penalties

A policy of rewards and penalties means rewarding the good and penalizing wrongdoers. Rewarding the good is to promote achievement; penalizing wrongdoers is to prevent treachery.

It is imperative that rewards and punishments be fair and impartial. When they know rewards are to be given, courageous warriors know what they are dying for; when they know penalties are to be applied, villains know what to fear.

Therefore, rewards should not be given without reason, and penalties should not be applied arbitrarily. If rewards are given for no reason, those who have worked hard in public service will be resentful; if penalties are applied arbitrarily, upright people will be bitter.

Clarity and Consistency

Generals hold authority over life and death. If they allow those who should live to be killed, or allow those who should be killed to live, or if they get angry without discernible reason, or their punishments and rewards are not clear, or commands are inconsistent, or they carry their private affairs over into public life, this is dangerous for the nation.

If their punishments and rewards are not clear, their directives will not always be followed. If they allow those who should be killed to live, treachery will not be prevented. If they allow those who should live to be killed, soldiers will defect. If they get angry without discernible reason, their authority will not be effective. If their rewards and punishments are not clear, the lower echelons will not be encouraged to achieve. If policies are inappropriate, orders will not be obeyed. If private affairs are carried over into public life, people will be of two minds.

If treachery is not prevented, it is impossible to last long. If soldiers defect, the ranks will be decimated. If authority is ineffective, the troops will not rise up in the face of the enemy. If the lower echelons are not encouraged to achieve, the upper echelons have no strong support. If orders are not obeyed, affairs will be chaotic. If people are of two minds, the country will be in danger.

Pleasure and Displeasure

Displeasure should not lead you to harm people who have done no wrong; pleasure should not lead you to go along with those who deserve to be executed.

Pleasure should not induce you to forgive those who have done wrong; displeasure should not induce you to execute the innocent.

Pleasure and displeasure should not be arbitrary; personal prejudices ignore worthy people. A general should not start a battle out of personal displeasure; it is imperative to go by the collective will. If he does go into battle because of personal displeasure, it will certainly result in defeat.

Culture and the Military

Culture takes precedence; the military comes after. If you put victory first, you will surely get beaten later; if you start out with anger, you will surely regret it later. One day's anger can destroy your whole life. Therefore a superior man is stern but not ferocious: he may get angry, but not furious; he may worry, but does not fear; he may rejoice, but is not overjoyed.

Organization

A policy to quell disorder involves minimizing offices and combining duties, getting rid of embellishment in favor of substance.

First organize directives, then organize penalties. First organize the near at hand, then organize the far removed. First organize the inner, then organize the outer. First organize the basic, then organize the derivative. First organize the strong, then organize the weak. First organize the great, then organize the small. First organize yourself, then organize others.

Instruction and Direction

A policy of instruction and direction means those above educate those below, not saying anything that is unlawful and not doing anything that is immoral, for what is done by those above is observed by those below.

To indulge oneself yet instruct others is contrary to proper government; to correct oneself and then teach others is in accord with proper government. Therefore true leaders first rectify themselves and only after that do they promulgate their directives. If they are not upright themselves, their directives will not be followed, resulting in disorder.

Therefore the Way of leadership puts education and direction before punishment. To send people to war without education is tantamount to throwing them away.

Thought and Consideration

A policy of thought and consideration means giving thought to what is near at hand and considering what is remote. As it is said, "If people do not consider what is remote, they will have trouble near at hand." Therefore "educated people think without leaving their positions." Thinking means correct strategy, consideration means thinking of plans for eventualities. One is not to plan policy when it is not one's place to do so, or consider the scheme of things that are none of one's business.

Major affairs arise in difficulty, minor affairs arise in ease. Therefore if you want to think of the advantages in a situation, it is imperative to consider the harm; if you want to think about success, it is imperative to consider failure.

Danger arises in safety, destruction arises in survival. Harm arises in advantage, chaos arises in order. Enlightened people know the obvious when they see the subtle, know the end when they see the beginning; thus there is no way for disaster to happen. This is due to thoughtful consideration.

Strength in Generals

Generals have five strengths and eight evils.

The five strengths are: noble behavior that can inspire the common people, social virtues that can elevate their reputations, trustworthiness and dutifulness in personal relationships, universal love encompassing all the people, and powerful action to succeed in their tasks.

The eight evils are: inability to assess right and wrong when formulating strategy, inability to delegate authority to the wise and the good in times of order, inability to mete out just punishments for incidents of disorder, inability to help the poor in times of plenty, insufficient intelligence to guard against threats before they have taken shape, insufficient thought to prevent subtle dangers, inability to express what is known intuitively, and inability to avoid criticism in defeat.

Sending Out the Armed Forces

In ancient times, when a nation was in trouble, the ruler would select a wise man and have him fast for three days in quiet seclusion before going to the gate of the national shrine, where he would stand facing south. He then took a high courtier to present a ceremonial axe to the ruler, who in turn would pass it by the handle to the general, saying:

"The military leadership settles matters outside the borders," and also directing him in these terms:

"Where you see the enemy to be empty, proceed; where you see the enemy to be full, stop.

"Do not look down on others because of your own elevated rank.

"Do not oppose the common consensus with personal opinions.

"Do not turn from the loyal and trustworthy through the artifices of the skilled but treacherous.

"Do not sit down before the soldiers sit; do not eat before the soldiers eat.

"Bear the same cold and heat the soldiers do; share their toil as well as their ease.

"Experience sweetness and bitterness just as the soldiers do; take the same risks that they do.

"Then the soldiers will exert themselves to the utmost, and it will be possible to destroy enemies."

Having accepted these words, the general led the armed forces out through the city's gate of ill omen.

The ruler, seeing the general off, knelt and said, "Advance and retreat are a matter of timing—military affairs are not directed by the ruler but by the general. Therefore 'There is no heaven above, no earth below, no adversary ahead, and no ruler behind.' Thus the intelligent think because of this; the mettlesome fight because of this."

Selection on Abilities

In military action, there are men who like to fight and enjoy battle, singlehandedly taking on powerful opponents; gather them into one squad and call them "the warriors who repay the nation."

There are mettlesome men with ability and strength, courage and speed; gather them into a squad and call them "the warriors who crash the battle lines."

There are those who are light of foot, good walkers and runners; gather them into a squad called "the warriors who capture the flag."

There are those who can shoot on horseback, swift as flight, hitting the mark every time; gather them into one squad and call them "the galloping warriors."

There are archers whose aim is accurate and deadly; gather them into one squad and call them "the warriors of the fighting edge."

There are those who can shoot heavy crossbows and catapults accurately at great distances; gather them into one squad and call them "the warriors who crush the enemy's edge."

These six kinds of skilled warriors should be employed according to their particular skills.

The Use of Knowledge

Generalship requires one to follow nature, depend on timing, and rely on people in order to achieve victory.

Therefore, if nature works but the timing doesn't work, and yet people act, this is called opposing the time.

If the timing works but nature isn't cooperating, and still people act, this is called opposing nature.

If timing and nature both work, but people do not act, this is called opposing people.

Those who know do not oppose nature, do not oppose the time, and do not oppose people.

Not Setting Up Battle Lines

In ancient times, those who governed well did not arm, and those who were armed well did not set up battle lines. Those who set up battle lines well did not fight, those who fought well did not lose, and those who lost well did not perish.

The government of the sages of old was such that people were comfortable in their homes and enjoyed their work, living to old age without ever attacking one another. "Those who govern well do not arm."

When King Shun (reigned 2255–2207 B.C.E.) organized rules and penalties for wrongdoing, he accordingly created knights, or warriors. But people did not violate the rules, and no penalties were enforced. "Those who arm well do not set up battle lines."

Later, King Yu (reigned 2205–2197 B.C.E.) made a punitive expedition against the Miao tribes, but all he did was demonstrate the martial and cultural arts, and the Miao people became more civilized. "Those who set up battle lines well do not fight."

King Tang (reigned 1766–1753 B.C.E.) and King Wu (reigned 1134–1115 B.C.E.) pledged armies for one military operation, by which the whole land was decisively pacified. "Those who fight well do not lose."

When King Zhao of Chu (reigned 515–488 B.C.E.) ran into disaster, he fled to Qin for help, and ultimately was able to get his kingdom back. "Those who lose well do not perish."

Sincerity in Generals

An ancient document says, "Those who are contemptuous of cultured people have no way to win people's hearts completely; those who are contemptuous of common people have no way to get people to work as hard as they can."

For military operations it is essential to strive to win the hearts of heroes, to make the rules of rewards and punishments strict, to include both cultural and martial arts, and to combine both hard and soft techniques.

Enjoy social amenities and music; familiarize yourself with poetry and prose. Put humanity and justice before wit and bravery.

In stillness be as quiet as a fish in the deep, in action be as swift as an otter. Dissolve enemies' collusion; break down their strengths. Dazzle people with your banners; alert people with cymbals and drums.

Withdraw like a mountain in movement, advance like a rainstorm. Strike and crush with shattering force; go into battle like a tiger.

Press enemies and contain them; lure and entice them. Confuse them and seize them; be humble to make them proud. Be familiar yet distant; weaken them by lending strength.

Give security to those in danger; gladden those in fear. If people oppose you, take what they say to heart; if people have grudges, let them express themselves.

Restrain the strong, sustain the weak. Get to know those with plans; cover up any slander. When there is booty, distribute it.

Do not count on your strength and take an opponent lightly. Do not be conceited about your abilities and think little of subordinates.

Do not let personal favor congeal into authority.

Plan before acting. Fight only when you know you can win.

Do not keep the spoils of war for your own possession and use.

If generals can be like this, people will be willing to fight when they give the orders, and the enemy will be defeated before any blood is shed.

PART TWO

Lessons of War

STUDIES IN STRATEGY

Liu Ji

TRANSLATOR'S INTRODUCTION

Liu Ji was born in 1311 C.E., during the Yuan dynasty. An exceptionally brilliant scholar, he earned an advanced degree in the state civil service examinations and was promoted to public office. While in office, Liu gained a reputation for integrity and honesty, but while these qualities endeared him to the local populace they made him a marked man among the ruling Mongol elite. As an alien dynasty that had to depend on the native Chinese bureaucracy, the Yuan regime was wary of close bonding between local officials and the people at large.

It had already been a long-standing policy of the Chinese government to appoint officials to posts outside of their own home areas, in order to prevent the growth of local factionalism. This in turn produced other problems, but in any event the whole syndrome of unease stemming from tension between central and regional interests naturally became aggravated under alien regimes like the Mongol Yuan. This tension is a pervasive thread of Chinese history, one that is clearly evident in the triumphs and trials of the great Liu Ji.

In 1348 Liu was appointed by the Yuan government to direct a containment action against an insurrection, for Liu was not only a brilliant scholar but also a distinguished strategist. Checked by Liu's masterful engineering, the leader of the rebellion attempted to save himself with a handsome bribe. Liu refused so the rebel went to Peking, the Mongols' capital in China, and succeeded in bribing his way into favor there.

Now the secessionist was given an office and a stipend for his trouble, while Liu Ji's relationship with the regime deteriorated further. Eventually he retired to his ancestral homeland. Here he attracted a following without really trying to do so, as many people came to him fleeing the depredations of that same rebel leader who had bought his way directly into the Yuan government. In 1366 Liu was invited to the headquarters of Zhu Yuanzhang, onetime follower of a warrior band of radical White Lotus Buddhists, now a leader of one of the popular anti-Yuan movements rising in the south of China.

Zhu was immediately impressed by the strategic thinking of the elder Liu, who was now fifty-five and well seasoned in political and military affairs. Under Liu's able guidance, in eight years Zhu established dominance over all the other insurrectionists in the south and moved north to overthrow the Mongol usurpers. When Zhu set up the Ming dynasty, restoring native rule to China, Liu Ji was one of his most trusted advisors and made perhaps the greatest contribution to the establishment of the new order.

Liu Ji's death in 1375 at the age of sixty-four has a ring of tragic irony to it, but from another point of view it would seem to be an outcome of his heroism and his final lesson to the world. Though he was the target of envious interlopers throughout his distinguished career, Liu Ji himself was known for impartiality in his judgments; this was one reason his advice was so highly esteemed, but it also cost him his life. One of the men whose proposed appointment to high office was rejected by Liu Ji contrived to effect Liu's downfall by convincing the emperor that Liu was plotting to establish his own power base. Liu was stripped of his emolument, and the whisperer was promoted.

The shock and outrage of the event destroyed Liu's health, and he soon passed away. He had told the emperor quite honestly that it was not impossible to find good men for government if he were really sincere, but none of those the emperor had with him were worthy. In particular, he warned the emperor that the individual who was to intrigue against him was like a chariot horse that may well break its harness. As it turned out, it was the interloper, now a high official of the new Ming dynasty, and not Liu Ji, who had been scheming to establish his own power base for a coup d'état. He even formed alliances with Mongolian nobles of the defunct Yuan dynasty, hoping to overthrow the Ming. When the plot was discovered, over thirty thousand people were convicted of conspiracy. So the final lesson of Liu Ji was that half of good advice is knowing when to take it. As he said to the emperor of Ming China, "Why worry that there is no talent in the country? Just let an enlightened leadership seek it wholeheartedly."

Liu Ji is famous not only as a warrior, strategist, and statesman, but also as a poet and writer. One of his early works, entitled *The*

Cultured One, written during his first retirement, illustrates his philosophy of life, society, and government. In a passage on conflict avoidance, Liu demonstrates his understanding of the Taoist attitude characteristic of the higher strategy extolled in Sun Tzu's classic *The Art of War:*

> Good warriors lessen opponents, bad warriors increase opponents. Those who decrease opponents flourish thereby, those who increase opponents perish.
>
> If you want to take other people's nations, then the people of those nations are all your opponents. Therefore those who are good at lessening opponents do not cause people to oppose them.
>
> The reason wise leaders of old had no opponents was that they used their opponents to oppose opponents. Only the most humane people in the world can use their opponents to oppose opponents; for this reason opponents did not oppose them, and everyone capitulated.

Further insights into Liu's political and practical thinking can be gleaned from his poetry. Several of his verses show his profound grasp of the contradictions of historical processes and the paradoxical strategy of *The Art of War* at its best:

> A nation does not prosper itself;
> If its people have enough, it is prosperous.
> Rulers are not powerful themselves;
> When they have many knights they are strong.
> So when those full of envy are in office,
> Knights retire to private life,
> And rulers just bleed them with taxes.
> When bureaucrats advance, people get hurt,
> And then the nation is wounded.

> When force brings loss of freedom,
> A little flexibility can overcome a great power.
> When there is stasis in formation,
> Even the mighty and ferocious
> Cannot conquer the small but secure.
> Thus a man-eating tiger cannot swallow a single porcupine,
> But a goat leash may be used to harness nine gelded bulls.

There are impasses and successes
As a matter of course:
One cannot prevail just by wits.
Fame may be gained or lost,
And cannot be achieved by force.
So even if you have no worldly ambitions,
You won't necessarily escape slander.
Even if you seek nothing from others,
Your advice won't necessarily be put into effect.

Those who save the world from chaos
Are not occupied with petty matters;
Those who accomplish the ongoing evolution of the world
Are not conceited over small accomplishments.
So that which cuts rotting flesh
Is not to be considered a sharp sword,
And that which penetrates a naked body
Is not to be considered a good bow.

Liu Ji's philosophy of war is epitomized in certain chapters from his neoclassic *Extraordinary Strategies of a Hundred Battles*. This book, based mainly on *The Art of War* and its congeners, is one of Liu's most famous and popular works; it is the source of the war tales translated in Part Two of this book. The following selections would seem to summarize both philosophical and strategic mainstays of his thinking on conflict management, showing his intimate connection with classic traditions.

FORGETTING ABOUT WARFARE

Sages are very careful not to forget about danger when secure, not to forget about chaos in times of order. Even when there is peace in the land, it will not do to abandon the military altogether. If you lack sufficient foresight, you will be defenseless. It is necessary to develop cultured qualities internally while organizing military preparedness externally. Be considerate and gentle toward foreigners, beware of the unexpected. Routine military exercises in each of the four seasons is the way to show that the nation is not oblivious to warfare. Not forgetting about warfare means teaching the people not to give up the practice of martial arts.

The rule is "Even if the land is at peace, to forget about warfare leads to collapse."

CAUTION IN WAR

In warfare, you should remain cautious. Go into action only when you see that it will be advantageous; if you see no advantage, then stop. Be prudent and do not act too readily. Then you will not fall into deadly situations.

The rule is "Be immovable as a mountain."

RELAXATION

In war, you should not relax when you have scored a victory. You should be even more strictly on guard against enemies, still diligent even while at ease.

The rule is "Be prepared, and you will have no trouble."

SECURITY

When enemies come from far off at the peak of their energy, it is to their advantage to fight right away; so increase your defenses, preserve your security, and do not respond—wait for them to wind down. Even if they try something to agitate you and pick a fight, do not move.

The rule is "Be still when in a secure place."

CHANGE

The essence of the principles of warriors is responding to changes; expertise is a matter of knowing the military. In any action it is imperative to assess the enemy first. If opponents show no change or movement, then wait for them. Take advantage of change to respond accordingly, and you will benefit.

The rule is "The ability to gain victory by changing and adapting according to opponents is called genius."

MILITARISM

Weapons are instruments of ill omen, war is immoral. Really they are only to be resorted to when there is no other choice. It is not right to pursue aggressive warfare because one's country is large and prosperous, for this ultimately ends in defeat and destruction. Then it is too late to have regrets. Military action is like a fire—if not stopped it will burn itself out. Military expansion and adventurism soon lead to disaster.

The rule is "Even if a country is large, if it is militaristic it will eventually perish."

Like the works of all the great philosophers of the East, Liu Ji's stories of strategy are primarily aimed at stimulating thought and analyzing situations. Even while example and anecdote are commonly used in the presentations of the classical thinkers, the questions of when and how to apply principles are by nature open. Confucius said, "If I bring up one corner and you cannot come back with the other three, I won't talk to you anymore." Symbolically, this famous statement is understood to mean that practical philosophy yields relatively little without context and reflection.

Because these tales from Chinese history are stories of war, there is horror in them. As an editor, Liu Ji does not say what should happen from an ethical point of view but observes what can and does happen to human thinking and behavior in the event of contention and conflict. On one level, the stories are meant to be viewed with detachment, as a method of understanding human behavior objectively. On another level, even the sensationalism of this horror is originally didactic, fortifying the traditional moral repulsion from warfare with direct emotional and physical repulsion. Nevertheless, in the final analysis the rational and ethical ingredients in the use of these tales on the art of war are inevitably supplied by the individual who uses them, even if only by default. According to legend, when Solomon was offered wisdom or riches, he chose wisdom and was granted riches as well.

Chronology of Historical Periods in Liu Ji's Tales

SPRING AND AUTUMN ERA (722–481 B.C.E.)

This era is generally cited to mark early to middle stages of the deterioration of the classical Zhou dynasty and the beginnings of militarism. Confucius lived in the last century of this period. The Taoist classic *Tao Te Ching* is also popularly believed to have been compiled around the end of this era.

WARRING STATES ERA (480–246 B.C.E.)

A period of prolonged civil war among the various states of the old confederation under the titular head of the Zhou dynasty. The Warring States era is generally cited to mark middle to late stages of the degeneration and demise of the Zhou dynasty. A great deal of classical literature from various schools dates from this period, including the works of Mozi and Mencius as well as *The Art of War*.

THE QIN DYNASTY (246–206 B.C.E.)

The first imperial dynasty, destroying the old system of feudal states in favor of uniform law administered by a central government. The name Qin (pronounced like the English word *chin*) would seem to be the root of the English word *China*, which bears no relation to what the Chinese call themselves. Bringing the Warring States era to a close and unifying China politically and culturally, the Qin dynasty was short but eventful.

THE HAN DYNASTY (206 B.C.E.–220 C.E.)

Under the wasteful and cruel regime of the second emperor of Qin there were widespread insurrections that eventually toppled the dynasty. The Han dynasty was established by the warrior party that emerged victorious in the subsequent power struggle. The Han dynasty lasted for nearly four hundred years, with one short interruption in the early years of the Common Era. The Han order left a profound mark on Chinese cultural consciousness, and the Chinese people call themselves and their language Han. The Taoist classic *Masters of Huainan*, heir to the political philosophy of *The Art of War*, dates from the first century of the Han dynasty.

THE ERA OF THE THREE KINGDOMS (190–265 C.E.)

The era of the Three Kingdoms refers to the extended struggle for dominion over the territories of the late Han. China was divided into three competing kingdoms—Wei, Shu, and Wu—vying to reconstruct the decayed empire under their own regimes. Many famous war tales and anecdotes on strategy are taken from this era, which was the time of Zhuge Liang and the notorious general Cao Cao. Cao Cao's own commentaries on *The Art of War* are included in the first book in this volume.

THE JIN DYNASTY (265–420 C.E.)

The Jin dynasty supplanted Wei, which had emerged victorious among the Three Kingdoms. The Jin dynasty was seriously challenged, and its imperial domains reduced, by other North and Central Asian peoples who set up numerous states collectively known as the Sixteen Kingdoms.

THE NORTHERN AND SOUTHERN DYNASTIES (420–589 C.E.)

The Northern dynasties were under non-Chinese rule, the Southern dynasties under Chinese rule. During this period there were conflicts both within and between the Northern and Southern dynasties. This period lasted for the better part of the fifth and sixth centuries.

THE SUI DYNASTY (558–618 C.E.)

The Sui dynasty reunified China in the late sixth century, then collapsed under the duress of rebellions against the government for the exorbitant costs of the policies and programs of the second emperor.

THE TANG DYNASTY (618–905 C.E.)

Supplanting the Sui, the Tang dynasty lasted for nearly three hundred years and is considered a peak in the cultural history of China. The Chinese empire expanded under the Tang and influenced the development of new nations in Japan, Korea, and Tibet. Buddhism flourished with increased input from India and Central Asia, which then diffused from China into the newer nations surrounding it. China also renewed contact with the West during the Tang dynasty through the entry of Christianity and Islam. As a global power China declined after the peak of the Tang dynasty, reentering centuries of conflicts with other Asian peoples. The tales of war recited by Liu Ji end at the Tang dynasty, ranging from the Spring and Autumn era to the beginning of the Tang.

LESSONS OF WAR

Calculated Battle

Liu Ji said:

The reasonable course of action in any use of arms starts with calculation. Before fighting, first assess the relative sagacity of the military leadership, the relative strength of the enemy, the sizes of the armies, the lay of the land, and the adequacy of provisions. If you send troops out only after making these calculations, you will never fail to win.

The rule is "Sizing up opponents to determine victory, assessing dangers and distances, is the proper course of action for military leaders" (Sun Tzu, *The Art of War*, "Terrain").

Liu Bei (161–223) was one of the warrior giants of Three Kingdoms fame. He established the kingdom of Shu, or Shu Han, envisioned as a continuation of the Han dynasty in the western part of the Chinese heartland, the ancient region of Shu.

In the last days of the Han dynasty, Liu Bei went three times to ask Zhuge Liang for advice on strategy. Zhuge Liang was to become one of the most famous strategists in history.

Zhuge Liang told Liu Bei, "Ever since the beginning of the current power struggle for what is left of the Han empire, many mettlesome men have arisen. Countless prefectures and districts have been taken over by such men. If you compare current contenders for national power, one of them—the notorious Cao Cao—was once an unknown with a small force, yet he was able to overcome another warlord with a much larger following. The reason the weaker was able to prevail over the stronger is not simply a matter of celestial timing, but also of human planning. Cao Cao now has a million followers; he controls the emperor and gives orders to the lords—he cannot really be opposed.

"Another warlord, in control of the area east of the river, is already the third generation hegemon there. The territory is rugged and the people are loyal to him; the intelligent and capable serve in his employ. He would be a suitable ally, but he cannot be counted on.

"Here there is ease of communication and transport. It is a land suitable for military operations. If its ruler cannot keep it, this would seem to be a boon to the general. Do you have any interest in it? To the southwest are precipitous natural barriers, beyond which lie vast fertile plains. That land is called the heavenly precinct, and it is where the Han dynasty really began.

"Now the governor of that region is ignorant and weak. To the north is the stronghold of the independent Taoist cult of the Celestial Masters. The people are robust and the land is rich, but they do not know how to take care of it. Men of knowledge and ability want to find an enlightened leader.

"General, you are a descendant of the imperial family, and are known everywhere for integrity and justice. You gather heroic men and eagerly seek the wise. If you occupy this whole region, guard the crags and defiles, establish good relations with the foreign tribes to the west and south, make friends with the warlord east of the river, and work to perfect internal organization, then when there is an upheaval in the total political situation and you mobilize your armies, the common people will surely welcome you with food and drink. If you can really do this, hegemony can be established, and the house of Han can be revived."

Liu Bei agreed, and it turned out as planned.

Fighting Schemes

Liu Ji said:

Whenever opponents begin to scheme, attack accordingly, foiling their plans so that they give up.

The rule is "The superior military artist strikes while schemes are being laid" (Sun Tzu, *The Art of War*, "Planning a Siege").

Around 500 B.C.E., in the Spring and Autumn era, the lord of Jin wanted to attack the state of Qi. He sent an emissary to Qi to observe the government there.

The lord of Qi wined and dined the emissary. The wine flowed freely, and the emissary asked to drink from the lord's cup. This is a gesture of familiarity, and such a request under such circumstances is an insult.

The lord said, "I offer my cup to my guest."

After the emissary of Jin had drunk from the lord's cup, one of the eminent nobles of the Qi court came forward, removed it, and personally continued to serve wine to the emissary in another cup.

Now the emissary, feigning inebriation, stood up in displeasure and said to the highest cabinet official at the court of Qi, "I desire the music of the duke of Zhou. If you can play it, I will dance it for you."

The duke of Zhou was the founder of the Zhou dynasty, which was beginning to disintegrate in the Spring and Autumn era.

The high official of Qi said, "I have not practiced it."

The emissary of Jin left.

The Lord of Qi said to the noble and the official, "Jin is a big state. Now you have angered the emissary of that great state, who came to observe our government. What shall we do?"

The eminent noble said, "I could see the emissary was not ignorant of etiquette, so I would not go along with him when he tried to shame our state."

The cabinet official said, "The music of the duke of Zhou is the music of the national leader. Only a ruler dances it. That emissary is the servant of another, yet he wanted to dance the music of leaders— that is why I didn't perform."

As for the emissary, he went back and reported to the lord of Jin. He said, "Qi cannot be attacked at this time. I tried to insult their lord, and a court noble knew it; I tried to violate their etiquette, and the highest official perceived it."

Confucius said of the court noble who took the lord's cup from the emissary that he "could stop a thrust from a thousand miles away without leaving the table."

Espionage and Warfare

Liu Ji said:

Whenever you move against anyone, before mobilizing the army first use spies to see whether the opponents are many or few, empty or full, active or quiet. Then you can be very successful and never fail to win in battle.

The rule is "Spies are useful everywhere" (Sun Tzu, *The Art of War*, "On the Use of Spies").

In the sixth century C.E., during the era of the Northern and Southern dynasties, General Wei of the court of Zhou was the military governor of Jade Wall City. General Wei was known for his exemplary behavior in his official capacity. He was skilled at management and able to win people's hearts. All of the spies he sent into the territory of the Qi court did their utmost for him, and certain people of Qi whom Wei had bribed sent him reports by letter. Therefore the Zhou court knew all about the movements of Qi.

Now the prime minister of Qi was a man of sagacity and courage. General Wei loathed him. One of Wei's officers, who knew quite a bit about divination, said, "Next year there will be slaughter in the east." The kingdom of Qi was to the east of Zhou. Wei had this officer compose a song with a double entendre suggesting that the prime minister of Qi was plotting a coup d'état; then he had his secret agents plant this song in the main city of Qi.

Subsequently there developed a rift between the prime minister of Qi and a certain general. When Wei heard of this, he further exacerbated it. The prime minister was eventually executed.

When the ruler of Zhou heard that the prime minister of Qi was dead, he issued an amnesty for that territory, then mobilized a large army to attack, ultimately destroying the kingdom of Qi.

Elite Fighters

Liu Ji said:

Whenever you do battle with opponents, it is imperative to select brave leaders and crack troops to be your vanguard. One purpose of this is the strengthen your own will; another is to break down the opponent's force.

The rule is "Those who do not sort out the levels of skill among their own troops are the ones who get beaten" (Sun Tzu, *The Art of War*, "Terrain").

In the year 207, two sons of a major warlord of the Three Kingdoms era fled to the north. There they joined forces with a northern tribal people, the Wuheng, who raided Chinese territory from time to time. Cao Cao set out on an expedition north to stop the tribal incursions, intending to strike down the sons of the Chinese warlord as well.

That autumn, with the roads north made impassable by heavy rains, Cao Cao's troops made their way two hundred miles through the hinterland, tunneling through mountains and filling in ravines. They reached north to the territory of the Turanian Xianbei tribes, then headed for the homeland of the Wuheng.

Before Cao Cao's army had gone much more than a hundred miles, they were discovered by the enemy. The brothers, together with several tribal chieftains, led a large force of mounted fighters against them.

Now Cao Cao's equipment was in transport behind him, and few of his soldiers were wearing armor. Everyone was worried.

Cao Cao climbed high up a mountainside to survey the situation. Seeing that their opponents' battle lines were disorderly, he allowed his soldiers to attack, appointing one of his best commanders to lead the vanguard.

The enemy troops were routed. A number of tribal leaders were killed, and many thousand mounted warriors surrendered to the Han Chinese.

Battling on Good Faith

Liu Ji said:

In any battle with an opponent, when soldiers face almost certain death without regret or fear, it is trust that makes them that way. When the leadership is trustworthy and honest, followers are earnest and free from doubt; so there is certain victory in battle.

The rule is "The trustworthy do not cheat" ("Six Secrets," "On Generalship").

During the Three Kingdoms era, the king of Wei personally directed an expedition against the kingdom of Shu. He sent a huge force of light troops under cover to proceed in stealth toward Shu.

Now Zhuge Liang, minister and general of Shu, had taken up a position in the mountains, guarding the passes with well-equipped troops. He had the troops replaced regularly, keeping a contingent of about one-half to one-third the size of the strike force now advancing from Wei to Shu.

The Wei army arrived and set up battle lines just as the Shu guard was in the process of changing. Zhuge's aides urged him to keep the departing troops there for another month to add their strength to the replacements in face of such a powerful enemy force.

Zhuge said, "My command of the military is based on trust and good faith. To lose trust by trying to gain an advantage is a mistake made by men of old. Those who are due to leave pack their gear quickly, waiting for their time to come, while their wives and children stand in their doorways back home, counting the days. Although we are facing a crisis, it will not do to abandon what is right and just."

Thus General Zhuge Liang urged all those whose tour of duty was done to leave the front and return home.

Now those who were scheduled to leave were all so pleased by this announcement that they asked to be allowed to stay for one more battle. They stirred up their courage, determined to fight to the death, saying to each other, "Even if we die, that is still not enough to repay the kindness of Master Zhuge."

On the day of battle, everyone in Zhuge's army rushed forward with drawn sword, each soldier taking on ten of the enemy. They killed one of the Wei leaders, drove off another, and won a great victory in a single battle. This was because of trust and good faith.

Instruction and Warfare

Liu Ji said:

Whenever you want to raise an army, it is necessary first to instruct it in warfare. When the soldiers are trained in ways of scattering and massing, and are thoroughly familiar with the signals for passivity and action, advance and retreat, then when they meet opponents they respond to direction by signals. Then you can do battle without failing to win.

The rule is "To have uninstructed people go into battle is tantamount to abandoning them" (Confucius, *Analects*).

In the Warring States era, the notorious martialist Wu Qi (d. 381 B.C.E.), general of the warring state of Wei, spoke in these terms: "People always die at what they cannot do and are defeated by what is not advantageous to them. The rule for military operations is to start with instruction and training. One person who learns to fight can teach ten people, ten people who learn to fight can teach a hundred people, a hundred can teach a thousand, a thousand can teach ten thousand, ten thousand can teach enough people for three armies.

"Let them learn all the adaptations: maximizing the distance traveled by opponents while minimizing your own, wearing opponents down while staying rested yourselves, starving opponents out while keeping yourselves well fed, knowing when to form a circle and when to form a square, when to sit and when to rise, when to move and when to stop, when to go right and when to go left, when to go ahead and when to fall back, when to split up and when to join, when to band together and when to spread out.

"When they have practiced all of this, then give the fighters weapons. To make them expert in this is called the business of a military leader."

Caring in War

Liu Ji said:

What makes soldiers in battle perfer to charge ahead rather than retreat even for survival is the benevolence of the military leadership. When the soldiers know their leaders care for them as they care for their own children, then the soldiers love their leaders as they do their own fathers. This makes them willing to die in battle, to requite the benevolence of their leaders.

The rule is "Look upon your soldiers as beloved children, and they willingly die with you" (Sun Tzu, *The Art of War*, "Terrain").

During the Warring States era, when the Wei general Wu Qi was military governor of West River, he wore the same clothes and ate the same food as the lowest of his soldiers. He did not use a mat to sit on, and he did not ride when traveling. He personally carried his own bundle of provisions and shared the toil and hardships of the soldiers.

Once, when one of the soldiers was suffering from a festering wound on his arm, the general himself sucked out the pus.

When that soldier's mother heard about this, she began to mourn.

Someone said to her, "Your son is a soldier, yet the general himself sucked the pus from his wound—what is there to mourn about?"

The woman said, "Last year General Wu did the same thing for my husband, and as a result my husband fought in battle without taking a backward step, finally dying at the hands of an enemy. Now that the general has treated my son in this way too, I have no idea where he will die. This is why I mourn him."

It was because Wu Qi was strict with himself while impartial toward others, and had won the hearts of his soldiers, that a Lord of Wei had made him military governor of West River. Wu Qi fought seventy-six major battles with lords of the other warring states, and gained complete victory sixty-four times.

Authority and Warfare

Liu Ji said:

When soldiers in battle forge ahead and do not dare to fall back, this means they fear their own leaders more than they fear the enemy. If they dare to fall back and dare not forge ahead this means they fear the enemy more than they fear their own leaders. When a general can get his troops to plunge right into the thick of raging combat, it is his authority and sternness that brings this about.

The rule is "To be awesome and yet caring makes a good balance" ("Dialogues of Li, Lord of Wei").

During the Spring and Autumn era, the state of Qi was invaded by the states of Jin and Yan. At first the invaders overcame the military forces of Qi.

One of the eminent nobles of the court of Qi recommended the martialist Tian Rangju to the lord of Qi. To this man, later called Sima Rangju, is attributed the famous military handbook "Sima's Art of War," or "Sima's Rules."

In recommending Rangju, the court noble said to the lord of Qi, "Although Rangju is an illegitimate descendant of a noble family of another state, his culture is attractive to people and his military prowess is awesome to opponents. Please try him."

The lord of Qi then summoned Rangju to discuss military matters with him. The lord was very pleased with what Rangju had to say, and he made him a general, appointing him to lead an army to resist the aggression of the forces of Yan and Jin.

Rangju said, "I am lowly in social status, yet the lord has promoted me from the ranks and placed me above even the grandees. The soldiers are not yet loyal to me, and the common people are not familiar with me; as a man of little account, my authority is slight. I request one of your favorite ministers, someone honored by the state, to be overseer of the army."

The lord acceded to this request and appointed a nobleman to be the overseer. Rangju took his leave, arranging to meet the nobleman at the military headquarters at noon the following day. Then Rangju hastened back to set up a sundial and a waterclock to await the new overseer.

Now this new overseer was a proud and haughty aristocrat, and he imagined that as overseer he was leading his own army. Because of his pride and arrogance, he did not see any need to hurry, in spite of his promise with Rangju the martial master. His relatives and close associates gave him a farewell party, and he stayed to drink with them.

At noon the next day, the new overseer had not arrived at headquarters. Rangju took down the sundial and emptied the waterclock. He assembled the troops and informed them of the agreement with the new overseer.

That evening the nobleman finally arrived. Rangju said to him, "Why are you late?"

He said, "My relatives, who are grandees, gave me a farewell party, so I stayed for that."

Rangju said, "On the day a military leader receives his orders, he forgets about his home; when a promise is made in face of battle, one forgets his family; when the war drums sound, one forgets his own body. Now hostile states have invaded our territory; the state is in an uproar; the soldiers are exposed at the borders; the lord cannot rest easy or enjoy his food; the lives of the common people all depend on you—how can you talk about farewell parties?"

Rangju then summoned the officer in charge of military discipline and asked him, "According to military law, what happens to someone who arrives later than an appointed time?"

The officer replied, "He is supposed to be decapitated."

Terrified, the aristocrat had a messenger rush back to report this to the lord and beseech him for help. But the haughty nobleman was executed before the messenger even returned, and his execution was announced to the army. The soldiers all shook with fear.

Eventually the lord sent an emissary with a letter pardoning the nobleman, who was, after all, the new overseer of the army. The emissary galloped right into camp on horseback with the lord's message.

Rangju said, " 'When a general is in the field, there are orders he doesn't take from the ruler.' "

He also said to the disciplinary officer, "It is a rule that there shall be no galloping through camp, yet now the emissary has done just that. What should be done with him?"

The officer said, "He should be executed."

The emissary was petrified, but Rangju said, "It is not proper to kill an emissary of the lord," and had two of the emissary's attendants executed in his stead. This too was announced to the army.

Rangju sent the emissary back to report to the lord, and then he set out with the army. When the soldiers made camp, Rangju personally oversaw the digging of wells, construction of stoves, preparation of food and drink, and care of the sick. He shared all of the supplies of the leadership with the soldiers, personally eating the same rations as they. He was especially kind to the weary and weakened.

After three days, Rangju called the troops to order. Even those who were ill wanted to go along, eager to go into battle for Rangju. When the armies of Jin and Yan heard about this, they withdrew from the state of Qi. Now Rangju led his troops to chase them down and strike them. Eventually he recovered lost territory and returned with the army victorious.

Reward and Battle

Liu Ji said:

For soldiers to strive to scale high walls in spite of deep moats and showers of arrows and rocks, or for soldiers to plunge eagerly into the fray of battle, they must be induced by serious rewards; then they will prevail over an enemy.

The rule is "Where there are serious rewards, there will be valiant men" ("Three Strategies," also in "Six Secrets").

At the end of the Han dynasty, whenever Cao Cao plundered a city and obtained rare and beautiful objects, he would always use them to reward achievement. To people who had worked hard and were worthy of reward, he would not begrudge even a thousand pieces of gold, while to those without merit he would give nothing. Therefore he was able to win battle after battle.

Punishment and Battle

Liu Ji said:

What will make soldiers in battle dare to go forward and not dare to retreat is a strict penalty for anyone who retreats even an inch. Thus it is possible to gain victory by this means.

The rule is "Punishment should be immediate" ("Sima's Rules," "Duties of the Emperor").

Yang Su (d. 606) was a great general of the brief but momentous Sui dynasty (589–617). His command was strict and orderly; anyone who violated military orders was immediately executed, with no exceptions.

Whenever General Yang was about to face an opponent, he would look for people to make mistakes so he could execute them. Sometimes over a hundred men would be killed; it was never less than several dozen. He himself would talk and laugh casually as the flowing blood flooded the ground before him.

Then when he faced the enemy on the battle line, he would first command three hundred men to attack. If they were able to break the opponent's battle line, they were all right; if they returned without being able to strike through enemy lines, they would all be executed, regardless of their number.

Then General Yang would send ahead another two or three hundred men, and again killed any who returned. As a result, the commanders and soldiers trembled in fear and were determined to fight to the death. Therefore they consistently won in battle.

Defensive Battle

Liu Ji said:

In any battle, if another is the aggressor and you are the defender, you should not be too quick to fight. If your army is at rest and the soldiers are watching over their homes, you should gather people to guard the cities and fortify the mountain passes, cutting off the aggressors' supply routes. When they do not succeed in drawing you into battle, and their supplies do not reach them, wait until they are worn out and then strike them. If you do this you will always win.

The rule is "Fighting on your own territory is called a ground of dissolution" (Sun Tzu, *The Art of War*, "Nine Grounds").

Wu Di (371–409) was the Martial Emperor of the Later Wei dynasty, a foreign regime in northern China under the rule of the Toba people. He personally led an expedition against the Later Yan dynasty, another foreign regime in northern China, this one under the rule of the Xianbei people, who had invaded Toba territory.

The Wei army failed in its action against Yan, and the Yan emperor wanted to strike back. A military aide came forth, however, and said, "The ancients would first be sure of victory in the planning before going on the offensive. Now there are four reasons why Wei cannot be attacked, and three reasons why Yan should not act."

The emperor of Yan said, "What are these reasons?"

The aide said, "The Wei army is deep inside our territory, and its advantage lies in battle on the open fields; this is one reason why it cannot be attacked. Indeed, it has penetrated so far that it is near our capital, so it is on deadly ground, where the invading soldiers know they have no choice but fight to the death; this is the second reason they cannot be attacked. Furthermore, the vanguard has already been defeated, so the rear lines must have been tightened up; this is the third reason not to attack. Finally, they are many while we are few; this is the fourth reason they cannot be attacked.

"As for the reasons why Yan should refrain from action: first of all, a government army is fighting on its own territory; so we should not act. Second, if it acts and does not prevail, it will be hard to make the hearts of the people resolute; so we should not act. Third, our defenses are not yet ready, and we are not prepared for the coming of an enemy; again, we should not act. These situations are all avoided by warriors.

"It would be best to secure our defenses and wait in ease for the enemy to tire. They have to transport grain over hundreds of miles, and there is nothing in the open fields to take. Eventually they will wear down, so that if they attack, many of their soldiers will die. When their army grows stale and discords develop, then rise up against them and you can overcome them."

The Yan emperor praised the strategic thinking of the military aide.

Offensive Battle

Liu Ji said:

In battle, if the adversary is the defender and you are the invader, just try to penetrate deeply. If you penetrate deeply into their territory, defenders cannot win. This is because of what is called the invader being on heavy ground while the defender is on light ground.

The rule is "Invaders become more intense the further they enter alien territory" (Sun Tzu, *The Art of War*, "Nine Grounds").

In the early Han dynasty, Han Xin (d. 196 B.C.E.) and Zhang Er (d. 202 B.C.E.) mobilized an army of several tens of thousands to attack the state of Zhao. Han Xin was an outstanding militarist involved in the wars waged to establish the Han dynasty. Zhang Er was one of a number of local feudal kings whose states were allowed to exist within the structure of the early Han empire.

Now the king of Zhao and the lord of Cheng-an massed an army of two hundred thousand men at a strategic pass, to defend against the invaders. One of the councillors of Zhao, however, said to the lord of Cheng-an, "I hear that Han Xin's army has been campaigning successfully, and now, reinforced by Zhang Er's army, he wants to descend on Zhao. His string of victories has taken him from his own land to fight far abroad; news of his power robs people of their courage, and it is impossible to stand up to him directly.

"I hear that Han Xin is transporting supplies from a great distance. The soldiers have the look of hunger; they eat irregularly and never sleep on full stomachs. Now the road through the pass is too narrow for two cars to travel abreast, or for a group of horsemen to ride in formation; so their supplies must be behind them.

"Please let me take a special force of thirty thousand to cut their supply lines off from the byways. You secure your fortifications and don't fight with them. They cannot go forward; they cannot return; they cannot plunder anything from the field. Before ten days are up, the heads of both leaders, Han Xin and Zhang Er, can be hanging from your flagpole. Please pay heed; otherwise you will be captured."

But the lord of Cheng-an was self-righteous and did not listen to this strategy. Eventually he was killed.

Strength and Battle

Liu Ji said:

Whenever you fight with opponents, if you are numerous and strong, you can feign weakness to entice opponents who will think little of coming to fight with you. Strike them with your best soldiers, and their forces will be defeated.

The rule is "Though effective, appear to be ineffective" (Sun Tzu, *The Art of War*, "Strategic Assessments").

Late in the era of the Warring States, a general of the state of Zhao named Li Mu (d. 228 B.C.E.) was permanently stationed on the northwest frontier to defend Chinese territory against incursions by the Huns. For convenience, he set up an office to collect taxes and forward them to his headquarters at the front, where he spent them on the soldiers. Every day he had cattle slaughtered to feed the troops well.

General Li had the soldiers practice mounted archery and watch over their signal fires, and he employed many spies and informants. Afterwards he made his commanders and soldiers promise to pull back into a closed defense and not to fight whenever the Huns came. Anyone who dared to take a Hun captive was to be executed.

They did this for several years, and although nothing was lost to the Huns, they considered Li Mu a coward. Even the Zhao frontier troops thought their leader was timid. The king of Zhao remonstrated with General Li, but the general continued to do as before.

Finally, the king recalled General Li and replaced him with someone else. Now, under their new leader, the Chinese garrison soldiers went out and fought whenever the Huns showed up. After little more than a year the Chinese had taken several beatings from the Huns and had suffered considerable loss. As a result, it was impossible to farm or raise animals in the frontier region.

Now Li Mu was asked to take over once again, but he claimed to be ill and refused to leave home. The king pressed him to lead the army, so Li finally agreed on the condition that he be allowed to pursue his former policy. The king accepted this provision, so General

Li went back and followed his original plan. The Huns came again, but though they didn't get anything, they thought General Li was a weakling.

The frontier soldiers won prizes every day, but prizes were not what they wanted. What all of them wanted was a fight. Now General Li had thirteen hundred specially selected chariots outfitted and picked out thirteen thousand horsemen, fifty thousand seasoned soldiers, and a hundred thousand archers. All of them drilled and practiced combat.

Now the military authorities allowed the local people to let their flocks and herds out. People filled the fields. When the Huns showed up, General Li pretended to be at a loss and even let them take several thousand captives.

When the Hun chieftain heard about this, he led a huge crowd on a mass raid into Chinese territory.

General Li set up many surprise battle lines and had his army fan out on both sides to attack. In this way the Chinese routed the Huns. They killed over a hundred thousand horsemen and put the tribal chieftain to flight.

For more than ten years after that the Huns did not dare to cross the border of Zhao.

Weakness and Battle

Liu Ji said:

Whenever you do battle with opponents who outnumber you and are stronger than you, you should set up many banners and increase the number of stoves you build, giving the appearance of strength to prevent opponents from figuring out your numbers and power. Then adversaries will not be quick to fight with you. If you can leave quickly, then your whole army can escape harm.

The rule is "Strength and weakness are a matter of formation" (Sun Tzu, *The Art of War*, "Force").

During the Later Han dynasty (25–219), a group of the seminomadic Qiang people of Central Asia, who were ancestors of the modern Tibetans, revolted against the Han Chinese empire. The Han empress dowager appointed a leading strategist to be the military governor of that area, but a horde of several thousand Qiang cut off the new governor's march.

The governor stopped his troops immediately and announced that he was going to send to the imperial court for reinforcements. Learning of this, the Qiang divided up to comb the surrounding countryside, looking for the Chinese messengers who had been sent to the Han court for help.

Now that the Qiang militia was scattered, the Chinese governor proceeded by forced marches night and day, covering over thirty miles a day. He had each mess sergeant make two stoves at first, and then increase the number of stoves each day. The Qiang did not dare to attack.

Someone said to the governor, "The famous martialist Sun Bin decreased his campfires, while you increased them. Also, you went more than three times the maximum daily march recommended in military classics. Why is this?"

The governor said, "The enemy had many soldiers, I had few. I increased the fire stoves to make them think the local militia was coming to welcome us. Thinking we are many and traveling fast, they hesitate to pursue us. Sun Bin saw weakness; I give the appearance of strength. The situations are not the same."

Hauteur and Battle

Liu Ji said:

When your opponents are strong and outnumber you, so that you cannot be sure of prevailing, you should use humility and courtesy to make them haughty, then wait for an opening that offers an opportunity of which you can take advantage, and you can beat them.

The rule is "Use humility to make them haughty" (Sun Tzu, The Art of War, "Strategic Assessments").

During the era of the Three Kingdoms, warlords of Wei in the north, Wu in the south, and Shu in the west struggled among one another for hegemony over the remains of the Chinese empire. At one point a leading general of Shu made a foray north, where he captured one Wei general and surrounded another.

Now the general of Wu who was stationed at the border with Wei and Shu left his post on account of illness. He was visited by another

Wu general, who said to him, "The Shu general is right on the border—why did you leave? There will be trouble if no one stands in his way."

The retired Wu general said, "You are right, but I am very ill."

The other Wu general said, "The Shu general is proud of his achievements, and his hauteur is overbearing. He has also heard of your illness, and is surely that more the lax in his precautions. If you attack now, when he isn't expecting it, you can capture or restrain him. This would be a good strategy to present to the king."

The retired Wu general said, "The Shu general is a brave and mettlesome man. He is already hard to oppose on this account. Furthermore, he has taken control of strategic territory, where he has won great prestige. With his recent successes and his growing boldness, it is not easy to plot against him."

When the retired Wu general got to the capital city, the king of Wu asked him, "If you are ill, who can replace you?"

The retired general recommended the other Wu general, with whom he had had the foregoing conversation, saying, "He is a deep thinker and has the ability to bear responsibility. Considering his orderly thinking, I regard him as suitable for this important post. Furthermore, he is not yet well known, so the general of Shu doesn't hate him. No one could be better. If you give him the job, have him conceal his actions outwardly while inwardly looking for opportunities to take advantage; then he can overcome the general of Shu."

So the king of Wu summoned the other general and promoted him. When this new Wu general of the border guard arrived at the frontier region, he sent a letter to the Shu general. The letter was fawning and obsequious, flattering the Shu general. The Wu general also wrote to the Shu general of his concern about the leading warlord of Wei and expressed hope that the general of Shu would contain this menace.

When the Shu general read this letter, he noted the humility expressed by the general of Wu and his desire for the good will of Shu. As a result, the general of Shu relaxed and was no longer hostile. Now the general of Wu reported this to the king of Wu, and explained how the Shu general could be captured.

So the king of Wu sent an undercover force up north, appointing two generals to lead the vanguard. In this way, the kingdom of Wu was able to wrest important territory from the grip of the warrior general of Shu.

Diplomatic Relations

Liu Ji said:

Whenever you go to war, establish cordial relations with neighboring countries. Form alliances to draw them into helping you. If you attack your enemies from the front while your allies attack from behind, your enemies will surely be vanquished.

The rule is "On intersecting ground, form communications" (Sun Tzu, *The Art of War*, "Nine Grounds").

During the era of the Three Kingdoms, at one point the top general of Shu had one of the Wei generals surrounded. The high command of Wei sent another general to the rescue. As it happened, the waters of the Han River rose violently, enabling the Shu general to capture the leader of the Wei reinforcements, with a large contingent of infantry and cavalry. The Shu general sent his own troops shooting down the swollen river in boats to strike the Wei forces.

Now at this time the puppet emperor of the dissolving Han dynasty had his temporary capital not far from the war zone. Cao Cao, the Wei warlord general who manipulated the puppet emperor, thought the capital was too close to enemy lines, and he wanted to move it out of reach.

One of the great ministers of Wei, however, objected to Cao Cao's plan. He said, "The reinforcements we sent were overcome by the river—it is not that they failed in defensive battle. As far as the overall policy of the state is concerned, nothing is lost; so if we move the capital now, this will come across to the enemy as a sign of weakness, and it will also make the local populace uneasy.

"The king of Wu and the king of Shu are outwardly close but inwardly distant; now that the top general of Shu is getting his way, the king of Wu is no doubt displeased. We should induce the king of Wu to stop the Shu general from behind—then the siege surrounding our Wei general will automatically be lifted."

Cao Cao followed this suggestion and sent an emissary to establish an alliance with the king of Wu. Subsequently the king of Wu sent one of his generals to attack the territory of the Shu warlord general, and the Wu general was able to wrest two districts from the grip of Shu. As a result, the general of Shu finally abandoned his siege of the Wei army and left the region.

Formation and Battle

Liu Ji said:

Whenever you do battle, if the enemy army is very large, then set up false formations as feints to divert and divide the enemy forces by inducing them to believe they have to divide their troops to defend against you. Once the enemy forces are divided, there will be relatively few troops in each contingent. You can concentrate your forces into one, so as to outnumber each group of enemy soldiers. Strike few with many, and you will not fail to win.

The rule is "Induce others to construct a formation while you yourself are formless" (Sun Tzu, *The Art of War*, "Emptiness and Fullness").

In the year 200, near the end of the moribund Han dynasty, the warlord Cao Cao faced off with one of his main competitors. His opponent sent two strategists with a top commander to lead an attack on an army led by one of Cao Cao's men, while he himself led another force to follow up.

As for Cao Cao, he went to rescue his men, who were now under siege. One of his advisors, however, warned him that he had too few troops with him to do battle, and that it would be necessary to divide the enemy's forces. Consequently, following the plan outlined by his advisor, Cao Cao led a contingent up behind his adversary, who thus had to send part of his own force back to deal with Cao Cao.

Now Cao Cao led his army on a forced march toward the position being held by his other troops under siege. When they were nearly there, the opposing commander took fright and turned around to fight Cao Cao's newly arrived reinforcements.

Now that the opponents' forces were divided, Cao Cao had two top generals launch a devastating attack, killing the enemy commander and lifting the siege.

Momentum and Battle

Liu Ji said:

In battle, momentum means riding on the force of the tide of events. If enemies are on the way to destruction, then you follow up and press them; their armies will surely collapse.

The rule is "Use the force of momentum to defeat them" ("Three Strategies").

In 265, the Martial Emperor of Jin founded the Jin dynasty, heralding the end of the era of the Three Kingdoms. Establishing himself by overthrowing the dynasty set up by Cao Cao in the northern kingdom of Wei, the Martial Emperor of Jin also had a secret plan to destroy the southern kingdom of Wu. Many of his courtiers, however, were opposed to the idea of attacking Wu.

Only three of the Martial Emperor's ministers were in favor of his plan to destroy Wu. One of them was ultimately appointed military director of the border region.

When the new military director of the border region reached his command outpost, he had the soldiers' armor and equipment repaired, and polished up their martial skills. Finally he selected a special force of elite troops, who then launched a successful assault against the army of one of the leading generals of Wu.

Now the military director petitioned the Jin emperor for permission to make a full-scale attack on the kingdom of Wu. The emperor sent back a message telling the director to wait until the following year for such a massive undertaking.

But the military director wrote a letter back to the emperor, explaining the situation in these terms:

"In any affair, it is imperative to compare gain and loss. With this invasion, the prospects of gain are 80 to 90 percent, while the prospects of loss are 10 to 20 percent. If we stop, nothing will be accomplished. The courtiers say we can be beat, but they cannot tell. It is just that they are not the strategists, so they get no credit for our military successes. The are all embarrassed at having spoken in error before, so they oppose this undertaking.

"Since autumn our movements against the enemy have become obvious; if we stop now, they might develop a scheme in fear—they may move the capital, increase fortifications, and relocate the populace. If their citadels cannot be attacked and there is no plunder in the countryside, next year may be too late to carry out our plans."

When this letter from the military director of the border region arrived at the capital, the emperor happened to be playing chess with one of the ministers who did approve of the emperor's plan to destroy the kingdom of Wu. The minister said, "Your Majesty is highly intelligent and has great military acumen. Your nation is rich and your armies are strong. The king of Wu is decadent and vicious, killing off the worthy and able. If you attack him now, the matter can be settled without much effort."

The emperor then gave his permission to move against the kingdom of Wu. Now the military director of the border region launched his campaign, scoring successive military victories and winning over the provinces of Wu as the provincial authorities defected from Wu and switched their allegiance to Jin.

That summer there was heavy flooding, and the commanders of the Jin army suggested to the military director that they wait until winter to go on the move again, as floods always brought epidemics. The director, however, said that a long entrenched enemy cannot easily be overcome, and insisted on riding the momentum of their victories all the way to the final overthrow of the king of Wu.

Pursuing this course of action, the Jin army encountered little further resistance. Finally, in the year 280, the Jin dynasty annexed the former kingdom of Wu.

Knowledge and Battle

Liu Ji said:

Whenever you mobilize an army to attack an enemy, it is imperative to know the location of battle. When your army gets there, if you can induce the enemy forces to come when you expect them, you will win in battle. If you know the place and time of battle, then your preparations will be concentrated and your defenses will be firm.

The rule is "When you know the place and time of battle, then you can join the fight from a thousand miles away" (Sun Tzu, *The Art of War*, "Emptiness and Fullness").

During the Warring States era, the states of Wei and Zhao attacked the state of Han, which appealed to the state of Qi for help in this emergency.

The government of Qi sent one of its generals with an army, which marched directly for the capital of Wei, the aggressor. When the invading Wei general heard of this, he left the state of Han and returned to Wei.

Now the Qi general received some advice from Sun Bin, a noted strategist and descendant of the famous Sun Wu (Sun Tzu), legendary author of *The Art of War.* Master Sun said, "The armies of Wei, Zhao, and Han are fierce and think little of Qi, which they regard as cowardly. A good warrior would take advantage of this tendency and 'lead them on with prospects of gain.'

"According to *The Art of War,* struggling for an advantage fifty miles away will thwart the forward leadership, and only half of those who chase prospects of gain twenty-five miles away will actually get there. Have the army of Qi enter Wei territory and make thousands of campfires; on the next day have them make half that number of campfires, and on the next day have them make half again that number."

The Qi army did as Sun Bin had advised. The Wei general was delighted to hear that the number of campfires was dwindling day by day, thinking that the men of Qi were defecting. He said, "I knew the soldiers of Qi were cowards—they've been in our territory for only three days now, and more than half the army has run away."

Consequently, the Wei general left his infantry behind and hastened in pursuit of the Qi army with only a personal force of crack troops. Calculating the speed of their pursuit, Sun Bin concluded that by nightfall the Wei force would reach an area of narrow roads and difficult passage, a place suitable for ambush.

Now Sun Bin had a large tree cut down and stripped of its bark. On the bare log he wrote, "The general Wei will die at this tree," and had it placed on the road where the Wei troops would pass that night. Then he had several thousand expert archers conceal themselves near the road.

When the Wei general came to the place where the stripped log had been set across the road, he lit a torch to read what had been written on it. Before he finished reading, the archers of Qi, for whom the kindling of the torch became a signal to fire, loosed their arrows all at once, throwing the Wei troops into a panic. Realizing he had been outwitted and his men were beaten, the Wei general killed himself.

Reconnaissance

Liu Ji said:

The first rule of maneuvering an army is to send out scouts for reconnaissance. Small brigades of scouts, keeping a fixed distance from the moving army, reconnoiter in all directions. If they see a hostile army, they relay this information back to the commander, who then directs the soldiers to prepare.

The rule is "Those who face the unprepared with preparation are victorious" (Sun Tzu, *The Art of War*, "Planning a Seige").

In the first century B.C.E., during the Han dynasty, one of the tribes of the ancient Qiang people rebelled against the Chinese empire. They broke into frontier fortifications, attacked cities, and killed officials.

At that time a certain Rear General Zhao (137–52 B.C.E.) was over seventy years old; the emperor considered him too old for warfare, and sent a message to ask the general to nominate a replacement.

The general said, "Hearing about something a hundred times is not as good as seeing it once. It is hard to predict the course of a military operation, so let me ride out to see conditions for myself so that I can present a plan."

He added, "The Qiang rebels are a small minority tribe and cannot last long in defiance of a major power. Please leave this up to me, old as I am, and don't worry about it.

The emperor smiled and gave him permission.

When the Chinese general reached the disturbed area, he commandeered a cavalry of ten thousand mounted warriors. To move against the Qiang they had to cross a river, but the general feared that the Qiang might cut them off, so he first sent three groups to cross by night. When they reached the other side, they set up a battle line, and the rest of the cavalry crossed over the next morning.

Hundreds of Qiang riders appeared, watching the Chinese cavalry from the side. The Chinese general said to his troops, "Our warriors and horses have just arrived and are tired out, so do not give chase to the Qiang. They are all expert horsemen, difficult to stop, and our soldiers might be tempted to pursue them. Our aim in striking this rebellious tribe is to exterminate them, so let us not be eager for small gains."

Thus commanding his men not to attack the Qiang, the general sent riders out to reconnoiter the mountain ahead. The scouts did not find any of the Qiang tribesmen, and the cavalry crossed the mountain in the middle of the night.

The general called his officers together for a conference and said, "I know the Qiang rebels cannot do anything. If they had sent several thousand men to guard the mountain, how could our troops have penetrated this far?"

So the general saw to it that there was constant reconnaissance, sending scouts out to considerable distances. Whenever he moved his troops he made preparations for battle, and when they stopped they built fortified camps. The old general was well able to bear this heavy responsibility, and he looked after his warriors very well. He never fought without strategic planning and eventually succeeded in pacifying the region.

Striving in Battle

Liu Ji said:

Whenever you engage in warfare with enemies, you should strive to be the first to occupy advantageous terrain, so that you can win in battle. If the enemy gets there first, do not attack; wait for a change such that you can strike advantageously.

The rule is "Let there be no attack on a ground of contention" (Sun Tzu, The Art of War, "Nine Grounds").

In the year 234, during the era of the Three Kingdoms, the kingdom of Shu sent an army out on the road north, toward the kingdom of Wei. One of the military leaders of Wei warned his people that the Shu army was intending to occupy the northern plain, but there were those who disagreed.

One of the great generals of Wei, however, thought that this advisor was correct, and he stationed a garrison in the northern plain before the Shu forces arrived. The Wei garrison had not yet finished building fortifications when a huge army from Shu showed up.

The Wei forces struck back, and after a few days the Shu general led his army west. Most of the Wei commanders thought the Shu army was going to attack the western provinces of Wei; one of them, however, disagreed, saying that the Shu general was just making things look that way as a strategic ruse to lure the Wei forces west, whereas the real intention of the Shu general was to attack the east.

That night the Shu army did in fact attack in the east. Because of the warning of the perceptive commander, however, the Wei army was prepared and did not suffer a loss.

Going on the Attack

Liu Ji said:

In warfare, attack is a matter of knowing the adversary. If you send out troops only when you know that the adversary is vulnerable for some reason and can be defeated, then you will not fail to win.

The rule is "Vulnerability is a matter of attack" (Sun Tzu, *The Art of War*, "Formation").

During the era of the Three Kingdoms, the warlord general Cao Cao of Wei sent one of his generals to be the military governor of a border area. This Wei general garrisoned his troops there, making many rice fields. He also sent secret agents into the kingdom of Wu to the south, to invite the cooperation of a group of dissidents within that kingdom.

One of the leading generals of Wu said, "The land where the Wei army is garrisoned is very fertile. Once they harvest a crop of rice there, their numbers will surely increase. If this goes on for a few years, Cao Cao will be hard to stop. We should get rid of them as soon as possible."

So the Wu general made a report on these conditions to the king of Wu, who then personally went on the expedition against Cao Cao's garrison. The Wu forces got there in a day and a night. The king asked his generals about strategy, and they all suggested making a high fortification, which they said could with effort be built rapidly.

But the leading Wu general said, "They have already fortified the city they occupy, and reinforcements are sure to be arriving, making it impossible to get at them. Now the rains are starting, and we should take this opportunity to attack; for if we stay a few days we will surely return exhausted, and the roads back will be difficult. I think that would be dangerous.

"Now as I see this city, it is not all that secure. If we attack it on four sides while our armed forces are at their keenest, the Wei occupation army can be thrown out in a short time, and we can get back home before the rivers swell. This is the way to complete victory."

The king of Wu followed this advice. The Wu forces staged an all-out attack on the city and very soon overthrew the Wei occupation. The leader of the Wei reinforcements was on the road when he heard the news that the city had fallen, and he promptly withdrew on learning of Wei's defeat.

As for the Wu general who had recommended this successful course of action, the king of Wu rewarded him for his achievement, making him military governor of the area.

Defense and Battle

Liu Ji said:

In warfare, the defender is the one who knows himself. If you know you have no reasonable chance of winning, then for the time being stay firmly on the defensive, waiting for a time when the adversary can be beaten. If you wait for the right time to attack, you will always win.

The rule is "Invincibility is a matter of defense" (Sun Tzu, *The Art of War*, "Formation").

Around the middle of the second century B.C.E., during the reign of the fourth-generation emperor of the Han dynasty, seven states—Wu, Chu, and five others—rebelled against imperial authority and tried to secede from the empire. The emperor appointed one of his distinguished generals to lead the reprisals against the rebellious eastern states.

The general made a petition to the emperor, stating, "The armed forces of Chu are highly mobile and hard to fight. Let us cede the state of Liang to them and then cut off their supply routes. If we do this, we can stop them."

The emperor agreed to this, and the general went out to join the army.

Right at that time, the Wu army was attacking the state of Liang, and the local government of Liang, in desperation, asked the imperial Han general for help.

But the general led his troops northeast to a walled city and took up a defensive position there. The king of Liang sent an emissary to plead with the imperial general, but the general kept to his ploy and did not go to the rescue.

Now the king of Liang sent an appeal to the emperor himself. The emperor ordered his general to rescue Liang, but the general did not obey the command; instead he fortified the city walls and refused to come out. In the meanwhile, he sent mounted commanders out to cut off the supply routes behind the armies of Wu and Chu.

When the armies of Wu and Chu ran low on supplies and were getting so hungry they wanted to go home, they tried to provoke the imperial general into a fight several times. The general, however, never came out.

One night there was a fearful commotion in the camp of the imperial general, as fighting started. The fighting spread to the skirts of the general's tent, but he lay there stoically and would not get up. After a while the disturbance died down.

The Wu army rushed the southeast corner of the city, so the imperial general had defenses built up on the northwest perimeter. Before long the Wu army did in fact rush the northwest wall, but they could not get in.

Now the armies of Wu and Chu were starving, so they withdrew and started back to their homelands. At this point the imperial general sent his best soldiers out to run them down, and his men routed the troops of Wu and Chu.

The king of Chu abandoned his armed forces and ran away with a few thousand bodyguards to hole up south of the Long River. The army of the Han empire now took advantage of this victory to chase the Chu armies down and catch them all, conquering the territories of Chu.

The imperial general of the Han sent out an order, saying, "Anyone who gets the king of Wu will be given a reward of a thousand pieces of gold."

In little more than a month, a man of Yue, a state neighboring Wu, showed up with the head of the king of Wu.

The whole civil war had taken seven months; Wu and Chu were completely pacified.

Postponing Battle

Liu Ji said:

In war, when adversaries are orderly in their movements and are at their sharpest, it is not yet time to fight with them; it is best to fortify your position and wait. Watch for their energy to wane after being on alert for a long time; then rise and strike them. You will not fail to win.

The rule is "Delay until others wane" ("Zuo Family Tradition on the Spring and Autumn Annals").

In the early days of the Tang dynasty (618–905), the founder of the dynasty campaigned against a warlord who had taken over territorial rule at the end of the preceding Sui dynasty (588–618). When the Tang founder surrounded the warlord in the ancient eastern capital, the leader of a concurrent peasant rebellion brought his whole following to rescue the Sui warlord. The Tang founder, however, blocked the peasant army at an outlying mountain pass called "Military Fastness."

When the peasant army massed east of the river, stretching over miles, all the commanders in the Tang founder's army looked frightened. The founder himself rode high up the mountain with a few horsemen to view the peasant army.

Seeing the masses, the founder of the Tang dynasty said, "This mob has never seen a major adversary, and now it is going through a narrow defile in a chaotic condition, without order in the army. The fact that they are massing near the city means they think lightly of us. I think that if our forces do not move, but wait for their spirits to wind down, after they have been in the field for a long time the fighters will get hungry and will surely withdraw on their own. If we then strike them as they are pulling out, we can surely overcome them."

The peasant army stayed in battle formation from before dawn until after noon. The fighters got hungry and tired, and began looking around and fighting over food and drink.

Now the Tang founder had one of his commanders lead three hundred mounted warriors south to gallop past the western flank of the mob, giving these instructions: "If the mob doesn't stir when you charge past, stop and come back. If you sense them stirring, turn and charge east."

When the horsemen galloped past, the peasants did stir, and the Tang founder gave the word to attack. They charged down the mountainside into the valley, following the valley east and attacking the insurgents from behind.

The leader of the peasants, once a military officer, led his fighters away, but before they could regroup, the Tang founder struck them with light mounted troops, mowing them down wherever they went. The mob scattered to the four winds, and their leader was captured alive, only to be killed later in the capital city of the new Tang empire, in the year 621.

Emptiness in Battle

Liu Ji said:

In warfare, if you are void of power, you feign the appearance of fullness in such a way the enemies cannot tell how empty or powerful you really are. Then they will be hesitant to engage you in battle, and you can keep your forces intact.

The rule is "When opponents are unwilling to fight with you, it is because they think it is contrary to their interests, or because you have misled them into thinking so" (Sun Tzu, *The Art of War,* "Emptiness and Fullness," Liu Ji's own paraphrase).

During the era of the Three Kingdoms, when Zhuge Liang, general of the kingdom of Shu, was stationed at one of the most critical strategic passes on the border of the kingdom of Wei, he was left alone to guard the fortress with ten thousand troops when the other Shu generals went south with their armies.

Now Sima Yi, general of the kingdom of Wei, led twenty thousand troops to attack Zhuge Liang. When they reached a point some twenty miles from the Shu outpost, Sima Yi sent scouts to reconnoiter. When the scouts returned, they reported that Zhuge Liang had little manpower in the citadel.

Meanwhile, Zhuge Liang also knew of the imminent arrival of the Wei army; he feared he might be hard pressed and wanted to recall one of the other Shu generals, who had left earlier with his troops. They were already too far away, however, and there was nothing they could do to help.

Now the defending Shu commanders and officers paled in fear, for none of them knew what to do. Zhuge Liang, however, remained composed. He ordered his soldiers to take down the banners, put away the war drums, and stay inside as much as possible. He also had all the gates of the walled city opened and the streets cleaned.

Sima Yi, the Wei general, had thought that Zhuge Liang was being cautious; and now that he saw this apparent weakness, he suspected that there were ambushers lying in wait. So he led his troops back up into the mountains to the north.

The next day at mealtime, Zhuge Liang was laughing with his assistants, saying, "No doubt Sima Yi thought I was only feigning weakness and must have had ambushers hidden, so he ran off through the mountains!"

Battling with the Full

Liu Ji said:

In warfare, if your opponents are full of power, be well prepared and they will not readily make any moves.

The rule is "When they are fulfilled, be prepared against them" (Sun Tzu, *The Art of War*, "Strategic Assessments").

In the early days of the era of the Three Kingdoms, when the first ruler of the kingdom of Shu originally established himself as a local king of a part of the region of Shu, he appointed a formidable warrior as forward general, handing him a ceremonial axe of authority. The same year the forward general garrisoned an army on the border of the kingdom of Wu; he also led a siege against the army of one of the generals of the kingdom of Wei.

Cao Cao, one of the leading warriors of Wei, sent a commander with some troops to rescue his brother general, now being besieged by the forward general of Shu. That autumn there were heavy rains, however, causing the Han River to flood, thus drowning the troops sent by Cao Cao. The chief commander of these troops surrendered to the forward general of Shu, and another of the Wei commanders was also captured.

Some dissident factions within the kingdom of Wei also accepted orders from the forward general of Shu and became his supporters. As a result, the power of the warrior of Shu shook all of China.

Fighting Too Readily

Liu Ji said:

Whenever you are going to fight with an enemy, you must measure the adversary carefully before you send out armed forces. If you sally forth recklessly and fight without a plan, you will surely be defeated by the enemy.

The rule is "The bold will readily clash, readily clash without knowing what is to their advantage" (Wu Qi, "On Generalship").

During the Spring and Autumn era, the state of Jin fought a war with the state of Chu. The lord of Jin knew that the Chu general was short tempered and impulsive; so he seized the Chu ambassador to anger the general.

Enraged, the Chu general did in fact attack the Jin army, and his forces were routed.

Using Profit to Fight

Liu Ji said:

Whenever you are at war, if the opponent's general is stupid and inflexible, he can be lured with the prospect of gain. When the opponent is so greedy to get something that he is not mindful of danger, you can overcome him by ambush.

The rule is "Draw them in with the prospect of gain" (Sun Tzu, *The Art of War,* "Strategic Assessments").

During the Spring and Autumn era, the state of Chu attacked the state of Jiao. One of the officials of Chu said, "Jiao is small but volatile. Being volatile, it is no doubt lacking in planning. Let us use unarmed men disguised as woodcutters for bait."

This plan was followed, and the Jiao side captured thirty men. The next day men of Jiao came out to fight and chased the men of Chu into the mountains.

Now there were Chu people sitting on the northern perimeter of the citadel of Jiao, and others lying in wait in the mountains; so when the men of Jiao chased the Chu agents into the mountains, they ran into the ambush and suffered a heavy defeat.

Fighting Attackers

Liu Ji said:

When you and your rivals are keeping to your respective borders, if rivals plunder your territory and thus disturb the populace in the outlying areas, you could set up ambushes at natural barriers, or you can construct artificial barriers against them, so that enemies will not readily try to invade.

The rule is "What discourages opponents from coming is the prospect of harm" (Sun Tzu, *The Art of War,* "Emptiness and Fullness").

Around the beginning of the eighth century, when the illustrious Tang dynasty (618–905) was nearly a hundred years old, there was a problem between the Chinese empire and a Turkic people known in Chinese as the Tuque. At one point the general overseer of the north, an officer of the imperial Chinese organization, was beaten in a battle with the Turks. He then summoned a high minister of the Tang court to lead an attack against the Turks.

The marauding Turks had already left the immediate vicinity when the imperial minister arrived. He led his troops after them, and attacked their camp that very night, routing them.

At first the Turks and the North Army of Tang China had recognized the Yellow River as the boundary between their territories. On the north bank there was a place where the Turks would go to pray at their shrine each time they were going to raid Chinese territory to the south.

Now at this time one of the Turkic khans, who was eventually to be khan of all the Turks, made a sudden all-out attack on the western Turks. The Chinese minister-general who had come from court to lead the punitive expedition took advantage of this drain on the Turks to seize territory north of the river to build a defensive fortress. The Chinese called this fortress "Citadel of Accepting Surrender," after the fortress built eight centuries earlier by the Han dynasty Chinese to stop the incursions of the Huns. This was the way the minister-general intended to stop the Turks from raiding Chinese territory to the south.

One of the Tang grandees objected that the line of defense against northern tribes was traditionally set south of the river, and if this citadel were built on the rangeland of the Turks, it would inevitably wind up in their hands. The minister-general, who had, after all, gone at the request of the general overseer of the north, insisted on having the fortress built, and the emperor of China finally gave his permission.

The minister-general proposed to keep the garrison troops there for a year to help with the work. Two hundred men ran away to go home, but the minister-general had them caught and killed at the wall of the fortress. The whole army shook in fear, and the draftees worked as hard as they could. As a result, three fortresses were built in sixty days.

The fortresses were over a hundred miles apart and bordered on the northern desert. The Chinese army opened up a hundred miles of territory and set up a watch post with eighteen hundred troops on a mountain further north.

From then on the Turks did not dare to come over the mountains to graze their horses, and there were no more yearly raids on the northern territories of Tang-dynasty China. Enormous expenditures were thus eliminated, and the garrison army was greatly reduced.

Fearlessness in Danger

Liu Ji said:

When you battle with opponents, if you fall into a situation where there is danger of destruction, you should inspire your soldiers to fight to the death, for they will win if they forget about surviving.

The rule is "When warriors are in great danger, then they have no fear" (Sun Tzu, *The Art of War,* "Nine Grounds").

The monumental Han dynasty of China lasted for more than four hundred years, with but a brief interruption in the middle, about two thousand years ago. During this hiatus after two centuries of the dynasty, a certain military commander set himself up as king of Shu in western China.

Now one of the loyalist generals of the Han dynasty invaded Shu to attack the warlord king. The Han loyalist overthrew a district of Shu, and all the fortresses in the area surrendered.

The emperor of China, however, warned the general, "There are over a hundred thousand troops in the capital of Shu, so it will not do to take them lightly. Just occupy the position you have taken; if they come to attack you, don't fight with them. If they don't come after you, then move your encampments up to pressure them. When they grow weary, then you may attack them."

But the loyalist general didn't listen to the emperor's advice. Taking advantage of the gains he had already made, he personally led a cavalry over two hundred thousand strong to ride against the capital city of Shu.

When he came within a few miles of the walled city, the general set up camp on the north bank of the river. Then he had pontoon bridges made and sent another general to garrison about seven miles away, south of the river.

Now the emperor was alarmed. He upbraided the loyalist general in a letter, saying, "After all my instructions, how can you disobey me? Now you have entered deeply into enemy territory, and you have set up separate camps. Your two camps won't be able to reach each other in an emergency. If the enemy sends a brigade to pin you down and attacks the other camp in force, once the others are defeated you will be beaten. Please take your army back to your stronghold."

But before the imperial message had reached his general, the self-proclaimed king of Shu actually did send a hundred thousand soldiers to attack one camp of Han loyalists, and another hundred thousand soldiers to block the other camp, preventing the two generals of the Han dynasty from helping each other.

The forces of the first loyalist general staged a tremendous battle that lasted all day, but they got the worst of it and ran inside the walls of the city they had occupied. Now the army of the king of Shu surrounded them.

At this point the Han general called his commanders together and tried to rouse their spirits, speaking to them in these terms: "We have crossed the most rugged territory together and have fought our way over hundreds of miles, winning everywhere. Now we have penetrated deeply into enemy territory and are near the capital city. But we and our ally camp are both under siege, and we can't join forces. It is hard to tell what might happen. I want to send an undercover force to join up with our ally camp south of the river. If we can cooperate with like minds, people will fight of their own accord, and much can be accomplished. Otherwise we will suffer a total loss. The chance to win or lose is in this one operation."

The commanders agreed.

So they closed the camp and stayed inside for three days while they feasted the soldiers and fed the horses. Then they set up a lot of banners and flags, and kept the fires burning constantly, leading the horses out by night to join up with the other camp of Han dynasty loyalists.

Unaware of this, the Shu general led an attack south of the river the day after the two camps of Han loyalists had secretly joined together. The loyalists fought back with their whole force. The fighting continued from morning until evening, but the loyalists finally routed the Shu army and killed its two generals.

Now the imperial Han general led his troops back to his base of operations and left the other camp of loyalists there to oppose the self-proclaimed king of Shu himself. The general reported everything to the emperor, severely blaming himself for not having followed the emperor's directions from the start.

The emperor replied, "You were quite right to return to your base of operations in Shu. The king of Shu will surely not dare to attack both you and the other loyalist army. If he attacks the others first, you send your whole infantry and cavalry at him from your base within Shu. When he finds he is in danger and at an impasse, you will surely beat him."

Now the Han loyalist general did battle with the king of Shu on the ground between the Han outpost and the capital of Shu. They fought eight times, with the imperial Han loyalists winning all eight battles, finally driving the Shu army back behind the walls of the capital city.

At this point, the king of Shu himself led ten thousand men out of the city for an all-out battle. The Han general sent two huge contingents of elite troops to attack the Shu forces. The army of the king of Shu took a thrashing and ran away. One of the Han commanders, charging right into the fray, stabbed the king of Shu to death.

The next day the city capitulated. The head of the self-proclaimed king of Shu was chopped off and sent to the imperial capital of China. Thus ended the civil war in the region of Shu in the early days of the renewed Han dynasty, the so-called eastern or latter Han, which lasted for another two hundred years.

Hunger and Battle

Liu Ji said:

Whenever you mobilize an army on a punitive expedition and penetrate deep into enemy territory, if you lack for provisions you will need to send troops out to plunder. If you take over enemy storehouses and stockpiles, using their supplies to feed your army, then you will win.

The rule is "By feeding off the enemy, you can be sufficient in both arms and provisions" (Sun Tzu, *The Art of War*, "Doing Battle").

During the period of the Northern and Southern dynasties, a general of the northern Zhou dynasty led an army across the river to take the territory of the Chen dynasty in the south. One of the generals of the Chen dynasty led an army to strike the Zhou invaders.

It was autumn, and the rains caused the river to flood, cutting off supply routes. The men of Zhou were worried, but their general sent out troops to plunder what they needed for the army.

Now the Zhou general was afraid that the Chen general would realize he was short of supplies, so he had a large mound of earth raised in his camp and had the mound covered with grain, to make it look like a huge pile of grain. He then invited people from the local villages on the pretext of asking after their welfare; he let the villagers see the artificial grain pile and then sent them away.

As a result, the Chen general heard about the great heap of grain and thought it was real. The Zhou general also built more fortifications and set up barracks, showing that he was ready for a protracted campaign.

Now agriculture was ruined in that area, and the Chen general was at a loss. At first local people rode fast boats with supplies of grain for the Chen army, but the Zhou general devised a scheme to put a stop to this. He sent boats to the Chen army, boats that had been disguised to look like the supply boats of the local people, but which in reality concealed ambushers.

The Chen soldiers, seeing the boats coming down the river and thinking they carried food, plunged into the current in their eagerness. Instead the ambushers hidden in the boats captured them.

There were some dissidents in the Zhou army who defected to the Chen side, and the Chen general took them all in. The general of Zhou took a horse to a boat, then had someone in the boat whip it; he repeated this several times, until the horse learned to fear boats and would not board. Then he stationed some ambushers along the river bank, and sent a pretended defector to the Chen general, mounted on the horse that feared boats.

When the Chen general sent some men to greet the defector, they vied with each other to get the horse. But the horse took fright and wouldn't board the boat with the soldiers; and in the commotion the Zhou ambushers rose from their hiding places along the river bank and killed every one of the men sent by the Chen general.

Later, when real supply boats or real defectors came along, the Chen general feared it was another Zhou ambush and wouldn't take them in. Thus there was a standoff for more than a year, and the Chen army was ultimately unable to stop the Zhou invaders.

Fighting on Full Stomachs

Liu Ji said:

When enemies come from far away and their supplies do not last, then they are hungry while you are well fed. In such a situation you should strengthen your defenses and not engage in battle. Hold them at a standoff so long that they wear out. Cut off their supply routes. If they retreat, send bushwhackers after them under cover to attack them by surprise on their way home; then you will not fail to beat them.

The rule is "Standing your ground awaiting those far away, awaiting the weary in comfort, awaiting the hungry on full stomachs, is mastering strength" (Sun Tzu, *The Art of War*, "Armed Struggle").

The Tang dynasty, during which China was a leader of world civilizations in the arts and sciences, lasted nearly three hundred years. It was formally established in the year 618, supplanting the Sui dynasty.

The Sui dynasty is distinguished for having unified China after the protracted civil wars of the era of the Northern and Southern dynasties. The heir of the founder of Sui, however, used his inherited power to undertake aggressive imperialist campaigns that alienated the people and brought the dynasty to a swift destruction. After the Sui collapsed, the warlord-administrators of the new empire, which had never been fully demilitarized, were foremost among those who scrambled for the power relinquished by the house of the Sui.

One of the Sui warlords continued to occupy a certain area even after the founding of the Tang dynasty had been formally proclaimed elsewhere. With the help of Central Asian Turks, the Sui warlord inflicted a series of defeats on the Tang armies. The warlord was so successful that he even sent one of his generals into Tang territory to expand his own bailiwick.

As a result, the founder of the Tang dynasty led an expedition against the Sui warlord in the year 619. The Tang warrior-prince, who established the dynasty and set his father on the throne, told his own generals, "The Sui warlord's general is deep in our territory, along with all their elite troops and best commanders. It seems to me, however, that while their army is large, they must really be short of supplies, seeing as how they are plundering to sustain themselves. Their intention is to do battle quickly. We should strengthen our fortifications and wait for them to starve. We shouldn't rush into a fight."

The Tang forces followed the reasoning of their leader, strengthening their defenses while cutting off enemy supply lines. Eventually they starved out the Sui army.

Fatigue and Battle

Liu Ji said:

In warfare, if there is an advantageous position but the enemy has already occupied it, if you then head into battle there you will be fatigued and therefore suffer defeat at the hands of the enemy.

The rule is "Those who are first on the battlefield and await opponents are at ease; those who are last on the battlefield and head into battle get worn out" (Sun Tzu, *The Art of War,* "Emptiness and Fullness").

After the civil wars of the Three Kingdoms period, the Jin dynasty was established, supplanting the victorious kingdom of Wei. The Jin dynasty lasted from 265 to 420, but it was challenged by a series of kingdoms ruled by non-Chinese peoples. These latter were called the Sixteen Kingdoms, and they were established by warlord-kings from among five Central Asian minorities who adopted elements of the cultures of East and South Asia in their rise to nationhood.

In the early fourth century, a high minister of the Jin dynasty sent an army of more than one hundred thousand troops to attack one of these kingdoms, which was ruled by a race of people known in Chinese as Jie, descendants of the ancient Xiongnu Huns.

The leader of the Jie intended to resist aggressively, but someone warned him, "The Chinese army is well trained and powerful; it is impossible to stand up to it. For now let us strengthen our defensive positions and thus 'break their edge.' There is a difference in the power of attack and the power of defense; if we remain on the defensive for now we will gain complete victory."

But the Jie leader said, "The Chinese army has come from afar; the soldiers are physically exhausted and in a ragged and disorderly condition. We can beat them in one battle—how strong can they be? How can we let them go, when we have the opportunity to attack them before reinforcements arrive? If we draw back now and the Chinese take advantage of our withdrawal to attack us once our army is in motion, it will be every man for himself—then how can we fortify our defensive position? What you are recommending is a way to self-destruction without even a fight."

And in the end the leader of the Jie killed the man who objected to aggressive defense against the Chinese.

Now the Jie warrior-king appointed a vanguard commander and ordered that any laggards be executed. He set up a dummy force on top of a hill, then stationed two ambush forces on either side. The warrior-king personally led a brigade to meet the Chinese in battle, and then pretended to flee.

The Chinese commander sent his men to chase the Jie warriors as they fled. Now hidden Jie ambushers rose up and attacked the pursuers. The Chinese were routed and had to retreat.

Victory in Battle

Liu Ji said:

When you defeat enemies in battle, it will not do to become haughty and rest on your laurels; you should be strictly prepared for adversaries at all times. Then even if enemies do attack, you will be ready and will not suffer harm.

The rule is "Once you have prevailed, be as if you had not" ("Sima's Art of War").

The brief but momentous Qin dynasty (246–207 B.C.E.) put an end to centuries of civil war and unified China for the first time in more than five hundred years. The founder of Qin supplanted the self-cannibalizing feudalism of ancient China with civil bureaucracy and rule of law, unifying both material and intellectual culture in China to an unprecedented degree. The Qin also expanded its influence beyond the realm of ancient China and established the first Chinese empire.

The second emperor, who did not have all of his father's qualities, exhausted the new empire very rapidly with his imperial schemes. Thus there was intense discontent in many parts of China, and the Qin dynasty was overthrown in its second generation by widespread rebellions.

One of the leaders of a major peasant uprising sent two of his most powerful allies against strategic Qin positions, and they scored a series of victories over the imperial armies. As a result, the rebel leader began to take the Qin armies lightly, and he became somewhat haughty.

Someone advised the rebel leader, "Having prevailed in battle, if the commanders become haughty and the soldiers become lax, they will inevitably suffer defeat. Now your soldiers are getting a bit lazy, while the Qin forces grow by the day. I fear them for your sake."

The rebel leader, however, would not listen. He sent this advisor as an emissary to another state. On the way, this emissary met an ambassador from that very state, and asked him if he were going to see the rebel leader.

When the ambassador replied in the affirmative, the emissary of the rebel leader said, "Our leader's army is now headed for certain defeat; if you go slowly you will escape death, but if you go quickly you will meet disaster."

As it turned out, the imperial Qin forces launched a total assault on the peasant army, inflicting a crushing defeat on the rebels. The leader of the uprising lost his life.

Defeat in Battle

Liu Ji said:

When you are defeated by enemies in battle, do not fear. You should think of how to find benefit in having suffered harm: service your equipment, rouse your soldiers, and watch for the enemy to slack off so that you can attack. Then you will prevail.

The rule is "Through injury trouble can be resolved" (Sun Tzu, *The Art of War*, "Adaptations," Liu Ji's own paraphrase).

In the early fourth century, there took place the infamous "Riots of the Eight Kings," civil wars among feudal kings of the Chinese empire under the Jin dynasty.

At one point, the king of Hojian sent one of his generals to attack the king of Changsha. The emperor of the Jin dynasty personally sent a force to oppose the Hojian army, but a division of Hojian guerrilla fighters broke through the imperial army. Then the Hojian army entered the ancient capital of China.

Now the emperor's general, following orders, went after the Hojian army in the capital city. When the Hojian soldiers saw the imperial cavalcade in the distance, they began to have fears, and their commander could not stop them. Ultimately the demoralized Hojian forces suffered a crushing defeat, with the dead and wounded filling the streets.

The Hojian general retreated to an outlying position. Everyone was broken in spirit and had no more will to fight. Many of them urged the Hojian general to flee by night.

The general, however, responded, "It is a matter of course for there to be victory and defeat in a military action. What is important is to use failure to achieve success. We will press further forward and construct fortifications, then attack them when they least expect it. This is how to use surprise tactics in a military operation."

So that very night the remaining Hojian forces advanced under cover to a position very near to the capital city. The leader of the imperial army, meanwhile, having just won a resounding victory, didn't pay much attention to these maneuvers. But then when he suddenly heard that siege fortifications had been built outside the city, he led his troops out to fight. In the end, the imperial army was soundly beaten and had to retreat.

Taking the Initiative

Liu Ji said:

In war, when you perceive a reasonable possibility of conquering the enemy, then it is appropriate to strike quickly. Then you can win every time.

The rule is "Proceed when you see it to be appropriate" (Wu Qi, "Assessing the Enemy").

In the early days of the Tang dynasty, one of the leading Tang generals dealt a telling blow to the Turks. The Turkish khan fled to safety in the mountains, then sent an ambassador to the Tang court to apologize and request that the Chinese empire accept the fealty of the Turks.

The Tang court sent the same general to welcome the Turks. But while the khan outwardly sought to have his allegiance accepted, he still had doubts in his mind, and the Chinese general sensed this. Meanwhile, the Tang court also sent an ambassador to the Turks to reassure them.

Now the Chinese general said to one of his chief assistant commanders, "When our ambassador arrives, the Turks will surely feel secure. If we send out a cavalry to attack them now, we will surely gain our desire."

The assistant commander said, "But the emperor has already accepted the Turks' surrender, and our own ambassador will be among them—what about that?"

The general said, "This is an opportunity not to be lost—why hold back just to spare the ambassador's life?"

Then the Chinese general quickly mobilized his troops and set out to ride on the Turks. They encountered over a thousand Turkish scouts on the way and took them all captive.

When the Turkish khan saw the ambassador of the imperial Tang court, he was very happy and did not worry about the Chinese army. The Chinese vanguard, meanwhile, took advantage of fog to advance, and the khan was not aware of their imminent attack until they were just a few miles away.

The Turks had not even had enough time to array their battle lines when the Chinese army struck them. The Chinese beheaded over ten thousand Turks and took more than a hundred thousand men and women captive, including the son of the khan himself.

The Chinese also caught and killed one of the princesses of the Sui dynasty, which had preceded the Tang as the ruling house of China. This princess had been actively encouraging the Turks to attack the Tang Chinese, hoping thereby to reestablish the Sui dynasty.

The Turkish khan fled, but he was subsequently captured and presented to the Tang court. Now Chinese territory was expanded all the way to the great desert.

Provocation and Battle

Liu Ji said:

In warfare, when your encampments and those of your enemies are far apart and your forces are of equal strength, you may send out light cavalry to provoke them, waiting in ambush for them to respond. By these tactics, their armies can be beaten. If enemies try the same strategy on you, don't attack them with your whole army.

The rule is "When the enemy is far away but tries to provoke hostilities, he wants you to move forward" (Sun Tzu, *The Art of War*, "Maneuvering Armies").

Concurrent with the Chinese Jin dynasty (third to fifth centuries) were sixteen kingdoms ruled by five different Central Asian peoples. These kingdoms included former Chinese territory within their domains and adopted certain elements of Chinese culture. This story concerns a conflict between two of these kingdoms, one under the leadership of the Qiang, ancient relatives of the modern Tibetans, and the Di, another ancient people who became increasingly Sinicized during the Jin dynasty.

The Di ruler sent two of his generals with infantry and cavalry to attack the Qiang, who were occupying a walled city in northern China. The Qiang, however, responded to this provocation by simply strengthening the city's fortifications, refusing to come out and fight.

One of the Qiang generals said, "The Di commander is a stubborn and inflexible man, easy to annoy. If we send a long line of troops to apply direct pressure to his defensive position, he will surely get angry and come out to oppose us. We can take him in one battle."

The other generals agreed, so they sent three thousand Qiang horsemen and soldiers to the very threshold of the Di encampment. The leader of the Di was infuriated and sent all of his best troops out to fight.

The Qiang brigade pretended to be overwhelmed and withdrew, with the Di in hot pursuit. Just as the Di overtook the Qiang, the Qiang turned around and lashed back. Now the main Qiang force also arrived, and there was a tremendous battle. The Qiang killed the Di commander and took all of his troops prisoner.

Slow-Paced Battle

Liu Ji said:

The general rule for besieging walled cities is that it is to be considered the tactic of last resort, to be done only when there is no other choice. Even if the city walls are high and the moats are deep, if there are many men defending it but few supplies and no reinforcements from outside, then it can be taken by stranglehold.

The rule is "Move slowly as a forest" (Sun Tzu, *The Art of War*, "Armed Struggle").

During the era of the Sixteen Kingdoms, the Early Yan dynasty was established by a leader of the Xianbei people in the year 337. At one point in this turbulent period, the king of Yan found it necessary to fight the self-proclaimed king of Qi, a warlord who had inherited his father's army and pledged fealty to Jin-dynasty China to the east. After proclaiming himself king of Qi, as a vassal of China the warlord-king made war on the Xianbei kingdom of Early Yan.

The Yan forces surrounded the king of Qi in a walled city in northern China. The Yan commanders wanted to attack the city as soon as possible, but their general said, "There are times when it is best to go slowly. If we are equal in power, but they have strong reinforcements outside, there is the possibility that we may get pinned between them, having trouble in front of us and behind us. In that case, if we were going to attack it would have to be done quickly.

"On the other hand, if we are stronger than they are, and they have no outside reinforcements, we should keep a stranglehold on them until they cave in. This is what *The Art of War* means when it says, 'Surround them if you have ten times their number, attack if you have five.'

"Now the army of the king of Qi is large, morale is still good, and they are occupying a secure citadel. If we all put forth every last bit of strength and attacked them with the greatest possible intensity, we could take the city in a month or two; but we would surely lose many of our soldiers.

"The essential thing is to be able to adapt."

So saying, the Yan general had a wall of bunkers built to keep watch over the city, until the Yan army finally strangled the stronghold and took it.

Swift Battle

Liu Ji said:

When you besiege a city, if the enemy has abundant supplies, few men, and outside reinforcements, it is imperative to attack quickly in order to win.

The rule is "In a military operation, extraordinary speed is valuable" *(Records of the Three Kingdoms)*.

During the era of the Three Kingdoms, when factions of the regions of Wei, Shu, and Wu competed for hegemony over the remains of the

Chinese empire after the fall of the Han dynasty, at one point a general of Shu defected to Wei and was subsequently made military governor of an area called "New City." Before long, however, the new governor established relations with the kingdom of Wu and transferred his allegiance back to Shu, rebelling against Wei.

Now Sima Yi, a leading general of Wei, sent a secret military force to strike the traitor. His commanders said, "Now that he is connected with Shu, we should observe from a distance before making our move." But the Wei general replied, "He is unreliable and lacks a sense of duty. This is a time when loyalties are in doubt, and we should hasten to resolve matters before he has settled down."

So the Wei troops traveled by forced marches day and night to arrive at the outskirts of New City. Both Wu and Shu sent reinforcements to help the defector, so the Wei general divided his forces to resist them.

At the outset of these events, the defector had written to the chief strategist of Shu, "New City is so far away from the center of Wei that I will have my fortifications all ready by the time the emperor in Wei is informed of my actions. My commanders are well prepared, and my location is protected by natural barriers. The great general of Wei will surely not come himself, and even if his commanders come they cannot trouble me."

But then when the Wei force arrived, the defector informed the Shu strategist, expressing his suprise: "It has only been eight days since I made my move, and the Wei army is already at the city wall. How extraordinarily swift they are!"

There was an outlying citadel surrounded on three sides by water, and the defector had a wooden barricade built outside for extra protection. The Wei troops, however, crossed the water and smashed the barricade, pressing right up to the city walls.

On the tenth day, several of the defector's own men assassinated him and opened the gates of the city, surrendering to the kingdom of Wei.

Orderliness and Battle

Liu Ji said:

In warfare, if the enemy's ranks are orderly on the move and the soldiers are calm, it will not do to enter into battle with them too readily. It is better to wait for a change or stir within them to strike; then you can win.

The rule is "Avoiding confrontation with orderly ranks and not attacking great formations is mastering adaptation" (Sun Tzu, *The Art of War*, "Armed Struggle").

This story is related to the preceding story, about the general of the Three Kingdoms era who defected from Shu to Wei, became a military governor in outlying territory, then defected back to Shu but also had ties with Wu. At one point he even declared independence, with the diplomatic recognition of the king of Wu.

According to this story, the great Wei general Sima Yi launched his expedition against the seceding defector when this took place. His forces came in secret across the river and surrounded the citadel of the traitor, but then they left that city and headed for the heartland of the region.

The Wei commanders said, "Surrounding the citadel without laying siege to it was not a good example to show the warriors."

The Wei general said, "The rebels are securely entrenched and want to take advantage of that to tire our army. If we besiege the city, we will be falling right into their trap. The rebels are massed here, so their homes are empty; if we head right for the local heartland, the people will be afraid. If they come to fight in fear, we are sure to beat them."

So the Wei army marched through in orderly ranks. When the secessionists saw the army, they came out after it and did actually try to face it. Then the Wei general had its own soldiers strike back at them, routing the rebels.

Energy and Battle

Liu Ji said:

Generals wage war through the armed forces, the armed forces fight by energy. Energy prevails when it is drummed up. If you can energize your troops, don't do it too frequently, otherwise their energy will easily wane. Don't do it at too great a distance either, otherwise their energy will be easily exhausted. You should drum up the energy of your soldiers when enemies are within a calculated critical distance, having your troops fight at close range. When enemies wane and you prevail, victory over them is assured.

The rule is "Fight when full of energy, flee when drained of energy" (Wei Liaozi, "Rigor of War").

During the Spring and Autumn era, the state of Qi attacked the state of Lu. The lord of Lu was about to go to battle when one of his warriors asked to accompany him. So the lord and the warrior rode to the battlefield in the same chariot.

Now the lord of Lu was about to give the signal for the war drums to stir up the soldiers, but the warrior said, "Not yet." Then when the men of Qi had drummed three times, the warrior told the lord of Lu, "Now!"

The Qi army was defeated, and the lord of Lu asked the warrior how this had come about. The warrior replied, "Bravery in battle is a matter of energy. Once energy is drummed up, a second try makes it wane, and it disappears at the third. They were exhausted while we were full, so we overcame them."

This story was later told as a classic case of the weaker successfully opposing the stronger through mastery of energy.

Fighting on the Way Home

Liu Ji said:

When you clash with enemies, if they withdraw and head home for no apparent reason, it is imperative to observe them carefully. If they are in fact exhausted and out of supplies, you can send commandos after them; but if they are an expedition on the way home, you cannot stand in their way.

The rule is "Do not stop an army on its way home" (Sun Tzu, *The Art of War,* "Armed Struggle").

In the year 198, near the end of the Han dynasty, the warlord Cao Cao, who was to become one of the most powerful competitors for the remains of the Han empire, had one of his rivals surrounded when another rival sent reinforcements to oppose him. The reinforcements took up a position behind Cao Cao, guarding the passes through the mountains to cut off his way back.

Cao Cao's army couldn't go forward, and now it had enemies before and behind it. That night Cao Cao's men tunneled through the defiles to give the appearance that they were trying to get away. In reality they lay in ambush, waiting for the enemies to come in pursuit.

Cao Cao's rival came after him with his entire army, and Cao Cao's soldiers destroyed it in a surprise attack. Later Cao Cao told one of his advisors, "The enemy tried to 'stop an army on its way home,' and also fought with us on 'deadly ground,' so I knew we would win."

Pursuit and Battle

Liu Ji said:

Whenever you pursue people on the run, chasing beaten soldiers, you must make sure whether they are really fleeing or just feigning. If their signals are coordinated and their orders are uniformly carried out, even if they are running away in apparent confusion and chaos they are not defeated. They surely have plans for surprise attacks, so you must take this into consideration.

If, on the other hand, their signals are disorderly and uncoordinated, if all sorts of different orders and directives are hollered and shouted, then this is the real fearfulness that is felt in defeat. In such a case you may pursue them vigorously.

The rule is "When you pursue people on the run, do not desist; but if the enemy stops on the road, then think twice" ("Sima's Art of War," "Deploying Groups").

In the year 618, the founder of the newly declared Tang dynasty moved against one of the last warlords of the preceding Sui dynasty. One of the Sui warlord's generals, opposing the Tang founder, was severely beaten and put to flight.

The Tang founder chased down the Sui survivors and surrounded them. Many of the Sui commanders surrendered right then and there on the battlefield. The Tang founder gave them back their horses and let them go.

Moments later, each of the Sui commanders came riding back. Now the Tang founder knew the real condition of the Sui warlord. As the leader of the new dynasty advanced his troops to close in, he sent a diplomat to the warlord to explain the advantages of capitulation and the risks of resistance. The warlord finally surrendered.

The generals of the young Tang founder congratulated him, and took the opportunity to ask, "When you had the enemy on the run, you left your infantry and rode right up to the city ramparts without even taking any siege equipment. We were all in doubt as to whether we could take the city, yet you did—how?"

The Tang founder said, "The men under the command of the Sui warlord's general are all outsiders, people from a completely different region. Although our army beat them, we didn't kill or capture too many. If we gave them time, they would all go into the city, where the warlord would take them in and treat them as his own—then they would not be easy to overcome. I knew that if we pressured them, the soldiers would all run away back to their homeland, leaving no one here to fight for the warlord.

"The warlord's spirit is broken with mortal terror; that is why he surrendered, out of fear."

Not Fighting

Liu Ji said:

When opponents in warfare outnumber you, or they are more powerful than you are, or when you are at a tactical disadvantage, or when they have come from far away but still have supplies, in any of these cases it will not do to fight with them. It is best to fortify your defenses and hold them off long enough to wear them down to the point of vulnerability.

The rule is "It is up to you not to fight" ("Dialogues of Li, Lord of Wei").

In the early years of the Tang dynasty, the founder of the new regime led an army against one of the warlords of the defunct Sui dynasty, a warlord who had joined forces with the Turks against the Tang armies.

One of the founder's cousins, a young man of seventeen who was later to be a minister of state, went with the Tang army. The two young men—the founder himself being only slightly older than his cousin—climbed the citadel of Gem Wall City, overlooking a deep valley, to observe the battle lines of the rebels.

The Tang founder looked at his cousin and said, "The rebels are coming to face me in battle counting on their numbers. What do you think?"

The younger warrior replied, "The thrust of this band of rebels is not to be met directly. They will be easy to foil by strategy, hard to contend with by strength. Let us secure our position so as to blunt their edge. They are a rag-tag mob and cannot last long. When their supplies start to run out, they will disperse by themselves. We can capture them without even fighting."

The Tang founder said, "Your perception accords with mine."

As it turned out, the Sui fighters fled by night when their food ran out. The Tang army chased them into the next country and put them to flight in one skirmish.

Avoiding Battle

Liu Ji said:

When you are at war with strong enemies, at first their energy is keen, while your momentum is weak, so it is hard to hold them off. Avoid them for the time being, and you can prevail.

The rule is "Avoid the keen energy, strike the slumping and receding" (Sun Tzu, *The Art of War*, "Armed Struggle").

In the year 189, one of the generals of the imperial armies of the Han dynasty was sent out to quell a group of dissidents who tried to secede from the empire. The secessionists had surrounded a walled city, and the general was appointed to put down their insurrection.

An imperial minister noted for his violent and cruel personality urged the general to proceed quickly, but the general said, "Even supposing victory in every battle, it is still better to win without fighting. Therefore Master Sun says in *The Art of War*, 'Skillful warriors first make themselves invincible, then watch for vulnerability in their opponents.'

"Now the city that the rebels have surrounded may be small, but it is well fortified and not easily taken. The secessionists have been making a powerful attack, yet the city has not fallen; so they must be tired. To strike them when they are fatigued is the way to complete victory."

The siege went on, but the city did not fall; completely worn out, at length the rebel army disbanded. Now the imperial forces went after them.

At this point, the imperial minister advised the general, "As Master Sun says in *The Art of War*, 'Do not press a desperate enemy,' and 'do not stop an army on its way home.' "

The general refused to listen to the minister and went in pursuit of the rebels on his own initiative, delivering a crushing blow.

Surrounding Enemies

Liu Ji said:

Whenever you surround enemies, you should leave an opening to make it appear to them that there is a way to survive, thus causing them to relax their determination to fight. Thus can citadels be taken and armies be beaten.

The rule is "A surrounded army must be given a way out" (Sun Tzu, *The Art of War*, "Armed Struggle").

In the last days of the Han dynasty, the warlord Cao Cao surrounded a certain city. Enraged when the city refused to capitulate, Cao Cao swore, "When the city falls, we will bury everyone in it alive!"

The siege went on for days, but the defenders of the city still did not give up. Now Cao Cao's brother said to him, "A surrounded city must be shown a way out, a way to survival. Now that you have announced your intention to bury everyone alive, this has caused all the people to defend it for their own sakes. What is more, the city walls are strong and their supplies are abundant. As we besiege the city, our soldiers are being wounded; and time is dragging on as they hold out. Now we have stationed our troops outside a well-fortified city and are attacking enemies who will fight to the death—this is not good strategy."

So Cao Cao followed his brother's advice, and in this way he finally captured the city.

Surrender

Liu Ji said:

In war, if enemies come to surrender, it is imperative to see whether or not their intention is genuine. Observe them and keep on guard at all times. Give your commanders strict directions to keep the troops in a state of readiness. Then you will prevail.

The rule is "Accept a surrender as you would take on an opponent" ("Book of the Latter Han Dynasty").

In 197, the warlord Cao Cao attacked one of his rivals, who surrendered to him. After that, however, the conquered rival attacked Cao Cao out of spite, killing Cao Cao's nephew and eldest son. Cao Cao himself was struck by a stray arrow during the assault.

Now Cao Cao moved his troops. His rival came with a cavalry to raid Cao Cao's army, but Cao Cao beat him back. Finally this rival ran away to join another warlord.

Cao Cao said to his commanders, "When I overcame this rival of mine, my mistake was not to take hostages right away. See what has happened as a result and do not make the same mistake again."

Hardship

Liu Ji said:

Essential to generalship is to share the pleasures and pains of the troops. If you encounter danger, do not abandon the troops to save yourself, do not seek personal escape from difficulties confronting you. Rather, make every effort to protect the troops, sharing in their fate. If you do this, the soldiers will not forget you.

The rule is "When you see danger and difficulty, do not forget the troops" ("Sima's Art of War").

During the era of the Three Kingdoms, when the warlord Cao Cao of Wei returned from his expedition against the king of Wu, he left a garrison of about seven thousand troops under three of his commanders. Cao Cao himself now went on an expedition against the leader of a semireligious popular militia, leaving the garrison chief with sealed instructions. On the outside of the instructions was written, "Open this if the enemy comes."

Before long, the king of Wu brought his troops to surround the Wei garrison. So the instructions of Cao Cao were opened and found to say, "If the king of Wu comes, let two of our commanders go out to engage him in battle; let one commander stay in the citadel to defend it. The garrison chief is not to fight."

Most of the Wei troop leaders were in doubt about these instructions, but one of the top commanders said, "With Cao Cao away on an expedition, the enemy is certain to beat us. This is why Cao Cao left those instructions. If we strike back at the Wu troops before they close in on us, breaking the force of their momentum, then we can calm the minds of our troops. Once that is accomplished, we can hold the citadel. The potential for victory or defeat is in this one action—how can any of you doubt it?"

That night the Wei commander called for volunteers to go with him. Eight hundred soldiers came forward. He killed some cattle to provide them with a hearty feast, for the next day there would be a major battle.

At dawn, the Wei commander put on his armor and went out to fight. He plunged first into the enemy battle line, killing dozens of men and cutting down two of their leaders. Shouting his name, the Wei commander crashed into enemy lines, fighting his way to the king of Wu.

With the Wei commander cutting his way toward him through the warriors of Wu, the king was terrified. Not knowing what to do, he and his bodyguards ran to high ground, the king defending himself with a halberd. The warrior commander of Wei called to the king of Wu to come down, but the king did not dare to move. Then the king regrouped his soldiers and surrounded the Wei commander.

The Wei commander struck at the surrounding Wu soldiers left and right, then charged straight ahead and broke through, so that he and several dozen of his men were able to get out.

Now the rest of the surrounded Wei force shouted to their commander, "Are you going to abandon us?" The commander then broke back in through the surrounding Wu soldiers and got his men out. None of the Wu fighters could stand up to the warrior of Wei.

The battle went on from morning until midday, until the men of Wu lost their spirit. Then the Wei troops went back to the citadel to fortify their defenses. Now everyone calmed down and gladly obeyed the Wei command.

When the king of Wu besieged the citadel, he continued his attack for ten days without success. Finally he withdrew. The Wei commander gave chase and nearly captured the king of Wu himself.

Easy Battle

Liu Ji said:

The rule of offensive warfare is that those who go the easy way prevail over their opponents. If your enemies are garrisoned in several places, there will inevitably be some places stronger and better manned than others. In that case, you should keep your distance from their strong points and attack their weak points; avoid places where they have many troops and strike where they have few—then you will not fail to win.

The rule is "Good warriors prevail when it is easy to prevail" (Sun Tzu, *The Art of War*, "Formation").

In the latter part of the sixth century, northern China was under the rule of the Xianbei, a northern Asian people culturally and politically influenced by centuries of contact with Chinese civilization. Two kingdoms formed by Xianbei leaders, the Northern Zhou dynasty and the Northern Qi dynasty, fought with each other to expand their territories.

The Martial Emperor of Zhou attacked a certain province of Qi, but one of his ministers said, "That province is a critical strategic area, where elite troops are massed. Even if we besiege it with all of our might it may not be possible for us to get our way. Let us attack another area, where there are few warriors and gentle terrain, a place that will be easy to take over."

The Martial Emperor refused to listen to this advice, and ultimately failed to succeed in his undertaking.

Battle in Extremity

Liu Ji said:

In war, if you greatly outnumber your enemies, they will fear your military strength and flee without putting up a fight. In such an event, do not chase them, for people will fight back in extremity. You should follow them slowly with an orderly army; then you will win.

The rule is "Do not press a desperate enemy" (Sun Tzu, *The Art of War*, "Armed Struggle").

In the first century B.C.E., during the Han dynasty, a Chinese imperial general moved against one of the tribes of the Qiang, an ancient relative of the modern Tibetan people. The Han general led his army up to the campgrounds of the Qiang, where they had been stationed for quite some time.

The tribal warriors, in fact, had been garrisoned there for so long that they had grown slack. Thus when they saw the huge Chinese army in the distance, they abandoned their equipment and ran away, intending to cross the river that formed a natural boundary to the area.

The road was narrow and cramped, and the Chinese general pursued the fleeing Qiang at a leisurely pace. Someone said to him, "We are going too slowly to follow up on our advantage." But the general replied, "This is a case where 'a desperate enemy is not to be pressed.' If we go easy, they will run without looking back; but if we rush them, they will turn around and fight to the death."

All of the officers of the imperial Chinese army agreed with the general.

When the Qiang tribesmen plunged into the river, hundreds of them drowned and the rest ran away.

Warring in Accord with Nature

Liu Ji said:

When you want to raise an army and mobilize it against criminals in order to give comfort to the people, it is imperative to do so according to natural timing. You will always win when you mobilize military forces against enemies under the following conditions: their leadership is benighted and their government policies are arbitrary; their armed forces are overbearing and their people are worn out; they drive out good and wise people; they judicially murder the innocent. Enemies like this can be beaten.

The rule is "You successfully carry out a punitive strike when you follow natural timing" (Sun Tzu, *The Art of War*, "Strategic Assessments," commentaries; also in "Sima's Art of War," "Determining Ranks").

The sixth-century Northern Qi dynasty was one of the short-lived reigns of the turbulent era of the Northern and Southern dynasties. It was founded by the younger brother of the assassinated king of Qi, a second-generation vassal of the Wei dynasty, which was a non-Chinese empire that included northern China in its territory. The Northern Qi dynasty lasted for only twenty-eight years, with six rulers of three generations.

The last emperor of Northern Qi was popularly called "The Sorrowless Emperor." He appointed dishonest and treacherous people to administer the rule of government and to sit on the board of his advisory council. All of these people had their own personal cliques, whose members thereby were given promotions that were out of order. Official posts were obtained by bribery, and people were oppressed and persecuted by arbitrary policies. There was also internecine conflict among the vassals, resulting in the judicial murder of innocent ministers.

The Martial Emperor of Northern Zhou (543–578) was also non-Chinese, a chieftan of the North Asian Xianbei people. Gradually seeing the signs that the Northern Qi dynasty was collapsing and going under, as soon as he saw its basis crumble like a landslide he took this opportunity to destroy it. The last emperor of Northern Qi capitulated to Northern Zhou, and his whole clan was exterminated.

Health and Warfare

Liu Ji said:

When you are at war, if your army has suffered a setback, it is imperative to examine the physical and mental health of the soldiers. If they are healthy, then inspire them to fight; if they are run down and low in spirits, then nurture their health for the time being, until they are again fit for service.

The rule is "Take care of your health and avoid stress, consolidate your energy and build up your strength" (Sun Tzu, *The Art of War,* "Nine Grounds").

The First Emperor of China, who united China in the third century B.C.E., was the founder of the imperial Qin dynasty. At one point in his conquests he planned to attack the ancient land of Chu and asked one of his commanders, a certain General Li, "I want to take Chu—how many troops will be needed?"

General Li replied, "No more than two hundred thousand."

Then the emperor put the same question to another commander, General Wang. General Wang said, "There have to be at least six hundred thousand."

The emperor said to General Wang, "You must be getting old! How can you be so timid?" And he appointed General Li to lead an army of two hundred thousand troops in an attack on Chu.

General Wang, not having gotten the job, announced that he was ailing and went into temporary retirement.

Now General Li attacked Chu and dealt the independent state a crushing blow. Then he withdrew his troops to take up a position to the west; but the men of Chu followed him, not pitching camp for three successive days, and finally routed the Qin army, killing seven captains and putting General Li to flight.

Hearing news of this, the emperor was wroth. He personally went to General Wang and insisted that he return to active duty. General Wang said, "I am a muddled old man; if you insist on employing me for this mission, I will need six hundred thousand men." This time the emperor agreed.

When the men of Chu heard of this, they mobilized all of their armed forces to resist the Qin army under General Wang. General Wang, however, just strengthened his fortifications and did not do battle. He gave his soldiers plenty of rest every day, allowing them to bathe and wash their clothing. He also fed them well and generally provided for their comfort, sharing in their lot.

After quite a while of this, General Wang asked if the soldiers were playing sports in camp. When he heard that they were, he declared, "Now they are fit for action!"

The men of Chu, unable to oppose the Qin army in battle, withdrew to the east. General Wang pursued them and struck them down, killing their leader and putting the soldiers of Chu to flight, achieving a settlement by military means.

THE LOST
ART OF WAR

Sun Tzu II

INTRODUCTION

Few things might seem as unlikely as ancient Chinese warriors rising up in modern American business schools, corporate boardrooms, and Hollywood movies, but there they are.

The rise of the new China, the power of the global marketplace, the intensification of international competition and rivalry—all of these elements of contemporary affairs may contribute in some way to present-day interest in ancient classics of strategy and conflict management.

This literature, however, may have yet another function—perhaps not as apparent, but no less important than what emerges from its use in business, diplomacy, and warfare. While the study and application of strategic thinking in these areas may be necessary to secure the economic, political, and territorial underpinnings of democracy, these cannot guarantee freedom unless individuals and peoples have the right and the opportunity to recognize and understand all of the operative influences in their lives and on their minds—not only those that happen to be, or are made to appear, most evident to everyday awareness. Only thus is true freedom of choice possible in a real, practical sense.

One of the most important functions of strategic literature in the public domain today, therefore, may be to enhance the general understanding of power and its uses and abuses. By understanding power—how configurations of power work, how masses of people are influenced, how individuals and peoples become vulnerable to internal contradictions and external aggression—it is possible to objectively and truthfully assess the operation of the world we live in—and, we might hope, to learn to avoid the abuses of power to which the massive, impersonal infrastructures of modern life are inherently prone.

The most famous of ancient Chinese strategic manuals is *The Art of War* by Sun Tzu, an outstanding military consultant of China's Warring States era. Somewhat more than a hundred years later, a lineal descendant of this Sun Tzu, or "Master Sun," also rose to prominence as a distinguished strategist. This was Sun Bin, whose name means Sun the Mutilated. He became Sun Tzu II, the second Master Sun, whose own *Art of War* was only known in part until a nearly complete, if somewhat damaged version recorded on bamboo strips was recently discovered in an ancient tomb.

It is not accidental that the great classics of Chinese political and military strategy emerged from the chaos and horror of the Era of the Warring States. The conditions of the time, and their effect on the morale and philosophy of the people, are graphically described in the traditional anthology known as *Strategies of the Warring States:*

> Usurpers set themselves up as lords and kings; states that were run by pretenders and plotters established armies to make themselves into major powers. They imitated each other at this more and more, and those who came after them also followed their example. Eventually they overwhelmed and destroyed one another, conspiring with larger domains to annex smaller domains, spending years at violent military operations, filling the fields with blood.
>
> Fathers and sons were alienated, brothers were at odds, husbands and wives were estranged. No one could safeguard his or her life. Integrity disappeared. Eventually this reached the extreme where seven large states and five smaller states contested each other for power. This all happened because the warring states were shamelessly greedy, struggling insatiably to get ahead.[1]

According to ancient documents, Sun Bin studied warfare along with a certain Pang Juan, who later became a high-ranking military leader. Their teacher was supposed to have been the mysterious sage Wang Li, known as the Master of Demon Valley, one of the most redoubtable strategic theorists of all time.

Reputedly the author of *The Master of Demon Valley*, the most sophisticated of all strategic classics, Wang Li was a Taoist recluse. According to Taoist records, while certain students of his became prominent strategists active in the melees of the Warring States, the Master of Demon Valley tried in vain to induce them to use their knowledge to convert the warlords to Taoism rather than to hegemonism.

Legend has it that the Master of Demon Valley lived for hundreds of years. While this sort of fable is ordinarily connected to esoteric Taoist life-prolonging theories and practices, in this case it may allude to the maintenance of a highly secretive hidden tradition. Such a pattern of esoterism in the preservation and transmission of potentially dangerous knowledge was typical, to be sure, of ancient Chinese schools, particularly under conditions of social disorder.

The book known as *The Master of Demon Valley* most certainly contains much that is not in the lore of the first Sun Tzu's popular *Art of War.*[2] The book of Sun Tzu II, Sun the Mutilated, also bears the stamp of extraordinary knowledge that may in fact derive from the school of the Master of Demon Valley. The reason for secrecy, which also explains the extremely cryptic language used in recording such texts, is made clear in the conclusion to *The Master of Demon Valley:* "Petty people imitating others will use this in a perverse and sinister way, even to the point where they can destroy families and usurp countries."[3] This is the tradition of Sun the Mutilated.

After completing his study of tactical strategy with the mysterious Master of Demon Valley, Sun Bin's schoolmate Pang Juan was hired by the court of the state of Wei, where he was appointed to the rank of general. Concerned that his own abilities were unequal to those of Sun Bin, General Pang Juan devised a plan to remove him from the scene.

To encompass his rival's downfall, Pang Juan had Sun Bin invited to Wei as if to consult with him. When Sun Bin arrived, however, Pang Juan had him arrested as a criminal. Falling victim to the plot and condemned as a convict, Sun Bin had both feet amputated and his face tattooed. This is why he came to be known as Sun the Mutilated. Such punishments were designed to reduce people to the status of permanent outcasts.

Sun Bin, however, was evidently undaunted by this setback. Perhaps he considered himself most at fault for having fallen into Pang Juan's trap. In any case, while he was a convict/slave, Sun Bin gained a private audience with an emissary of the state of Qi who was passing through Wei en route to the state of Liang. Taking advantage of his opportunity, Sun Bin astounded the ambassador with his extraordinary knowledge of strategy and warfare.

Recognizing the value of such a mind, the emissary smuggled Master Sun out of Wei into his own state of Qi. Now the ruler of Qi wanted to make Sun Bin a general, but he pleaded infirmity on account of having been judicially maimed. As a result, the strategist was instead appointed military consultant to the great general Tian Ji.

Sun Bin's skill in the classical strategy of his ancestor Sun Wu and his teacher Wang Li is illustrated by a famous story of his service to Qi, immortalized in the popular *Extraordinary Strategies of a Hundred Battles* by the great Ming dynasty warrior-scholar Liu Ji:[4] When two states attacked a third, the victimized state appealed to the state of Qi for help. The general of Qi asked Sun Bin for advice. Master Sun said, "The aggressor armies are fierce and think little of your army, which they regard as cowardly. A good warrior would take advantage of this tendency and 'lead them on with prospects of gain.'

"According to *The Art of War*, struggling for an advantage fifty miles away will thwart the forward leadership, and only half of those who chase prospects of gain twenty-five miles away will actually get there. Have your army enter enemy territory and make thousands of campfires; on the next day have them make half that number of campfires, and on the day following that have them make half again that number."

The general had his army do as Sun Bin advised. The enemy general was deceived by this maneuver, delighted to hear that the number of campfires was dwindling day by day, assuming that the men of Qi were defecting. He said, "I knew the soldiers of Qi were cowards—they've only been in our territory for three days now, and more than half their army has run away!"

As a result of this misperception, the enemy general left his own infantry behind and rushed in pursuit of the Qi army with nothing but a personal force of crack troops. Calculating the speed of their pursuit, Master Sun the Mutilated concluded that by nightfall his opponents would reach an area of narrow roads difficult to pass through, a place suitable for ambush.

Now Master Sun had a large tree felled and stripped of bark. Then he wrote on the bare log, "The general of Wei will die at this tree," and had it placed on the road where the aggressor troops of Wei would pass that night. Then Master Sun had several thousand expert archers conceal themselves near the road.

When the general of Wei, Sun Bin's opponent, came to the place where the stripped log lay across the road, the general had a torch kindled for light to read the writing on the log. Before he had finished reading the inscription stating that he himself would die right there that night, the archers placed by Sun Bin loosed their arrows at the sight of the torch, throwing the enemy into a panic. Realizing he had been outwitted and his troops beaten, the general of Wei committed suicide.

Thus the tactics of Master Sun the Mutilated encompassed victory at minimal cost. This is one of the cardinal principles of the science.

Sun Bin's book of strategy, long known by fragments and only recently discovered in the same ancient tomb in which the previously unknown version of Sun Tzu's *Art of War* was found, was most likely compiled by disciples. Like other works of pre-imperial China, this text appears to be a collection of aphorisms and analects, largely organized in a lateral associative manner rather than in a linear progressive order.

The book begins with a cryptic story of Sun Bin's ultimate triumph over his old nemesis, Pang Juan, using the strategy of misdirection advocated by his ancestor Sun Wu. This account, which is intrinsically obscure and subject to different readings and interpretations, mainly serves to establish the superior mastery of Master Sun the Mutilated. Undoubtedly, it was for this purpose that the followers of Sun Bin introduced their account of their master's teachings with this story.

The text goes on to record some of master Sun Bin's conversations with the king and the general Tian Ji of Qi, to whom he acted as consultant. After that, the book proceeds to deal with a series of related topics, focusing on hard-core issues of tactics and strategy. The book of Sun Bin is a composite text, based on a Chinese sense of holistic order rather than a Hellenic sense of logic. Thus it covers a wide range of subjects as a totality, without the linear progression familiar to scholastic Western thought. As an esoteric work of military strategy, furthermore, it is by nature highly secretive, recorded in extremely difficult language, often substituting homonymic characters in a kind of cryptic code.

A century deeper into the chaos of Warring States China, while retaining the ancient moral foundations of Sun Wu's *Art of War*, Sun

Bin went that much further than his distinguished ancestor in detailing practical tactics. Like what can be found in other strategic manuals, moreover, Sun Bin's methods are represented by structures that operate as metaphors for events and activities other than warfare, in the domains of government, diplomacy, business, and social action.

There is a Chinese saying, "The wise see wisdom, the good see goodness." How people interact with powerful and secretive lore like *The Art of War* is held to reveal something about their inner character—and this function itself is a classic maneuver of strategic art.

Notes

1. Cited in *The Art of War* in this volume. It has often been noted how much the highly competitive contemporary international marketplace resembles the Era of the Warring States.
2. For a complete translation of the esoteric classic of strategy known as *The Master of Demon Valley*, see Thomas Cleary, *Thunder in the Sky: On the Acquisition and Exercise of Power* (Boston: Shambhala, 1993). *The Master of Demon Valley* contains much more of the psychological, social, and political dimension of strategy in action than does Sun Tzu's renowned *The Art of War,* which is more strictly military. *The Master of Demon Valley* illustrates the Taoist ideas and techniques in traditional strategy more prominently than do either of the Suns, Sun Tzu I (Sun Wu) or Sun Tzu II (Sun Bin). Taoist legend about Wang Li, the Master of Demon Valley, has the maestro weeping over his wayward disciples who became famous military strategists but failed to convert the lords to the moral dimensions of the Tao.
3. Clearly, *Thunder in the Sky,* 76.
4. For Liu Ji's own commentary on how this story illustrates the art of war, see *Mastering the Art of War* in this volume, pages 277–278.

Sun Bin's Art of War

THE CAPTURE OF PANG JUAN

In the past, when the ruler of Liang was going to attack Handan, the capital of Zhao, he sent his general, Pang Juan, to Chuqiu with 80,000 armed troops.

*Sun Bin's *The Art of War* begins, appropriately enough, with the story of how he vanquished his arch rival, Pang Juan. The shifting alliances of China's Era of the Warring States created enormous confusion and uncertainty; and the chaotic and unpredictable nature of the political scene was ruthlessly exploited by civil and military leaders as well as by freelance consultants. To read ancient Chinese war stories like this, which do not necessarily follow a straight line, and whose action is inherently and perhaps deliberately confusing, observe the relationships and interactions as well as the overall "plot."

When King Wei of Qi (B.C.E. 356–320) heard of this, he had his general, Tian Ji, lead 80,000 armed troops to the rescue.

Pang Juan attacked the capital of Wey. General Tian Ji asked Master Sun Bin, "What should I do if I do not rescue Wey?"

When Sun Bin was offered a generalship by King Wei, he refused the honor; ostensibly he did so on account of his physical disabilities, but perhaps for other strategic reasons as well. Instead, he was appointed military adviser to the top general, Tian Ji.

Master Sun said, "Please attack Rangling to the south. The walled city of Rangling is small, but its province is large, populous, and well armed. It is the essential military zone in eastern Wei; it is hard to besiege, so I would make a show of confusion. Were I to attack Rangling, I would have the state of Song to my south and the state of Wey to my north, with Shiqiu right in the way, so my

*Commentary on Sun Bin's text is provided by the translator.

supply lines would be cut off; I would thus make a show of incom-petence."

Two essential principles of conflict outlined by Sun Bin's distin-guished ancestor Sun Wu are illustrated here. One concerns the way to draw an enemy out of a secure position by attacking a place of strategic value, somewhere that the opponent is sure to go to the de-fense. The Master of Demon Valley, another Warring States–era strat-egist, also described the practice of drawing people out in interactions by observing their structures of psychological defense. The exercise of tact, as well as apparent lack of tact, may both be used in strategic encounters as means of observing reaction patterns in actual or po-tential allies or adversaries, either from a "closed" undercover posi-tion (disguised as tact) or from the shifting, roving, deceptively "open" position of the provocateur (disguised as lack of tact).

The second principle illustrated here is the use of deceit for strate-gic advantage in hostile situations. In this case, the particular avenue of deception employed is that of deliberately giving the appearance of confusion and lack of skill in order to make an enemy contemptuous, complacent, and therefore careless, rendering the enemy vulnerable to counterattack. Thus, in situations where strategy is the paramount guide of affairs, it is customary not to take anything naively at face value; yet it is therefore crucial to attain the intelligence and balance to avoid becoming excessively imaginative and lapsing into self-defeating paranoia.

So General Tian broke camp and raced to Rangling.

Subsequently, General Tian summoned Master Sun and asked, "Now what should I do?"

Master Sun said, "Which of the grandees of the cities are ignorant of military affairs?"

General Tian replied, "Those in Qi-cheng and Gao-tang."

Here, the least competent are being selected because they are to be pawns in a larger game. Their role, which they are to play unawares, is to keep up the appearance of lack of skill and intelligence on the part of the leadership. They are also being set up to be sacrificed for a larger cause; this is one of the notorious Thirty-Six Strategies.

Master Sun said, "Get these grandees to take charge of defense of their cities. Fan out and then close in on all sides, circling around. Fanning out and then closing in with a battlefront, circle around to station camouflaged soldiers. With your vanguard forceful, have your main force continuously circle around and strike the opponent from behind. The two grandees can be sacrificed."

So Qi-cheng and Gao-tang were separated into two units, and a direct assault on Rangling was made in an attempt to swarm the city. Camouflaged ambushers circled around and struck from behind; Qi-cheng and Gao-tang were routed, succumbing to the strategy.

Master Sun advised General Tian to draw the opponent in by this show of incompetence, then come upon the enemy from behind with a sneak counterattack. In this case, the opposing side added another layer of the same strategy, thereby succeeding in gaining an immediate aim, yet also falling into the trap of Master Sun Bin.

The master strategist had already taken this possibility, or indeed likelihood, fully into account; the purpose of the siege ordered by Sun Bin was not to win its ostensible aim, but to render his opponent vulnerable. When you see a target, and you see people aiming for the target, try to see what the actual purpose—in effect, that is—might be: the target, the aiming, the attention of onlookers, whatever might possibly be gained from a combination of some or all of these under prevailing conditions, or possibly something else again.

General Tian summoned Master Sun and said, "I failed in the siege of Rangling, and also lost Qi-cheng and Gao-tang, which were defeated strategically. Now what should I do?"

Master Sun said, "Please send light chariots galloping west to the city of Liang, to enrage them; follow up with your troops split up to make it look as if they are few in number."

It may seem dangerous to enrage an enemy; and indeed it may be, so it is imperative to examine the specific conditions of the moment. The purpose of strategic use of anger in this way is to blunt the effectiveness of an opponent by making him lose his head and expend his energy wildly, without deadly concentration. The great heavyweight champion boxers Jack Johnson and Muhammad Ali were particularly renowned for their consummate skill in this art. In some cultures, what Americans call "in your face" manners or mannerisms are in fact either active examples or not-quite-dead relics of this type of strategic behavior, developed within the context of social conditions that tend to force people to assume such behavior, if for no other reason than instinctive self-preservation.

There is another function of anger noted in classics of Chinese strategy, that of enraging one's own forces against a powerful enemy in order to add to the psychological momentum of one's attack and surety of one's defense. Ancient Norse berserkers, from whom we derive the word *berserk*, practiced this on themselves.

In American pugilism, the legendary middleweight boxing champion Stanley Ketchel was famous for this berserkerlike practice. Powerful enough in his rage to floor the great heavyweight champion Jack Johnson himself, Ketchel seems to have been one of the few truly violent young men who ostensibly succeeded in this profession. His habitual indulgence in his own passions, however, and his consequent forgetfulness of passion as a double-edged sword—capable of making men killers as well as buffoons—was precisely what led to his own early death. One of the most murderous of men ever to box under the Marquis of Queensbury rules, Stanley Ketchel was only twenty-four years old when he was shot to death by an angry cuckold.

Nowadays, the practice of enraging one's troops against an enemy seems to be widely used. Film clips of such training procedures are even to be seen on national educational television from time to time. The use of such tactics on soldiers of a highly diverse nation with ancestral roots all over the world has very serious drawbacks. Already evident on the battlefield, these drawbacks are particularly glaring when viewed in the total context, including the relationship between civil society and its own military. It may be for this reason that strategic lore in China, a land of great regional diversity, generally speaks more of enraging others than enraging one's own minions or allies against others.

In this connection, it may be noteworthy that Sun Bin's book on strategy does not vilify his arch enemy Pang Juan, the man responsible, out of paranoid jealousy, for having Sun Bin's feet amputated and his face tattooed as a criminal. The book contains no hint, for example, of Sun Bin attempting to enrage his advisee General Tian against Pang Juan; nor does he leave a string of uncomplimentary epithets in his work to curse his malefactor until the end of time. This does not mean Sun Bin had no feelings, of course; only that he kept his professional cool in spite of what emotions he might have felt at heart. In such cases, it should be noted, this virtue is not necessarily a moral virtue; it may not be any more than a strategic virtue. To make this distinction clearly is itself a strategic advantage, for it diminishes vulnerability to confusion, which can occur and can also be exploited in any domain, dimension, or form.

General Tian did as Master Sun recommended, and General Pang did in fact come by forced march, leaving equipment behind. Master Sun attacked him relentlessly at Guiling, and captured General Pang.

All along, Sun Bin's strategy had been aimed at getting General Pang to overreach and expose himself carelessly, in the process also tiring his troops out and tricking them into coming to the fray too lightly equipped.

That is why it was said that Master Sun was a consummate expert at his business.

In sum, Sun Bin got General Tian to employ classic tactics of misdirection, inward and outward deception, giving up something in order to get something more valued, strategically exploiting the quirks, weaknesses, and shortcomings of human neurological, perceptive, and emotional functions to achieve a specific purpose. The Taoist classic *Tao Te Ching* says, "The Tao is universal; it can be used for the right or the left." This means that natural laws can be caused to operate in ways that may be amoral or even immoral as well as in ways that may be moral. It is for this reason that development of both character and perceptivity was in ancient times a traditional Taoist requisite for learning to practice the Tao in one's own life.

[2]

[Title Lost]

When Master Sun met King Wei, he said, "A militia is not to rely on a fixed formation; this is the way transmitted by kings of yore."

The reasons for not relying on a fixed formation are both defensive and offensive. In terms of defense, predictability means vulnerability, since an adversary who knows how you will react to a given situation will be able to take advantage of this knowledge to scheme against you. If you are not so predictable, on the other hand, not only will adversaries be unable to pinpoint their targets, but their attention will be weakened by dispersal.

When opponents cannot predict what you will do, they cannot act against you with inevitable effect; and when they realize they cannot predict what you will do, they have to be more watchful without knowing quite what they are watching for, thus exhausting the energy of attention and progressively diluting its effectiveness.

This leads naturally into the offensive aspect of unpredictability; enemies who cannot tell when or where you might act are thereby prevented from preparing a sure defense. Their attention is thus necessarily spread more thinly, and their mental energy naturally wanes on account of the added burden. The buildup of constantly mounting anxiety accelerates this process, and aggressively unpredictable behavior that is fundamentally intended to increase tension succeeds doubly in its function by the added tension inherent in futile reactions to misdirection.

"Victory in war is a means of preserving perishing nations and perpetuating dying societies; failing to win in war is how territory is lost and sovereignty threatened. This is why military matters must be examined."

In her small but powerful book *Prisons We Choose to Live Inside* (1987), Doris Lessing observes the tragedy of those who believe in freedom and peace but inhibit their own liberation and fulfillment by refusing to examine the mechanisms of oppression and war. If we wish to remedy malignant conditions, she argues, we need to understand those conditions and how they affect us. This is precisely the logic of the ancient *Art of War:* Know your enemy, know yourself, know where you are, know what is going on.

The idea of smashing the mechanisms of oppression and war may be emotionally stimulating, but it is both childish and exactly contrary to strategic common sense because it falls into the simplest of traps. Dismantling these mechanisms, not dreaming of smashing them, is a sounder and more intelligent approach—provided it is not just a calmer dream and is actually empowered with knowledge and understanding of their designs and operations.

These reasons for studying the art of war are already set forth with simple clarity by classical philosophers of China, whom Sun Bin is informally citing here. In sum, the logical purpose of learning about the workings of conflict is to be able to preserve innocents from aggression, oppression, and destruction. This is considered to be an intelligent and civilized extension of the natural instinct of self-preservation.

This applies not only to warfare in a literal sense, but to all fields of competition and contention, all domains of hostility and conflict. Before we can fairly understand what we might be able to do about anything, we need to see what aims are being served and what means are being employed. Without this mental equipment, we are likely to become unable to react to trying situations in any but emotionally overcharged but pragmatically inefficient ways.

"Those who enjoy militarism, however, will perish; and those who are ambitious for victory will be disgraced. War is not something to enjoy, victory is not to be an object of ambition."

The Taoist classic *Tao Te Ching* says, "Fine weapons are implements of ill omen: People may despise them, so those who are imbued with the Way do not dwell with them." The pacifism expressed here is not sentimental or naive; note that the text says people "may despise" weapons, not that people "do" despise weapons, or that people "all" despise weapons. Weaponry fetishes are well documented throughout the world from ancient to modern times, and contemporary sociological and psychological researchers have testified to forms of this phenomenon so comparatively subtle as to be normally unidentified as such. Not being adequately described or identified as such in everyday consciousness, these influences therefore pose a more insidious threat to human stability than grosser and more readily identifiable forms of weaponry fetishism.

The *Tao Te Ching* continues, "Weapons, being instruments of ill omen, are not tools of the cultured, who use them only when unavoidable. They consider it best to be aloof; they win without beautifying it. Those who beautify it enjoy killing people." Also, "The good are effective, that is all; they do not presume to grab power thereby. They are effective but not conceited, effective but not proud, effective but not arrogant. They are effective when they have to be, effective but not coercive." These passages of the quintessential Taoist classic reflect with ample clarity the pristine Taoist inspiration of Sun Bin's concept of the proper place of warfare in human affairs as illustrated in the introduction to this chapter of his classic manual, on strategic advice to a king.

"Act only when prepared. When a citadel is small and yet its defense is firm, that means it has supplies. When there are few soldiers and yet the army is strong, that means they have a sense of meaning. If they defend without supplies or fight without meaning, no one in the world can be firm and strong."

To act only when prepared is the cardinal rule of all martial arts and strategic action, and indeed of all business and creative endeavor. This perennial admonition is followed by a series of diagnostic guidelines, because proper preparation is only possible with knowledge of conditions for or against which preparation is being made.

In this particular case, insofar as his remarks are introductory, Master Sun takes a general approach and summarizes the main parameters according to which conditions can be usefully described: the material and the mental or moral. As is often the case, this is simply a matter of common sense, not only in warfare, but in any constructive activity. It is necessary to have a concentrated sense of purpose to make effective use of material resources, and it is necessary to have adequate wherewithal to sustain the effort to actualize the aim.

"When Yao ruled the land in antiquity, there were seven instances where royal decrees were rejected and not carried out; two among the eastern tribes, four in the heartland of China, . . . Nothing could be gained from just letting things go, so Yao fought and won, and established himself strongly, so that everyone submitted.

"In high antiquity, Shennong warred against the Fusui tribe, the Yellow Emperor warred on the region of Shu-lu. Yao struck down the Gong Gong people, Shun struck down . . . and drove off the San Miao tribes. Tang banished a despot, King Wu struck down a tyrant. The Yan tribe of the old Shang confederacy rebelled, so the Duke of Zhou overcame it.

"Therefore it is said that if your virtue is not comparable to the Five Emperors of Antiquity, your ability is not comparable to the Three Kings of old, and your wisdom is not comparable to the Duke of Zhou, even if you say you are going to build up humaneness and justice and use ritual and music to govern peacefully, thus putting a stop to conflict and depredation, it is not that Yao and Shun did not want to be thus, but that they were not able to do so; that is why they marshaled warriors to rectify matters."

Here Master Sun is also following classical tradition in citing events from the legends of ancient cultural heroes to underscore the need to understand the art of war even in just and peaceful societies. Shennong was a prehistorical leader, associated with the development of agriculture, horticulture, and herbal medicine. The Yellow Emperor, who is supposed to have reigned in the twenty-seventh century B.C.E., is one of the most important figures of Taoism, believed to have studied and collected a broad spectrum of esoteric knowledge. Yao and Shun, ancient kings of the twenty-fourth and twenty-third centuries B.C.E., are depicted as paragons of just rulership. King Tang was the founder of the Shang/Yin dynasty in the eighteenth century B.C.E.; King Wu and the Duke of Zhou were founders of the Zhou (Chou) dynasty in the late twelfth century B.C.E. Yao, Shun, Tang, Wu, and the Duke of Zhou were particularly revered in the Confucian tradition, which emphasized justice and humaneness in government and public service.

The Five Emperors and Three Kings, although differently named and listed in various traditional sources, collectively refer to legenday leaders symbolizing prototypes of wisdom and humanity in Taoist,

Confucian, and other Chinese political traditions. The reasoning Sun Bin is using here in citing these images, echoed in eminent Taoist classics such as *The Masters of Huainan* and *Wen-tzu*, is this: Since even great leaders of the past renowned for the benevolence of their regimes were not able to avoid hostilities, it follows that rulers of later times, no matter how good their intentions, cannot afford to ignore the science of conflict management and ignore the arts of strategy. *The Masters of Huainan*, a comprehensive Taoist classic of the second century B.C.E., illustrates this humanistic approach to the issue of military preparedness: "Those who used arms in ancient times did not do so to expand their territory or obtain wealth; they did so for the survival and continuity of nations on the brink of destruction and extinction, to settle disorder in the world, and to get rid of what harmed the common people."

[3]

QUESTIONS OF KING WEI

King Wei of Qi asked Master Sun about military operations in these terms: "When two armies are a match for each other and their commanders are at a standoff, with both sides holding firm and neither willing to make the first move, what should be done about this?"

Master Sun replied, "Test the other side by means of light troops, led by a brave man from the lower echelons. Aim to cause a setback, not to gain a victory. Create a hidden front to harass their flanks. This is considered great success."

The purpose of aiming to cause a setback rather than gain a victory is to test the strength of the opponent without revealing the depth of one's own resources. The hidden front stands behind the dummy test front, awaiting the adversary's reaction.

This sort of maneuver takes places in all sorts of interactions. In Japanese, the overt content of an interpersonal transaction is called the *omote*, which means "front," or *tatemae*, which means "setup"; while the ulterior motive is called the *ura*, meaning "back," or *honne*, meaning something like "true voice." While the strategic use of gaps between overt expression and covert intention is probably universal negotiating practice, cultural differences in the manner of its operation and perception may obscure relevant parallels in apparently different behaviors.

Description of this tactic is useful for defensive purposes, because alertness and perceptivity can be enhanced simply by keeping it in mind. When in adversarial, disadvantageous, or simply unfamiliar circumstances, it is useful to remember that one and the same conversation or confrontation can simultaneously accomplish two or more purposes. What it all really means in actual effect depends on the way in which the total transaction is understood and the manner in which each party perceives and reacts to the other's overt moves and covert intentions. Sun Bin's distinguished predecessor, Sun Wu, wrote, "If you know yourself and also know others, you will not be endangered in a hundred battles."

King Wei asked, "Are there proper ways to employ large and small forces?"

Master Sun replied, "There are."

King Wei asked, "If I am stronger and more numerous than my enemy, what should I do?"

Master Sun answered, "This is the question of an intelligent king. When your forces are larger and more powerful, and yet you still ask about how to employ them, this is the way to guarantee your nation's security. Give the command for an auxiliary force. Disarray the troops in confused ranks, so as to make the other side complacent, and they will surely do battle."

Complacency undermines strength, so the powerful can retain their power by avoiding complacency, while encompassing the downfall of adversaries by projecting such an image of incompetence as to induce complacency and contempt. Sun Wu wrote, "Even when you are solid, still be on the defensive; even when you are strong, be evasive."

King Wei asked, "When the enemy is more numerous and stronger than I, what should I do?"

Master Sun said, "Give the command for a retractable vanguard, making sure to hide the rear guard so the vanguard is able to get back safely. Deploy the long weapons on the front lines, the short weapons behind, with mobile archers to help the hard-pressed. Have the main force remain immobile, waiting to see what the enemy can do."

The function of the vanguard is to harass the adversary, whether to induce exasperation, to draw a counterattack that would leave the opponent vulnerable, or to induce the enemy to divide and split off or otherwise abandon a position or configuration of power. The rear guard, naturally, is there to cover and back the vanguard up, while the main force lies in wait to follow up on any confusion or weakening of the opponent's power.

This passage also provides a useful metaphor for resource allocation in challenging situations, or when dealing with intractable problems. The vanguard is research, the rear guard is development, the main force is the existing infrastructure and resource allocation already in place.

The vanguard has to be "retractable" in that effective research needs to be flexible and adaptive, ready to start anew in fresh directions as conditions require. Fixed commitments that are unresponsive to changing conditions, like a vanguard that cannot be withdrawn, are more vulnerable to being compromised by the vagaries of the unpredictable and the unforeseen.

In a highly competitive environment, development as the "rear guard" backing up vanguard research is kept "hidden," or secret, so that everyone is not doing the same thing at the same time. This makes constructive, evolutionary competition possible, while helping to maintain a relatively open space in which public opinion can be expressed.

The "main force" of existing infrastructure (including abstract, conceptual infrastructures of culture) remains immobile in the sense that it requires a degree of stability in order to function effectively, yet must "see what the enemy will do" in order to evolve the organs and operations needed by the society, the company, and the individual to manage challenging or threatening situations.

King Wei asked, "Suppose the enemy comes out when I go out, and I do not yet know whose numbers are greater; what should I do?"

The reply to this question is missing. Based on relevant materials in this and related texts, it might be surmised that Master Sun would be likely to have recommended tactics designed to feel out the opponent while concealing one's own strengths.

King Wei asked, "How should one attack desperadoes?"
Master Sun answered, ". . . [Wait] until they find a way to live."

The most ancient Chinese classic, the *I Ching*, or *Book of Changes*, is the first to outline this particular strategy of not driving opponents to deadly desperation. There, this is symbolized by a king on a hunt using only three chasers, leaving one corner of the dragnet open in order to give the prey a fighting chance to escape.

The principle is that a "cornered rat" may turn on its pursuer with inconceivably deadly force if it is driven to a frenzy in absolute despair. Given a chance to escape, the reasoning goes, vanquished opponents will not become embittered diehards and need not be imprisoned, suppressed, or exterminated to achieve and maintain peace and social order in the aftermath of conflict.

King Wei asked, "How do you attack equals?"

Master Sun replied, "Confusing them and splitting them up, I concentrate my troops to pick them off without the enemy realizing what is going on. If the enemy does not split up, however, settle down and do not move; do not strike where there is doubt."

Confusing and splitting an opponent's force is done in order to diffuse and blunt the enemy of an attack as well as to compromise the security of the enemy's defense. Striking the diffuse with concentrated force is a way to shift the balance of strategic factors in one's own favor when facing an adversary of equal size and strength. Concentration and diffusions are both mental and physical, applying to attention, momentum, force, numbers, and material resources. The existence of doubt means that there is diffusion of attention, resulting in loss of concentration; therefore it is recommended that no action be initiated in doubtful situations.

King Wei asked, "Is there a way to strike a force ten times my size?"

Master Sun replied, "Yes. Attack where they are unprepared, act when they least expect it."

This tactic is taken directly from *The Art of War* by Sun Wu (Sun Tzu). The idea is that greater power and resources do not guarantee tactical superiority if they are not effectively employed. The purpose of deception as a strategic art, therefore, is to prevent adversaries from using their aggressive and defensive capacities accurately.

King Wei asked, "When the terrain is even and the troops are orderly, and yet they are beaten back in an engagement, what is the reason?"

Master Sun said, "The battlefront lacked an elite vanguard."

The function of an elite vanguard is to harass, split up, confuse, and otherwise soften up the adversary.

King Wei asked, "How can I get my people to follow orders as an ordinary matter of course?"

Master Sun said, "Be trustworthy as an ordinary matter of course."

If ever there was a golden key to the art of leadership, perhaps this is it: To get people to follow orders as a matter of course, be trustworthy as a matter of course. The practical philosopher Confucius is on record as observing that people will not obey leaders they do not trust, even if they are coerced; whereas they will follow leaders they do trust, even when nothing is said.

King Wei exclaimed, "Excellent words! The configurations of warfare are inexhaustible!"

Inexhaustibility of configurations means endless adaptation. When surprise tactics are repeated over and over, they become conventionalized and lose their strategic value. When conventional tactics are altered unexpectedly according to the situation, they take on the element of surprise and increase in strategic value. Thus it is said that the surprise becomes conventional, while the conventional becomes a surprise.

General Tian Ji asked Master Sun, "What causes a militia trouble? What thwarts an opponent? What makes walls impregnable? What makes one miss opportunities? What makes one lose the advantage of the terrain? What causes disaffection of people? May I ask if there are underlying principles governing these things?"

Master Sun replied, "There are. Terrain is what causes militias trouble, narrow passages are what thwart opponents. Thus it is said, 'A mile of swamp is a commander's nightmare; . . . to cross over, they leave their full armor behind.' That's why I say that it is the terrain that troubles an army, narrow passages that thwart an opponent, barbed wire that makes walls impenetrable, ..."

In the original, parts of Sun Bin's reply are missing. The master's explanations of how opportunities are missed and how disaffection occurs are lost, but similar themes appear elsewhere in classical strategic lore, being critical issues of leadership.

Generally speaking, opportunities are lost through misinformation or lack of information, faulty evaluation of intelligence, lack of courage or initiative, indolence, preoccupation, or similar flaws in basic management. The great civil and military leader Zhuge Liang said, "There are three avenues of opportunity: events, trends, and conditions. When opportunities occur through events but you are unable to respond, you are not smart. When opportunities become active through a trend and yet you cannot make plans, you are not wise. When opportunities emerge through conditions but you cannot act on them, you are not bold." He also said, "Of all avenues of seeing opportunity, none is greater than the unexpected." Disaffection arises from arbitrariness and unfairness, particularly in matters of rewards and punishments, privileges and opportunities. Citing ancient tradition, Zhuge Liang wrote in his advice for commanders, "Do not turn from the loyal and trustworthy because of the artifices of the skilled but treacherous. Do not sit down before your soldiers sit down, do not eat before your soldiers eat. Bear the same cold and heat as your soldiers do; share their toil as well as their ease. Experience sweetness and bitterness just as your soldiers do; take the same risks that they do. Then your soldiers will exert themselves to the utmost, and it will be possible to destroy enemies."

Tian Ji asked, "Once a moving battle line has been established, how does one get the warriors to obey orders without fail when going into action?"

Master Sun said, "Be strict, and indicate how they can profit thereby."

The effort inspired by commonality of purpose is by nature greater, more genuine, and more reliable than the effort inspired by authoritarian demands or fixed wages alone. This point is underscored in the following question and answer.

Tian Ji asked, "Are rewards and punishments critical to warriorship?"

Master Sun said, "No. Rewards are means of encouraging the troops, to make the fighters mindless of death. Punishments are means of correcting disorder, making the people respect authority. These can enhance the odds of winning, but they are not what is most crucial."

There are inherent limits to rewards and punishments. Excess in presentation of rewards can be ruinous because of material cost, and by the creation of secondary competition. Excess in punishments can be ruinous because of cost in personnel, and by the creation of an atmosphere of fear and suspicion.

Tian Ji asked, "Are planning, momentum, strategy, and deception critical to warriorship?"

Master Sun answered, "No. Planning is a means of gathering large numbers of people. Momentum is used to ensure that soldiers will fight. Strategy is the means of catching opponents off guard. Deception is a means of thwarting opposition. These can enhance the odds of winning, but they are not what is most crucial."

An inspiring plan can magnetize attention and galvanize efforts, but this cannot guarantee positive environmental conditions. Momentum can join a multitude of smaller energies into a stream of major force, but this cannot guarantee the accuracy of aim and direction needed to overcome an intractable obstacle. Strategy can enable one to outwit adversaries when it works, but that cannot prevent them from regrouping and counterattacking. Deception may throw opponents off your trail or off their guard, but that does not guarantee an effective offense to put an end to the conflict. All of these things may have their place in tactical action, in short, but no one of them is sufficient to be in itself quintessential to victory.

Flushed with anger, Tian Ji retorted, "These six things are employed by all experts, and yet you, Maestro, say they are not crucial. If so, then what is crucial?"

Master Sun replied, "Sizing up the opposition, figuring out the danger zones, making sure to survey the terrain, . . . are guiding principles for commanders. To make sure you attack where there is no defense is what is crucial to warriorship. . . ."

Part of Sun Bin's reply is also missing here, but the overall sense of the passage emphasizes preparedness and surprise. Both of these factors are stressed throughout classical strategic literature.

Tian Ji asked, "Is there a principle according to which a deployed army should not engage in combat?"

Master Sun answered, "Yes. When you occupy a narrow strait and have further increased defensive fortification of this fastness, be quiet, be on the alert, and do not move. Let nothing seduce you, let nothing anger you."

When you are in a secure position, if you rise to an enemy's bait and let yourself be drawn out through greed or rage, then you give up your security to expose yourself to indefinite risks.

Tian Ji asked Master Sun, "Is there a principle according to which one should not fail to engage in combat even if the opposition is numerous and powerful?"

Master Sun said, "Yes. Fortify your ramparts to enhance determination, solidify group cohesion with strict uprightness. Evade them to make them haughty, lure them to tire them, attack where they are unprepared, act when they least expect it, and make sure you can keep this up."

Evading a powerful enemy to give the impression of weakness or lack of confidence is a tactic to induce arrogance, complacency, and overconfidence in order to weaken the enemy's tension and attention. Luring the enemy on fruitless chases is a tactic to wear down the enemy's stamina and patience. Acting outside of expectation and striking where there is no defense are general principles of strategy, but they are particularly recommended in cases where there is so much difference in relative strength that direct confrontation is unfeasible.

Tian Ji asked Master Sun, "What is the Awl Formation for? What is the Goose Formation for? What are elite troops for? What is rapidfire shooting with powerful bows for? What is a whirlwind battle line for? What are common soldiers for?"

Master Sun replied, "The Awl Foundation is for piercing tight defenses and breaking edges. The Goose Formation is for sniping on flanks and responding to changes. . . . Elite troops are for crashing through battle lines to capture commanders. Rapid-fire shooting with strong bows is for ease of battle and the ability to hold out for a long time. A whirlwind battle line is for . . . Common soldiers are for sharing the work to bring about victory."

The Awl Formation may be thought of as an intense, acute concentration of energy, especially adapted to breaking through obstacles and breaking down resistance. The Goose Formation may be envisioned as still having a concentrated focus, but also maintaining a broader peripheral consciousness and capacity; the expanded scope of its breadth of action is particularly useful for picking off opponents from the side, while the combination of sharply focused and evenly distributed concentration is especially suitable for effective adaptivity in action.

The elite vanguard, supporting artillery, and common soldiers may be translated into civil terms as research, development, and production. Research may be likened to an elite vanguard, which must break through the barriers of existing convention to seize the potential of the unknown. Development supports research by pragmatic follow-up, through which the potential advantages brought to light by research can be tested and proved through transformation into concrete practicalities, so that research continues because of demonstrations of its utility in development of what is useful. Production rationally follows proof of utility, enabling the benefits to be actualized on a public scale.

Master Sun added, "Enlightened rulers and knowledgeable commanders do not expect success by common soldiers alone."

In both martial and productive endeavors, success is obtained through the cooperation of people of different skills, talents, and capacities. When the potentials inherent in these different capacities are each activated and deployed in such a way as to bring about their maximum collective effect, then they may be said to be cooperating. Cooperation is not simply a matter of everyone doing the same thing regardless of their individual capacities.

To extend this remark of Master Sun to the previous simile of research, development, and production, it may be observed in modern history that economies based on production without research and development have been or become more dependent and more vulnerable than those that have combined research, development, and production within themselves.

It may be, of course, that all economies have, somewhere within them, all three of these elements in some measure. The fact is, however, that in the modern currency/credit-based global economy, research and development can be and have been both forced to and allowed to become more vestigial in many economies at various times than is really healthy—either for the local economy in question or, in the long run, for the global economy itself.

These observations include all tiers of an economy. Ongoing research and development are as important in relation to production in such apparently diverse domains as animal husbandry, agriculture, and the service sector as they are in science, technology, and manufacturing industries.

When Master Sun emerged from these interviews, his disciples asked him about the questions of King Wei and his general, Tian Ji. Master Sun said, "King Wei asked about nine matters, Tian Ji about seven. They are close to knowledge of warriorship, but they have not yet reached the Way.

"I have heard that those who are always trustworthy as a matter of course will flourish, and those who act justly . . . Those who use arms without preparation will be wounded, while armed desperadoes will die. The third generation of Qi is a worry!"

Master Sun Bin's fears for Qi were in fact borne out by history in three generations. Although Qi had become one of the most powerful of states in the aftermath of the breakup of the old Zhou dynasty federation, eventually it fell through intrigue and poor judgment. Five smaller states applied to Qi for help against the depredations of the rapacious state of Qin (Ch'in), which eventually would take over all of ancient China and establish the first empire. As it happened, one of the chief advisors of the reigning king of Qi sold out to Qin, accepting bribery to advocate the Qin cause at the Qi court. Siding with Qin on the advice of this traitor, Qi was betrayed and annexed by its supposed ally. The mighty Qin armies then overthrew the five smaller states with ease.

It may seem like sound strategy, if not sound morality, to help the powerful against the weak; and this may have been a reason for the king of Qi to accept and pursue what turned out to be a ruinous tactic recommended by a traitor. Not only did the king of Qi violate the traditional Taoist morality of warfare teaching that the weak should be protected against the strong; from a purely strategic point of view, he also overlooked the tactical potential latent in the very desperation of the five smaller states appealing for assistance against a powerful common enemy.

[4]

TIAN JI ASKS ABOUT RAMPARTS

[*Tian Ji asked Sun Bin, "Would it be effective if my troops in the field keep strengthening their barricades?"

Master Sun replied, "This is the question of an enlightened commander, one which people overlook and do not stress. It is also one detested by opponents."

It is one thing to place a task force in the field and expect it to get the job done; it is another to see to the ongoing development and adaptation of this force to emergencies and changing conditions.

Tian Ji said, "Can I hear about it?"

Master Sun answered, "Yes. This is used to respond to sudden changes, or when in confined, closed-off deadly grounds. This is how I captured Pang Juan and Prince Shen."

It is strategically necessary to provide for the ability to handle unforeseen developments, unpredicted shifts in the action, and unexpected impasses. The capacity to strengthen defenses under such adverse conditions is essential to mount an effective offense.

Tian Ji said, "Fine, but those events are already past, and I have not seen the formations involved."]

Master Sun said, "Barbed wire can be used to serve the function of a moat, wagons can be used to serve as a barricade. Shields can be used to serve the function of rampart blinds. Long weapons come next, as a means of helping out in danger. Small spears are next, to back up the long weapons. Short weapons are next, to inhibit the enemy's return and strike him when he flags. Bows are next, to serve in place of catapults. The center has no one in it, so it is filled with . . . When the soldiers are set, the rules are fulfilled.

*Brackets enclose reconstructions.

"*The code says, 'Place the bows after the barbed wire, then shoot as is proper. Atop the ramparts, bows and spears are half and half.'* "

A basic principle of practical adaptation is to employ whatever is available at hand to accomplish the task. This includes the art of substituting what one has for what one lacks, and the ability to organize resources in such a way as to maximize the effects obtained from their combination and cooperation.

"*A rule says, 'Act after having seen what spies sent out come back and say . . . Keep watchers at intervals where they can be seen. On high ground, have them arrayed rectangularly; on low ground, have them arranged circularly. At night, let them signal with drums; during the day, let them signal with flags.'* "

Self-knowledge and knowledge of the opposition are considered critical to successful prosecution of the art of war. The main infrastructures connected with these tasks are a system of external intelligence gathering and a system of internal communications.

[5]

ELITE TROOPS

Master Sun said, "The victory of a militia lies in its elite corps, its courage lies in order, its skill lies in configuration and momentum, its advantage lies in trust, its effectiveness lies in its guidance, its richness lies in quick return, its strength lies in giving the people rest, its injury lies in repeated battle."

The elite corps is the vanguard that breaks through or smashes down the edge of an enemy's line of attack or defense, thus creating a loss of momentum or a gap of vulnerability.

Courage is said to be a matter of order in that an orderly formation or organization unites the efforts of people having diverse physical and psychological capabilities, thereby evening out individual disparities; the bold and mettlesome bolster and encourage the less robust, while the presence of weaker and more cautious elements restrains the overly rambunctious.

Skill in configuration and momentum is a matter of organizing people in such a way that they operate as one unit, the force of which can then be directed coherently to achieve an intense focus of power and impact.

Advantage and effectiveness lie in trust and guidance because trust in leadership unifies the people and empowers the leadership. Without guidance, trust is blind; without trust, guidance is powerless.

Richness lies in quick return because this is the way to avoid excess expenditures of constructive energy and material resources. Strength lies in rest because this is the way to avoid useless waste and recover from exertion. Injury lies in repeated battle because continued expenditure of energy and material resources inevitably wears down the strength of a force, even a winning force, ultimately making it vulnerable to loss of capacity to avoid, resist, or withstand antagonistic factors.

Master Sun said, "Acting with integrity is a rich resource for warriors. Trust is a distinguished reward for warriors. Those who despise violence are warriors fit to work for kings. Those who win many cohorts overcome . . ."

Acting with integrity is what wins the trust of leaders, commanders, colleagues, and subordinates, as well as the people at large. Trust solidifies and empowers working relationships, enabling the individual to operate at full personal potential, with the effective cooperation of others.

Warriors who despise violence are fit to work for kings in two important senses. One of the most ancient principles of the art of war is that the best victory is won with the least violence; those who despise violence and yet are warriors are those who are most efficient at their work. Warriors who are fond of violence, furthermore, have a private motivation and cannot be trusted to fight for a public cause; it is those who despise violence who can only be moved to go into battle under conditions of objective necessity. The *Tao Te Ching* says, "Those who enjoy killing cannot get their will of the world." Also, "When you win a war, you celebrate by mourning."

Master Sun said, "There are five conditions that always lead to victory. Those who have authorized command over a unified power structure are victorious. Those who know the Way are victorious. Those who win many cohorts are victorious. Those whose close associates are in harmony are victorious. Those who take the measure of enemies and size up difficulties are victorious."

A unified power structure can be expected to be more effective than one that is internally ruptured or fragmented. The Way, according to Sun Bin's predecessor Sun Wu, means "inducing the people to have the same aim as the leadership," thus achieving internal unity of aspiration as well as external unity of organization.

Winning support is naturally conducive to success, but disharmony and lack of integrity within an inner circle of leadership will undermine effectiveness. Knowledge of conditions, of adversaries as well as of critical environmental circumstances, is essential to effective employment of capacities and resources.

Master Sun said, "There are five things that always lead to failure. Inhibiting the commander leads to failure. Not knowing the Way leads to failure. Disobedience to the commander leads to failure. Not using secret agents leads to failure. Not winning many cohorts leads to failure."

The skills of a directorate cannot materialize in action without an effective organizational structure and chain of command responsive to its initiatives. Inability to achieve this degree of order, by the same token, not only thwarts leadership but is also a failure of the directorate itself. Poor leaders and recalcitrant followers earn each other's mistrust, perhaps because their common cause does not really motivate them, or because their private interests are originally too strong and too disparate to achieve unity of purpose and effort.

The use of secret agents is for the purpose of collecting vital information and the purpose of disseminating crucial misinformation. Secrecy is involved in gathering information because knowledge is power and therefore guarded; secrecy is involved in spreading misinformation to maintain the effect of illusion.

Master Sun said, "Victory lies in consummation of . . . , a clear system of rewards, selecting elite troops, and taking advantage of enemies. . . . This is called the security of a great military."

A clear and reliable system of rewards is established to create a unified motivational structure capable of effectively directing the attention and effort of personnel.

Elite troops, whose function and importance as vanguard forces were defined earlier, need to be chosen expertly, based on actual capacity, training, and accomplishment.

The real point of taking advantage of enemies is to win by superior tactical skill rather than by overwhelming violence or force. It is based in the first place, of course, on the premise that the situation has already reached the point where enmity exists and conflict can no longer be avoided by any means.

Master Sun said, "There is no command without leadership.

"[There are three elements of] order: First is trust, second is loyalty, third is willingness. Wherein is loyalty? Loyalty to the govern-

ment. *Wherein is trust? In reliable rewards. Wherein is willingness? Willingness to get rid of the bad.*

"*Without loyalty to the government, one may not presume to employ its military. But for reliability in rewards, the peasants will not be virtuous. But for the willingness to get rid of the bad, the peasants will not be respectful.*"

A militia, or a special task force of any kind, may accomplish something with its resources and skills, but if the effect is not in harmony with the legitimate underlying aims of the nation or the organization—which include the policies of the rulership or directorate as well as the aspirations of the citizens or the workers—it will be impossible to maintain lasting success and build upon successive achievements.

[6]

TIMING COMBAT

Master Sun said, "Between sky and earth, nothing is as noble as humanity. . . . The right seasonal timing, the advantages of the terrain, harmony among personnel—if these three things are not gained, there is calamity even in victory. Therefore it is better to give before fighting, only doing battle when there is no choice."

Even victory is calamitous without the right seasonal timing, the advantages of the terrain, and harmony among personnel, because under these conditions victory will have been won at the cost of loss of productive labor, environmental destruction, and excessively high casualty rates. The Taoist classic *Tao Te Ching* says, "If one were bold but had no mercy, if one were far-ranging but not frugal, if one went ahead without deference, one would die."

The conclusion that it is "better to give before fighting, only doing battle when there is no choice" is also reflected in the *Tao Te Ching*, which claims that this is ancient philosophy: "There are sayings on the use of arms: 'Let us not be aggressors, but defend.' 'Let us not advance an inch, but retreat a foot.' "

"Thus when you have fought for the tranquility of the time, then you do not work the masses anymore. Those who do battle wrongly or unmethodically gain small victories by attrition."

The special effects and allocations needed to meet emergencies become ruinous if continued compulsively after the job has been one. The *Tao Te Ching* says, "Calculated sharpness cannot be kept for long. . . . When one's work is accomplished honorably, to retire is the natural way."

The victories of the unjust and unmethodical are attained by attrition because they are gained by fighting when honest and innocent people need to be about their business.

Master Sun said, "Those who win six out of ten battles go by the stars. Those who win seven out of ten battles go by the sun. Those who win eight of ten battles go by the moon. . . . Those who win ten out of ten battles have skilled commanders yet give rise to calamity. . . ."

Those who win all the battles can give rise to calamity by draining resources through continued prosecution of warfare; by creating an aggressive momentum, an appetite for conquest; and by falling prey to complacency and carelessness. There is an ancient saying that repeated victory in repeated warfare produces a haughty leadership commanding an exhausted populace, eventually thereby ruining a nation.

". . . There are five things that make for failure; with even one of these five, you won't win. Thus among ways of war, there are cases where many people are killed but the commanders and troops are not captured, there are cases where commanders and troops are captured but their base camp is not taken, there are cases where a base is taken but the general is not captured, and there are cases where the army is overthrown and the general killed. So, if you find the Way, no one can survive against you."

The ancient text is broken, so it is not clear what is intended here by the "five things that make for failure." There appears later in the text, however, an extensive list of failures in commanders.

The sense of the text that does remain is that there are many grades of victory and defeat, many shades of gray. Part of the art of war is understanding how final the outcome of a particular defeat or victory is, seeing how gains might be lost and how losses might be regained, using this knowledge to plan for security or recovery. Only with comprehensive perspective and fluidly adaptable strategy is it possible to deal unfazed with all sorts of contingencies, even those seeming most desperate.

7

EIGHT BATTLE FORMATIONS

Master Sun said, "One who leads a militia with inadequate intelligence is conceited. One who leads a militia with inadequate courage has an inflated ego. One who leads a militia without knowing the Way and does battle repeatedly without being satisfied is surviving on luck."

Unless one has adequate information and also the intellectual ability to process it usefully, one cannot willfully exercise command without an inflated opinion of one's abilities; thus defect is added to lack, providing for a perilous situation. One who takes on leadership in spite of such dangers is foolhardy, not courageous; and one who takes on leadership in psychological compensation for inner lack of fortitude is supremely egotistical, endangering others for personal pride. One who takes on leadership with nothing but witless ambition may get somewhere by dint of perseverance, but no gain attained in this manner can be stabilized safely on a permanent and peaceful basis.

"Bringing security to a large country, expanding a large dominion, and safeguarding a large populace can only be done by knowing the Way. Knowing the Way means knowing the pattern of the climate and the lay of the land, winning the hearts of the people, knowing the conditions of enemies, knowing how to set up the eight battle formations, engaging in combat only when it is obvious you will win, otherwise keeping your peace; this is the kind of commander appointed by a successful ruler."

The secret of the master warrior is knowing when to fight, just as the secret of the artist is knowing when to perform. Knowledge of technical matters and methods is fundamental, but not sufficient to guarantee success; in any art or science of performance and action, direct perception of the potential of the moment is crucial to execution of a master stroke.

Master Sun said, "The use of eight battle formations in combat is based on the advantages of the terrain, using whichever of the eight formations is most suitable. Deploy a battle formation in three parts, each with a vanguard and a backup, each awaiting orders to act, acting only on orders. Use one to fight, two to defend; use one to invade, two to rally.

"When an opponent is weak and confused, send your elite troops in first to take advantage of this. When an opponent is strong and orderly, send your lesser troops in first to lure them.

"When chariots and cavalry are involved, divide them into three groups; one to the left, one to the right, and one in the back. On even ground, use more chariots; in narrow gorges, use more cavalry. On perilous ground, use more archers.

"Whether the ground is rugged or easy, it is imperative to know what ground is viable and what ground is deadly; occupy the viable and attack the deadly."

8

TERRAIN AND SECURITY

Master Sun said, "Generally speaking, a course over terrain through sunny ground is called 'outside,' while one through shady ground is called 'inside.' "

In metaphorical terms, the "outside" is the obvious, the evident, the open and aboveboard; the "inside" is the subtle, the concealed, the ulterior or underhanded. The "outside" in this sense may also refer to common consensus, the "inside" to private or covert power. The point of defining these distinctions as they apply to a given situation is to match the nature of a feasible approach to fit the character of an accessible route in the process of pursuing chosen aims.

"The straight and direct is called 'rope,' while the crooked and tortuous is called 'string.' When properly organized according to the character of the route, a battle formation does not get confused. Those on a straight way thrive, while those on a tortuous course half die."

It may be wondered why anyone would take a tortuous course with this understanding. The answer, aside from real or feigned incompetence, may simply be lack of choice, one of the primary motivations of warriors following the tradition of *The Art of War.*

This aphorism applies to the moral dimension of behavior as well as the strategic aspect. Truth or honesty may seem inconvenient under certain circumstances, but the compensation is freedom from confusion and conservation of energy. The whole process of creating and maintaining false appearances to conceal and foster ulterior motives requires so much time and energy for its own operation that this preoccupation alone can become a motivation in itself that is powerful enough, however secondary it may be, to turn into a compulsive mode of behavior.

"In general, when it comes to the matter of a battle ground, the sun is the essential element."

On an actual battlefield, the most advantageous position to occupy in relation to the sun is to have it at your back and in your opponent's eyes. In metaphorical terms, as the source of light that makes it possible to maneuver, the sun stands for intelligence. Strategically, intelligence means reconnaissance and information as well as the specific means and methods of gathering, processing, and applying knowledge. The question that needs to be considered first is what sources and techniques of intelligence are practical under given conditions.

"Wind may come from eight directions, and must not be forgotten."

Depending on its direction in relation to the direction of tactical maneuvers on a battlefield, wind affects vision, hearing, coordination, and stamina. Symbolically, wind is traditionally used to represent external influences that affect states of mind. The "eight winds" are gain and loss, censure and praise, honor and disgrace, pain and pleasure. Insofar as psychological states influence personal interaction and professional performance, the action of the "eight winds" must be considered in the course of organizing and managing a group work situation or developing and implementing an operational strategy of any kind.

"Crossing water, heading up an incline, or going against the current of a river, camping on deadly ground, or facing woods, are equally worthy of note because these are not conducive to victory."

Crossing water is perilous because the process of the passage creates inherent vulnerability to attack, difficulty of defense, and inhibition of movement. A maneuver is not conducive to victory if it puts one even temporarily in the position of a "sitting duck" to adversaries, if it requires an excessive expenditure of effort and attention, or if it involves placing oneself in the midst of compromising obstacles under pressure, or even under fire.

By heading up an incline, going the hard way, not only do you lose the advantages of momentum and gravity for movement or offense, you also turn these forces against your own defensive interests.

Going against the current not only saps your strength, it also puts you directly in the firing line of whatever comes down the current from upstream, by chance or by hostile design. Going against the current of affairs not only drains your energy, it places any results of effort beyond the pale of contemporary relevance.

Camping on deadly ground means occupying an indefensible and inescapable position, sitting in an open trap, waiting for someone to shut it. Facing woods is situating yourself in a milieu where malefactors and interlopers can readily conceal themselves in the surroundings.

"Mountains stretching southward are viable mountains, mountains stretching eastward are deadly mountains. Water flowing eastward is viable water, water flowing northward is deadly water. If it does not flow, it is stagnant water.

"The order of superiority of five terrains is as follows: Mountains are superior to high hills, high hills are superior to low hills, low hills are superior to rolling ground, rolling ground is superior to wooded flatlands.

"The five outstanding kinds of vegetation are thickets, brambles, hedges, reeds, and sedges.

"The order of superiority of five kinds of earth is as follows: Green overcomes yellow, yellow overcomes black, black overcomes red, red overcomes white, white overcomes green.

"The five deadly terrains are: natural wells, natural bowls, natural entanglements, natural clefts, and natural pitfalls. These five graveyards are deadly ground, so do not stay there.

"Do not go downhill in spring, do not go uphill in autumn. The main body of the army and the battle formations should not be arrayed to the forward right; they should circle to the right, not the left."

The advantage or disadvantage of a particular element or configuration of a situation depends not only on its own specific characteristics, but also on its interrelationship with other factors and its place in the total context. Factors to examine in making strategic assessments include elements of protection versus vulnerability, concealment versus exposure, freedom of movement versus impediment and restriction, clarity of perspective and vision versus obstruction and partiality, fertility or supportiveness versus aridity or hostility. When the measures of these various factors and their interplay have been assessed, then it is possible to develop a more objective picture of the potential and limitations inherent in a given situation.

9

CONFIGURATIONS OF FORCE
AND STRATEGIC PLANNING

Master Sun said, "Fangs and horns, claws and spurs, harmonizing when pleased, fighting when angry—these are in the course of nature and cannot be stopped. Therefore those who have no natural defenses plan strategically for themselves; this is the business of wise leaders.

"The Yellow Emperor invented the sword, symbolizing it by the battle line. Hou Yi invented the bow, symbolizing it by a rush of force. King Yu invented boats and chariots, symbolizing these by adaptive change. King Tang and King Wu invented spears and halberds, symbolizing standard signals. These four are functions of weaponry."

While traditional Taoist military science condemns militarism as both immoral and inefficient, nevertheless, defensive, protective, peacekeeping, and punitive capabilities are considered rational and natural. Sun Bin follows tradition here in naming the martial actions and contributions of a variety of ancient sage kings and culture heroes to justify the judicious use of arms for pacification and order.

"In what sense is a sword a battle line? You may wear a sword all day without necessarily using it; hence the saying, 'Set out a battle line, but without fighting.' Consider a sword as a battle line: If the sword has no sharp point, even the bravest warrior will not dare . . . ; if a battle line has no elite vanguard, anyone who dares lead it forward with exceptional courage is extremely ignorant of military science. If a sword has no handle, even a skilled warrior cannot go ahead . . . ; if a battle line has no backup, anyone who dares to lead an advance without being a skilled warrior is ignorant of military affairs."

A sword must have a point, a cutting edge, a handle, and a ridge. A task force must have direction, skills, maneuverability, and backbone. Direction means the relationship between objective aims and active leadership. Skills need to be deployed selectively, according to conditions, and applied to precise objectives. In order to effect accurate and useful direction of skills, a mechanism of command and control is necessary. In order to carry out directions, an organization needs an adequate degree of inner cohesiveness, such as can be achieved by a commonly shared moral backbone.

In these senses, a sword can be a symbol or a metaphor for a battle line, which can in turn represent a task force of any kind. To wear a sword without necessarily using it means to be prepared but not anxious; the force is not there for its own sake, but for a specific purpose. To operate the force when it is not necessary is a wasteful mistake in itself, and can also evoke undesirable reactions from the political, social, economic, and natural environments.

"Thus when you have a vanguard and a backup with unshakable trust in each other, opponents will flee. If you have neither vanguard nor backup, ..."

The vanguard is needed to make the initial cracks in the facade of aggressors; the backup is needed to finish the job of breaking down and through the enemy front. The key expression here is "with unshakable trust in each other." This inner cohesion is the element that fortifies a group to the degree that it can make opponents flee; one of the critical elements of good leadership is evoking and strengthening mutual trust and internal harmony among members of the group.

"In what sense is the bow a rush of force? Shooting from between shoulder and arm, killing people a hundred paces away without their knowing where it is coming from—this is why the bow is said to be a rush of force."

A rush of force may be envisioned as a force of movement initiated or "launched" within a relatively small compass that goes on to exert a wide-ranging effect by the force of that initial momentum. In this sense it may be symbolized by the bow and arrow.

"In what sense are boats and chariots adaptive changes? When high, ..."

Boats rise and dip with the waves and the tide, chariots travel up and down hills and around curves. These symbolize adapting responsively to changes in circumstances in the course of progress.

"In what sense are spears and halberds signal standards? . . . Signal standards are mostly flags by day and mostly drums by night, used as means of directing the battle."

Spears and halberds are models for signal banners because of their frontline position as well as their length and consequent visibility. Sound is used when visual signals are ineffective. Metaphorically, vanguard weaponry representing signal standards reflects the use of outstanding indicators—such as economic indices, technological developments, or progressive sociopolitical adaptations—to evaluate the state of a nation or community.

"These four things are functions of weaponry. Everybody considers them useful, but no one knows the right way to use them.

"Overall, there are four military sciences: battle formation, force, adaptation, and direction. Thorough understanding of these four is a means of destroying powerful enemies and capturing fierce commanders."

Battle formation represents the disposition and deployment of resources. Force represents the energy and momentum of an endeavor or a movement. Adaptation represents the capacity to respond effectively to changes. Direction represents the aim and guidance of energy and effort.

10

MILITARY CONDITIONS

Master Sun said, "If you want to know the conditions of a military force, archery is an appropriate model. The arrows are the soldiers, the bow is the commander, and the archer is the ruler."

The arrows are the power, the bow concentrates and releases the momentum, while the archer takes aim.

"An arrow is tipped with metal and fletched with feathers so that it will be sharp and fly straight. . . . If you organize soldiers so that the rear guard is heavy while the front is light, they may be orderly when arrayed in battle formation, but they will not obey when ordered to charge the enemy. This organization of soldiers is not in accord with the model of the arrow."

Insufficient force in the vanguard makes it impossible to open up enough of a gap in the resistance to allow a telling follow-through.

"The commander is the bow: if the grip is not right when the bow is drawn, there will be an imbalance of strength and weakness, resulting in disharmony, such that the force imparted by the two ends of the bow will be unequal, and thus the arrows will not hit the target even if they are properly weighted and balanced. If a commander does not harmonize . . . successfully, they will still not overcome the enemy."

A commander has to motivate a group of people uniformly enough to get them to operate in harmony. If some are highly enthused while others are cynical and recalcitrant, the energy of the group cannot be focused accurately and released effectively.

"If the arrows are properly weighted and balanced, and the bow draws true and sends arrows with uniform force, yet if the archer is

not right, he still won't hit the target. If the soldiers are balanced [and the commander is competent, if the civil leadership is awry,] they still cannot overcome enemies. . . ."

Even the best resources, human and material, however superbly coordinated, cannot consummate a successful operation if the overall aim of the total force and its momentum are off target.

"Thus it is said, 'The way a militia overcomes an opponent is no different from the way an archer hits a target.' This is the way of warfare."

11

PRACTICING SELECTION

Master Sun said, "The guiding principle for mobilizing warriors and moving people is the balance scale. The balance scale is the means of selecting the wise and choosing the good. Yin and yang are the means of rallying the masses and meeting opponents. When an accurate scale is restacked . . . as long as it is faithful, it is called inexhaustible."

The balance scale is used to represent leadership, because a leader must above all be able to weigh and measure, to assess and evaluate all human and environmental factors relevant to an enterprise or an undertaking. The ability to select appropriate personnel for a specific job is a particularly valuable asset in the exercise of leadership.

As for the use of "yin and yang" to rally people and face adversaries, this has a wide range of meanings, based on the broad spectrum of associations of yin and yang. In basic terms relevant to this discussion, yin may have the meaning of self-effacement, docility, or conformity, complemented by yang as self-assertion, initiative, or activity; these refer to harmonizing with allies (yin) and striking out against enemies (yang).

"When articulating direction and establishing a standard of measure, focus only on what is appropriate."

If would seem to be a truism to say that focus should be only on what is appropriate, but the idea of inexhaustibility of an accurate scale mentioned in the text above suggests that there is, as the Chinese say, an "eye" in the word "appropriate." The main idea is that what is appropriate depends on the situation and cannot be determined in a dogmatic or peremptory fashion. Thus with the successive arising of new situations and new realities, reexamination of aims and measures is necessary to ensure the maintenance of effective alignments of efforts with actualities.

"Private and public wealth are one. There are those who have too little life and too much money, and there are those who have too little money and too much life: only enlightened rulers and sages recognize them, and thus can keep them in place. When those who die are not bitter, those who are bereft are not resentful."

Private and public wealth are one from the point of view of the totality of the economy; the manner in which wealth circulates back and forth between the private and public sectors defines the economy in certain ways, of which enlightened leadership must be aware in order to understand the real and potential effects of programs and policies.

To have too little life and too much money means to have more wealth than can be effectively used under these conditions; to have too little money and too much life means to have more energy or talent than can be constructively employed under these conditions. The wealth of a society that can balance these two extremes does not leak away.

When people die without bitterness and leave no resentment behind them, that means they did the best they could under the conditions in which they lived.

"When there is an abundance of money and goods, things are easy. When things are easy, the people do not attribute the merit to their rulers. . . . Therefore to accumulate wealth for the people is the means whereby you may accumulate wealth yourself; this is how warriors last. . . ."

This key idea of Sun Bin is based on traditional philosophy. In his commentary on the classic *I Ching,* or *Book of Changes,* the educator Confucius wrote, "Those above secure their homes by kindness to those below." Also, "Leaders distribute blessings to reach those below them, while avoiding presumption of virtue." According to the later Taoist Masters of Huainan, who compiled a great deal of ancient philosophical and scientific lore, "When people have more than enough, they defer; when they have less than enough, they contend. When people defer, courtesy and justice are born; when they contend, violence and disorder arise."

12

KILLING SOLDIERS

Master Sun said, ". . . When you know soldiers are trustworthy, don't let others alienate them. Fight only when you are sure to win, without letting anyone know. In battle, don't forget your flanks, don't . . ."

Most of this chapter is missing or corrupt.

Even when people are known to be trustworthy, their loyalty should not be taken for granted. Interlopers may attempt to alienate them, and complacency or arrogance on the part of leadership makes it easier for divisiveness and recalcitrance to take root in the lower echelons.

Fighting only when sure to win is standard wisdom in the philosophy of the art of war transmitted by Sun Wu and Sun Bin. This policy helps to eliminate conflict management to the greatest possible degree. Even the *Thirty-Six Strategies*, full as it is of draconian maneuvers, says at the end, "Of the thirty-six strategies, flight is best."

Flanks should not be forgotten, because otherwise you might be outflanked. In general terms, this means that peripheral awareness should be deliberately maintained along with centrally focused awareness, so that the power of the essential thrust of an effort or undertaking is not undermined by lack or failure of coordinated backup and support measures.

[13]
PROLONGING ENERGY

Master Sun said, "When massing troops to assemble armed forces, the thing to do is stimulate energy. When breaking camp and consolidating forces, the thing to do is keep the soldiers orderly and sharpen their energy. When on a border near an enemy, the thing to do is intensify energy. When the day of battle has been set, the thing to do is stabilize energy. On the day of battle, the thing to do is prolong energy.

". . . , thus awing the soldiers of the armed forces, is means of stimulating energy. The general commands . . . , which command is means of sharpening energy. The general then . . . wears simple clothing to encourage the warriors, as a means of intensifying energy. The general gives an order commanding every soldier to muster three days' rations, and the people in the homes of the nation make . . . ; this is a means of stabilizing energy. The general summons his guard and declares, 'Food and drink should not . . .' Thus energy is prolonged."

The process of stimulating, sharpening, intensifying, stabilizing, and prolonging energy needs to be rationalized so that it can be repeated when necessary. The original meaning of the word *energy* used here in the text includes mental and physical aspects of energy, and both mental and physical momentum are considered critical to the success of an action. The timing of each stage in the process is crucial, so the key to effective leadership is to coordinate the psychological and physical inspiration and readiness of participants in an action with the timing of developments in the unfolding of actual events.

[14]

OFFICIAL POSTS

*Master Sun said, "Whenever you set out troops, make battle forma-
tions efficient, and organize armed forces, when setting up official
posts you should do so in a manner appropriate to the individual,
indicate ranks by means of insignia, promote and demote to grade
people, march in an orderly fashion to . . . , organize soldiers by
homeland, delegate authority to those who are leaders in their own
localities. Clarify confusion by signal flags and chariots, dissemi-
nate orders by means of gongs and drums."*

Setting up official posts in a manner appropriate to the individual
means assigning people to duties and responsibilities matching their
capacities and talents.

Ranks are indicated by insignia so that organizational order and
chain of command can be made clear in an impersonal manner.

Personnel are graded by promotion and demotion to adjust their
positions to their abilities and achievements, and to provide a system
of rewards and punishments fully integrated into the functional operation of the organization.

Soldiers are organized by homeland for the sake of the inner cohesion of a unit; authority is delegated to local leaders who already have
standing in the eyes of their own people.

*"To keep soldiers in line, use the method of following tracks.
Camps are to be guarded by the strongest men. Overtake armies
by means of a continuous line formation; adjust the formation to
contain disorder. Position your army on high ground, use a cloudlike formation for arrow and missile combat. To avoid being surrounded, use a formation like a winding river. To take out a
vanguard, shut off the road; when it is on the verge of defeat, circle
around. When going to the rescue, put on pressure from outside. In
a hectic battle, use mixed lines. Use heavy arms to face a concen-*

trated force, use light arms to face a scattered force. To attack a secured position, use a moving battlement."

The method of following tracks means that each successive individual in a line of movement follows in the tracks of the preceding individual. In general representative terms, this means using available forces of internal cohesion to keep a group action focused on collective aims.

Guarding camp does not offer the glamour, excitement, or opportunity for exploit found on the front lines. Untutored thinking might expect the most powerful or most heroic personnel to be strictly elite vanguard material, but the security of the base of operations is essential if the action is to succeed. If a camp is poorly defended, those in the field can be cut off from behind and isolated; they will have no resort in defeat and no backup in victory.

The configuration of an operation, the disposition of resources and personnel, depends on the aim, the terrain and environmental conditions, and the situation and condition of adversaries. This is why it is said that a successful force has no constant configuration.

High ground is preferred because it is easier to command a view of the terrain, and because it puts attacking opponents at a gravitational disadvantage and makes it possible to launch an assault with extra momentum. The same things could also be said of moral high ground, provided the position is authentic and effective, not a mere posture.

A diffuse cloudlike formation is used for arrow and missile attack because it is thereby possible to rain projectiles over a wide area while minimizing casualties under return fire by spreading out rather than clustering.

A formation like a winding river is used to avoid being surrounded, by repeatedly outflanking adversaries and thereby thwarting attempts to encircle your force.

A vanguard is stopped by blocking off its route of advance and then circling around to isolate it and attack from behind.

When going to the rescue, pressure is put on from outside in order to divert the adversary's attention and energy away from the beleaguered party, thus making it easier to secure escape from a difficult situation.

Using mixed lines in a hectic battle means arraying forces so that they are not restricted by their formation but are able to move in any direction, thus being in a position to give and receive support from all sides in the midst of a chaotic fray.

Heavy arms are used against a concentrated force because of its density, and because of the kind of target it affords; intensely focused assault with heavy arms maximizes the power and efficacy of an attack. Light arms are used against a scattered force for the sake of the mobility needed to oppose a relatively diffuse target.

A moving battle line is used against a secured position to take advantage of the limitations imposed on the maneuverability of an occupying force by the requirements of security and defense.

"Use square formations on level ground, use pointed formations when setting out battle lines facing higher ground.

"Use round formations on rugged ground. Use your forces strategically with alternating aggressiveness and withdrawal. Against an orderly battle line, use a square formation with wings; in a more spread-out battle, close in like a bird's bill shutting. When trapped in rugged territory, open up a way out by outcircling the enemy; on grass and sand, you have to cut through out in the open. When you have won in war and yet still maintain troops in the field, it is to keep the nation on the alert."

A square formation is suited to level ground because it is easy to set out a tight battlefront with a matching backup and flanks poised to either circle or spread out. Metaphorically speaking, on a level field of action—when conditions are fair, being functionally similar or equivalent on all sides—it is appropriate to proceed in a "square" or conventional manner.

A pointed formation is used when facing higher ground because of the need for a sharp edge to resist and break through the momentum of a downhill charge. An overwhelming force should not be met with direct resistance, unless the resistance can be focused so sharply and aimed so adroitly that it does not absorb the full force but rather splits it apart.

A round formation is used in rugged territory because in a circle the positions in the front, rear, and flanks can be spaced in such a way that communication and contact can be maintained in spite of natural barriers, and the formation can expand, contract, or modify its shape as a coherent whole. In metaphorical terms, emphasis is on "roundness" or strategic adaptability when conditions are uneven and unfair, because conventional methods are not sure to work with predictable efficacy in such a situation.

Alternating aggressiveness and withdrawal are used to confuse and mislead opponents; retreat after an assault is a common tactic to draw an adversary into a compromised position. The notorious "hard cop, soft cop" method of interrogation is an application of this principle. The same tactic was used against prisoners of war by communist Chinese agents in Korea.

A square formation with wings is used to outflank and engulf a contained battle line. Against a more scattered force, individuals or squads can be picked off by closing in from two sides, like a bird of prey snatching an animal in its bill.

When on rugged territory, it is necessary to use the difficulty of the terrain to your own advantage, using natural obstacles to help you to outmaneuver adversaries rather than letting them keep you trapped. Where the ground is flat and open, in contrast, it is necessary to cut right through because there is no natural cover. Here again there is a metaphorical contrast between the use of subterfuge and deviousness when at an unfair disadvantage and the use of a more open and direct approach on an even ground where no one has an unfair advantage.

Maintaining troops in the field after a war is won is normally not indicated because of the drain on the economy. It is only justified tactically when the situation has not been completely stabilized and it is imperative to keep on the alert.

". . . In thick undergrowth, move like a snake; to make it easy when weary, travel in a Goose Formation. In dangerous straits, use a medley of weaponry; when retreating, dissolve into the underbrush."

Zigzagging through obstacles like a snake rather than plowing through them like a bulldozer has the advantages of conserving energy, minimizing environmental destruction, and leaving a less obvious trail. Traveling in a Goose Formation makes it easy when weary by positioning people where they can easily keep in contact with each other and come to each other's assistance and yet not stumble over one another. A medley of weaponry is used in dangerous straits because different weapons have different effective ranges and usages, so having a variety of arms at hand increases resources and enhances adaptability. Dissolving into the underbrush when retreating means relying on concealment rather than speed of flight, which is naturally compromised by the fatigue and stress of battle.

"When circling mountains and forests, use circuitous routes and go by stages; to attack cities, use their waterways, Organize night retreats by memo; use relay signals for night alarms. Use talented warriors for double agents. Place troops armed with close-range weaponry where convoys are sure to pass."

One may take a circuitous route to outflank an opponent's position, or to weary an opponent in pursuit. The purpose of going by stages is to avoid debilitating weariness. Waterways are convenient for attacking cities because their functional relationship to cities makes them ideal delivery systems for assault forces; waterways can also be blocked or poisoned. Night retreats are organized by memo for security reasons, so that the orders and plans for retreat do not leak out. Relay signals are used for night alarms to compensate for limited visibility. Talented warriors are used for double agents because their talents can win them the confidence of adversaries for whom they appear to be working. Ambushing convoys reduces defensive expenditures by diminishing the enemy's fighting capacity with minimal effort.

"For incendiary warfare, deliver the fuel in wagons. When setting out a battlefront of blades, use a pointed formation. When you have few soldiers, deploy them with a combination of weapons; a combination of weaponry is a way to prevent being surrounded."

The best firepower delivery system to use in a given situation depends on the nature of the particular form of firepower to be employed and the local and temporal environmental factors affecting transport.

The use of a pointed formation in a battlefront of bladed weapons is recommended to maximize the effective range of the weaponry while minimizing the dangers of accidental injuries in a crush.

Deploying a small force with a variety of weaponry is a way to enhance the efficiency and adaptability of each individual warrior. In particular, arming everyone with both long- and short-range weapons increases their chances of preventing a larger enemy from surrounding them by holding the enemy at bay or breaking through attempts to outflank and encircle them.

"Patching up the lines and linking fragments is a way to solidify battle formations. Swirling and interlacing is a means of dealing with emergencies. A whirlwind kicking up dust can be used to take advantage of unclarity. Hiding out and hatching schemes is a way of provoking a fight. Creeping like a dragon and positioning ambushers is a way to fight in the mountains. . . ."

Patching lines and linking fragments means regrouping your forces. A mediocre commander, or a mediocre force, is one that does this only after being routed; the true warrior, in contrast, is constantly solidifying in this way, grooming power under all conditions. One of the reasons Turkish captives in North Korea were able to resist communist Chinese brainwashing techniques was because they continually regrouped in spite of all efforts by their captors to destroy group cohesion and leadership.

Swirling and interlacing work together as a way of meeting emergencies. Swirling is a technique of dodging direct onslaughts while simultaneously launching one's own assault from constantly changing angles; interlacing reinforces the swirling lines without compromising their fluidity.

A whirlwind kicking up dust, or mass distraction or confusion of any sort, can be used as a cover for covert operations or sneak attack. It is widely used by thieves, especially pickpockets.

Hiding out and hatching schemes is a way of provoking fights because it arouses the suspicions and fears of enemies. For this reason, the appearance of being open and aboveboard is also used as a diversionary tactic, presenting adversaries with a nonsuspicious front while plotting against them under the cover of their own false sense of security.

Guerrilla tactics are recommended for mountain warfare because of the inherent difficulties of mountainous terrain. Once in such a situation, the most practical way out is to use the difficulties to one's advantage against adversaries.

"Sneaking up unexpectedly on soldiers is a way of fighting in the dark. Taking a stand on the opposite side of a river is a way of clashing with a smaller force."

Sneaking up on enemies unawares is more precise, efficient, and economical than random bombardment. Forcing an opponent to cross a
natural barrier, rendering itself vulnerable to attack as it does so, is a
way of keeping expenditures to an absolute minimum.

*"Tattering banners is a way to fool enemies. A chariot train in swift
formation is a way to pursue remnant forces."*

Tattering banners means giving the appearance of fatigue and distress
in order to make opponents contemptuous, haughty, and therefore
careless and unprepared for a hard fight.

More ancient work on strategy draws limits to the distances to
which a fleeing enemy should be pursued by foot soldiers and by cava-
liers. The reason for this is to limit expenditure of time and energy,
and to avoid being lured into ambushes. The use of a chariot train to
chase down remnant forces provides for greater swiftness and stamina in advance and withdrawal than can be achieved on foot, and
more powerful defensive and offensive capabilities than horseback
fighters alone.

*"Ability to move an army at a moment's notice is a way to be pre-
pared against those who are stronger. Spreading out over water or
swampland is a way to fight with fire."*

When strength is overbearing, it can be neutralized by yielding; the
flexibility to change at an impasse is one variety of this maneuver.
Lao-tzu said, "The softest can drive the hardest."

The use of environmental or other ambient factors inherently antagonistic to specific kinds of force is another mode of softness overcoming hardness; here this manner of defense is typified by using
water to control fire.

*"Retreating under cover of darkness, like a cicada leaving its shell,
is a means of luring an enemy on. A light, mobile task force of specially trained troops is used to oppose a blitz attack."*

The image of a cicada leaving its shell is a traditional representation
of strategic maneuvering whereby a semblance or facade is left in
place to convey a misleading impression, while the real power or

force has been moved elsewhere, poised for a surprise assault on the opponent who had been deceived by appearances.

In the case of a blitz attack, the nature of the action makes it inherently costly to mount direct opposition. Mobility is therefore essential to counter such an attack, so that the most dangerous and destructive waste of a head-on collision may be avoided while more patient and more effective defensive measures are arranged and carried out by strategically harrying, diverting, and splitting up the oncoming force.

"A stiffened and thickened battle line is used to attack fortifications. Making breaks in surrounding ground cover is a way to create confusion."

The precise manner in which a battle line is stiffened and thickened with extra weaponry and personnel depends on the characteristics of the fortifications under siege. The general idea is to provide for the flexibility to concentrate or dilute manpower and firepower freely enough to adapt successfully to rapidly changing needs and challenges.

Ground cover providing camouflage under which to maneuver is undoubtedly useful, but unmitigated cover may frustrate an opponent so much as to incite random fire or blanket fire. When breaks are made in the ground cover, in contrast, tactical movements of troops through these breaks can be staged so as to create concrete but false impressions of the strength and disposition of those under cover. Thus instead of the risk of an uncontrolled release of fear, it is possible to take advantage of a calculated manipulation of apprehension.

"Pretending to leave behind a small loss is a way to bait an opponent. Heavy weaponry and severe violence are used in active combat. To maneuver at night, use signals opposite to those used during the day."

Appearing to make a concession in order to bait an adversary is a tactic that may be useful when trying to lure an enemy out of a fastness, or when trying to slow down an advancing force without putting up direct opposition.

It seems redundant to say that heavy weaponry and severe violence are used in active combat, but this is an indirect way of teaching, somewhat like making a noise to produce an echo. The point of making such an apparently obvious statement is to emphasize the basic tactical principle that combat is a last resort, that it is better to win by strategy than by violence.

The reason for varying signals is to make them more difficult for the enemy to read. This is an example of the principle that "the unconventional becomes conventional, the conventional becomes unconventional." Surprise tactics and secret usages become routine if they are employed too much; routines have to be changed if the element of surprise is to be exploited.

"Excellent salaries and useful supplies are means of facilitating victory. Firm and strong warriors are needed to repel assaults. . . ."

Excellent salaries are means of facilitating success when they are used to attract and maintain superior personnel and dependable loyalty.

The usefulness of useful supplies is another self-evident tautism used as a sound to produce an echo. In this case, the echo is the idea that the utility of supplies is not only a matter of quantity, but also of quality. The question of useful qualities is one that changes according to situations, so every operation needs to be considered in terms of its particular needs.

Firmness and strength are qualities proper to all warriors. The point of saying that such warriors are needed to repel assaults is another way of expressing the principle that these qualities are not properly used for aggression but for defense and prevention.

[15]

STRENGTHENING THE MILITARY

There are significant lacunae in every sentence of this chapter, such as to make it impractical to attempt to produce an accurate and meaningful translation.

16

Ten Battle Formations

Generally speaking, there are ten kinds of battle formations. There are square formations, round formations, sparse formations, dense formations, pointed formations, formations like a flock of geese, hooklike formations, confusing formations, fire formations, and water formations. Each of these has its uses.

Square formations are for cutting off, round formations are for massing solidly. Sparse formations are for bristling, dense formations are for being impossible to take. Pointed formations are for cutting through, formations like goose flocks are for handling barrages. Hooklike formations make it possible to adapt and change plans, confusing formations are for deceiving armies and muddling them. Fire formations are used for rapid destruction, water formations are used for both offense and defense.

The rule for square formations is to make the center thin and the sides thick, with the main line at the back. The sparse array in the center is used for bristling.

"Bristling" refers to giving the illusion of being bigger and stronger than one really is, just as an animal bristles when faced with a natural enemy.

The rule for sparse formations is for added strength and firmness in cases where there is little armor and few people. The warrior's technique is to set up banners and flags to give the appearance that there are people there. Therefore they are arrayed sparsely, with space in between, increasing the banners and insignia, with sharpened blades ready at the flanks. They should be at sufficient distance to avoid stumbling over each other, yet arrayed densely enough that they cannot be surrounded; this is a matter for caution. The chariots are not to gallop, the foot soldiers are not to run. The general rule for sparse formations is in making numerous small groups, which may advance or retreat, may strike or defend, may intimidate enemies or may ambush them when they wear down. In this way a sparse formation can successfully take an elite corps.

The rule for a dense formation is not to space the troops too far apart; have them travel at close quarters, massing the blades yet giving enough room to wield them freely, front and rear protecting each other. . . . If the troops are frightened, settle them down. Do not pursue opponents in flight, do not try to stop them from coming; either strike them on a circuitous route, or break down their elite troops. Make your formation tightly woven, so there are no gaps; when you withdraw, do so under cover. In this way, a dense formation cannot be broken down.

A pointed formation is like a sword: if the tip is not sharp, it will not penetrate; if the edge is not thin, it will not cut; if the base is not thick, it cannot be deployed on the battlefront. Therefore the tip must be sharp, the edge must be thin, and the main body must be thick; then a pointed formation can be used for cutting through.

In a hooked formation, the front lines should be straight, while the left and right flanks are hooked. With gongs, drums, and pipes at the ready, and flags prepared, the troops should know their own signal and flag. . . .

A confusing formation must use a lot of flags and insignia, and drum up a racket. If the soldiers are in a commotion, then settle them down; if the chariots are disorderly, then line them up. When all is in order, the battle lines moves with a shocking commotion, as though it had come down from the sky or emerged from the earth. The foot soldiers come on unstoppably, continuing all day long inexhaustibly.

The rules for incendiary warfare are as follows. Once moats and ramparts have been made, construct another moat. Pile kindling every five paces, making sure the piles are placed at even intervals. A few men are needed to set the fires; they must be fast and efficient. Avoid being downwind; if the fire has overwhelmed you, you cannot fight a winning battle, and you will lose whether you stay put or go into action.

The rule for incendiary warfare is that the ground should be low and grassy, so that enemy soldiers have no way out. Under these conditions, it is feasible to use fire. If it is windy, if there is plenty of natural fuel, if kindling has been piled up, and if the enemy encampment is not carefully guarded, then a fire attack is feasible. Throw them into confusion with fire, shower them with arrows, drum and yell to encourage your soldiers, using momentum to help them. These are the principles of incendiary warfare.

The rule for amphibious warfare is to have a lot of infantry and few chariots. Have them fully equipped so that they can keep up when advancing and do not bunch up when withdrawing. To avoid bunching up, go with the current; make the enemy soldiers into targets.

The rule for warfare on the water is to use light boats to guide the way, use speedboats for messengers. If the enemy retreats, pursue; if the enemy approaches, close in. Be careful about advancing and withdrawing in an orderly manner, according to what is prudent under prevailing conditions. Be on the alert as they shift positions, attack them as they set up a front, split them up as they organize. As the soldiers have a variety of weapons and chariots, and have both mounted troops and infantry, it is essential to find out their quantities. Attack their boats, blockade the fords, and inform your people when the troops are coming. These are the rules of amphibious combat.

17

TEN QUESTIONS

In this chapter, classical tactics are defined according to their usefulness in given situations. All of these strategies are to be found in *The
Art of War*, the earlier manual by Sun Bin's distinguished predecessor,
Sun Wu. Typical examples include feigning flight to split up opponents and set them up for a counterattack; dividing and regrouping to
confuse and overwhelm enemies; seeking the advantage of the terrain
according to conditions; feinting to mislead opponents and create
openings; attacking where there is no defense; inducing laziness and
arrogance in adversaries by appearing irresolute; seducing opponents
into ambushes; striking unexpectedly with such speed that there is
no time to mount a defense.

*Someone asked, "Suppose two armies are facing off with equal fod-
der and food, comparable personnel and weaponry, both aggressor
and defender wary. If the enemy uses a round battle formation for
security, how should we attack it?"*

*[Master Sun Bin replied,] "To strike an opponent like this, divide
your forces into four or five groups, one of which closes in and then
feigns defeat and flight to give the appearance of fear. Once the opponents see you to be afraid, they will unthinkingly split up to give
chase. Thus their security will be disrupted. Now mobilize your
cavalry and drummers, attacking with all five groups at once. When
your five divisions get there together, all of your forces will cooperate profitably. This is the way to strike a round formation."*

*"Suppose two armies are facing off, and our opponents are richer,
more numerous, and more powerful than we are. If they come in a
square formation, how do we strike them?"*

*"To strike such a force, [using a sparse] formation to [assault]
them, contrive to split them up. Clash with them, then appear to
run away beaten, then come kill them from behind without letting*

them know what is going on. This is the way to strike a square formation."

"When two armies face off, suppose the enemy is numerous and powerful, forcefully swift and unyielding, waiting with a battle line of crack troops; how do we strike them?"

"To attack them, it is necessary to divide into three. One group stretches out horizontally. The second group . . . so that the enemy leaders are afraid and their troops are confused. Once both lower and upper echelons are in disarray, the whole army is routed. This is how to strike a battle formation of elite troops."

"When two armies face off, suppose the enemy is numerous and powerful, and stretches out in a horizontal battle line; meanwhile, we set out our front to await them, but we have few troops, and even these are unskilled. How do we strike?"

"You must divide your troops into three battalions. Train a suicide squad; have two battalions stretch out a battlefront, extending the flanks, while the elite specially trained group attacks the enemy's strategic points. This is the way to kill commanders and crash horizontal battle fronts."

"When two armies face off, suppose we have a lot of infantry but ten times fewer chariots than the enemy; how do we strike?"

"Keep to rugged terrain, carefully avoiding wide-open level ground. Level ground is advantageous for chariots, rugged terrain is advantageous for infantry. This is the way to attack chariots."

"When two armies face off, and our side has plenty of chariots and cavalry, but the enemy has ten times as much personnel and weapons as we have, how do we attack them?"

"To attack them, be careful to avoid constricting land formations; induce them to pass through to level, open ground, where your chariots will have an advantage and be able to strike even if the enemy has ten times the men and weaponry you have. This is the way to attack infantry."

"When two armies face off, suppose our supplies are irregular and our personnel and weapons are inadequate, so we have to make an all-out attack on an enemy ten times our size, how do we strike?"

"To strike in this case, once the enemy has occupied a fastness, you . . . turn around and attack where they have no strength. This is a strategy for aggressive contention. . . ."

"When two armies face off, suppose the enemy commander is

brave and cannot be intimidated, the enemy's weaponry is powerful, their troops are numerous, and they are in a secure position.
Their soldiers are all brave and unruffled, their commander is
fierce, their weaponry is powerful, their officers are strong and their
supplies are regular, so that none of the local leaders can stand up
to them. How do we strike them?"

"To strike in this case, let them think you lack resolve, feign lack
of ability, and appear to have a defeatist attitude, so as to seduce
them into arrogance and laziness, making sure they do not recognize the real facts. Then, on this basis, strike where they are unprepared, attack where they are not defending, pressure those who
have slacked off, and attack those who are uncertain or confused.
As long as they are haughty and warlike, when the armies break
camp the front and rear battalions will not look out for each other;
so if you strike them precisely at this point, it will be as though you
had a lot of manpower. This is the way to strike a large and powerful force."

"When two armies face off, suppose the enemy holds the mountains and occupies the defiles, so that we cannot get to them if we
are far off yet have nowhere nearby to take a stand; how do we
strike them?"

"To strike in this case, since the enemy has withdrawn to a fastness . . . then put them in danger; attack where they are sure to go
to the rescue, so as to get them to leave their fastness, and thus find
out their intentions; set out ambushers, provide reinforcements to
back them up, and strike the enemy troops while they are on the
move. This is the way to attack an opponent occupying a fastness."

"When two armies face off, aggressor and defender both arrayed
in battle lines, suppose the enemy takes a basketlike formation, so
it seems they want us to fall into a trap; how do we strike them?"

"To strike in this case, move so quickly that the thirsty haven't
time to drink and the hungry haven't time to eat; use two thirds of
your forces, and aim for a critical target. Once they . . . have your
best and most well trained soldiers attack their flanks. . . . Their
whole army will be routed. This is the way to strike at a basket
formation."

[18]

[TITLE LOST]

This chapter is so fragmentary that even the order of the strips is uncertain.

19

DISTINCTIONS BETWEEN AGGRESSORS AND DEFENDERS

In warfare, there is an aggressive party and a defensive party. Aggression requires more troops than defense; when there are twice as many aggressors as defenders, it is still possible to oppose them.

The defender is the one who is first to get set up, the aggressor is the one who is last to get set up. The defender secures the ground and settles his forces to await the aggressor, who comes through narrow passes. . . .

The terms *aggressor* and *defender* here are not defined in reference to invasion and defense of the homeland of one of the parties by another, but in reference to confrontation on mutually contested ground. The first to get set up is the defender, in terms of defending a claim or a conquest; while the last to get set up is the aggressor, in terms of challenging that claim or conquest.

When soldiers retreat even in face of the threat of decapitation, and refuse to oppose the enemy as they advance, what is the reason? It is because the configuration of forces is unfavorable and the lay of the land is not advantageous. If the configuration of forces is favorable and the lay of the land is advantageous, people will advance on their own; otherwise, they will retreat on their own. Those who are called skilled warriors are those who take advantage of configurations of forces and the lay of the land.

The point of these statements, which may seem repetitive truisms, is that authoritarian coerciveness is not ultimately effective, whether in war or in peace, if for no other reason than that there will always be people who follow natural intelligence whatever others may say. True leaders are not those who force others to follow them, but those who are able to harmonize the wills of others and unify the overall direction of their energies.

If you keep a standing army of 100,000 troops, they won't have enough to eat even if the populace has surpluses. . . . There will be more soldiers in camp than in action, and those in camp will have plenty while those in action will not have enough.

Standing armies were a comparatively recent development in the time of Sun Bin, but here it is evident that the civil and military economic pressures and imbalances resulting from such a system were quite apparent to him.

If you have an army of 100,000 troops and send them out in battalions of 1,000, the enemy may repel you with battalions of 10,000 each. So those skilled at warfare are skilled at trimming enemies down and cutting their forces apart, like a butcher dismembering a carcass.

Those who are able to split up others' armies and control others' forces are adequate even with the smallest quantity; those who are unable to split up others' armies and control others' forces are inadequate even if they have several times the firepower.

Taking on too much at once can sap any amount of energy and thwart the successful completion of any undertaking. Parceling tasks into manageable portions without losing sight of the overall design of the whole endeavor is one of the arts of leadership at all levels, from personal self-management to corporate, community, and political domains of action.

Do you suppose that the side with the most troops wins? Then it is just a matter of going into battle based on head count. Do you suppose the wealthier side wins? Then it is just a matter of going into battle based on measurement of grain. Do you think the side with sharper weapons and stronger armor wins? Then it would be easy to determine the victor.

Therefore the rich are not necessarily secure, the poor are not necessarily insecure, the majority do not necessarily prevail, minorities do not necessarily fail. That which determines who will win and who will lose, who is secure and who is in peril, is their science, their Way.

According to *The Art of War* by Sun Bin's distinguished predecessor Sun Wu, the "Way" is that whereby the wills of those above and those below are united. In other words, the Way is the guiding ideal, principle, or means of accomplishing collective goals, that which subtends the order and morale of an organization. Without this cohesion, the superiority of numbers, supplies, or equipment cannot guarantee success.

If you are outnumbered by opponents but are able to split them up so they cannot help others . . . the stoutness of their armor and efficiency of their weapons cannot assure them strength, and even soldiers having courage and power cannot use them to guard their commanders, then there is a way to win.

Conversely, if it is possible to undermine the cohesion of a more powerful opponent, it is thereby possible to compensate for disadvantages of numbers, arms, or other formal and material factors.

Therefore intelligent governments and commanders with knowledge of military science must prepare first; then they can achieve success before fighting, so that they do not lose a successful accomplishment possible after fighting. Therefore, when warriors go out successfully and come back unhurt, they understand the art of war.

In making preparations for struggle, it is not only necessary to consider how best to prevail, but also how best to handle the aftermath of struggle, how to safeguard the fruits of victory, and how to make the best of further opportunities that arise as a result of success. It is also imperative, of course, to include due consideration of problems, difficulties, and the chances of defeat, in order to be able to "go out successfully and come back unhurt."

20

EXPERTS

Even though an enemy army has many troops, an expert can split them up so that they cannot help each other while being attacked.

Therefore the depth of your moats and the height of your ramparts do not make you secure, the strength of your chariots and the effectiveness of your weaponry do not make you awesome, and the bravery and strength of your soldiers do not make you powerful.

Therefore experts take control of mountain passes and take account of obstacles; they take care of their troops, and are able to contract and expand fluidly. If enemies have many troops, experts can make them as if few; if enemy stores of food are enough to fill their troops, experts can make them starve; if enemies stay in their places unmoving, experts can make them tire. If enemies have won the world, experts can cause division; if enemy armies are harmonious, experts can break them up.

Following on the preceding chapter, this one begins by emphatically restating the critical importance of group cohesion, beyond even that of sheer material and energetic factors. One of the essential elements of cohesion, furthermore, is a comprehensive and coherent strategy that can outwardly adapt to all situations while inwardly maintaining integrity of purpose and morale in pursuing goals.

So military operations have four routes and five movements. Advance is a route, and withdrawal is a route; to the left is a route, and to the right is a route. To go forward is a movement, to retreat is a movement; to go to the left is a movement, and to go to the right is a movement. To stay put silently is also a movement.

Experts make sure to master the four routes and five movements. Therefore when they advance, they cannot be headed off in front; and when they withdraw, they cannot be cut off behind. When they go to the left or right, they cannot be trapped on treacherous ground. When they stay put silently, they are not troubled by opponents.

Thus experts drive their enemies to their wits' end in all four routes and five movements. When enemies advance, experts press them in front; when enemies retreat, experts cut them off from behind. When enemies move left or right, experts trap them in rough terrain. When enemies silently stay put, their troops cannot escape trouble. Experts can make enemies put aside their heavy armor and rush long distances by forced double marches, so they cannot rest when they get tired and sick, and cannot eat and drink when they get hungry and thirsty. Thus do experts press enemies to ensure that they cannot win at war.

You eat to your fill and wait for the enemy to starve; you stay put comfortably and wait for the enemy to tire; you keep perfectly still and wait for the enemy to stir. Thus will the people be seen to advance without retreating, tread on naked blades without turning on their heels.

Relentless pressure is one way to thwart an opponent's strategy at every step and thereby systematically undermine morale. Made from a position of relative security, unremitting pressure is supported and strengthened by the specific psychological effects visited upon both parties by this sort of tactic.

FIVE DESCRIPTIONS AND FIVE COURTESIES

There are five descriptions of military forces. The first is called awesome and powerful. The second is called proud and arrogant. The third is called adamant to the extreme. The fourth is called greedy and suspicious. The fifth is called slow and yielding.

An awesome and powerful force you treat with humility and softness. A proud and powerful force you keep waiting with courteous respect. An extremely adamant force you take by seduction. A greedy and suspicious force you press in front, harass at the sides, and use deep moats and high barricades to make it hard for them to keep supplied. A slow and yielding force you terrorize by harrassment; shake them up, surround them, and strike them if they come out. If they do not come out, then encircle them.

Military actions have five courtesies and five harsh actions. What are the five courtesies? If it invades a territory and is too courteous, a militia loses its normal state. If it invades a second time and is too courteous, a militia will have no fodder. If it invades a third time and is too courteous, a militia will lose its equipment. If it invades a fourth time and is too courteous, a militia will have no food. If it invades a fifth time and is too courteous, a militia will not accomplish its business.

Violently invading a territory once is called aggression. Violently invading a second time is called vanity. A third violent invasion, and the natives will be terrorized. A fourth violent invasion, and the soldiers will be given misinformation. A fifth violent invasion, and the militia will be worn out.

Therefore, courtesy and harshness must be intermixed.

An invasion or a takeover has to command respect and collaboration without causing terror and disaffection if it is to avoid either absorption and vitiation of its power on the one hand, or resistance and repulsion on the other.

MISTAKES IN WARFARE

*If you want to use unrest among the people of an enemy state . . .
to inhibit the strengths of the enemy state's military, you will wear
out your own military.*

Fanning flames of unrest among a people is one way to attack their
government and also inhibit the strength of their military by preoccupation with civil disturbance. This does not guarantee, however, that
people aroused by such provocations will necessarily side with your
cause. This tactic is thus as likely to result in an overall increase in
resistance to outside control, thus wearing down the mechanisms by
which the attempt to assert control is made.

*If you want to strengthen and increase what your state lacks in
response to the abundance of an enemy state, this will quickly frustrate your army.*

Competing with a rival on a sheerly quantitative basis leads to excessively narrow funneling of enemy and resources along lines determined too rigidly by fixation on fear of the competition. This results
in frustration through lack of flexibility, foresight, and discretionary
resources needed to adapt to changing circumstances in the environment at large.

*If your preparations are all set, and yet you cannot thwart the ene-
my's equipment, your army will be disrespected. If your equipment
is not effective, while your enemy is well prepared, your army will
be crushed. . . .*

The unspoken point of these apparent truisms is that when objective
assessments indicate that you are in such a position, it is better to
avoid engagement with the opponent. This is not simply because of

the immediate likelihood of defeat, but because of the long-term strategic disadvantages of humiliation and demoralization.

If you are skilled at arraying battle lines, and you know the odds for and against, and know the lay of the land, and yet your army is thwarted time and again, that means you do not understand both diplomatic victory and military victory.

Purely military or strategic factors are not considered sufficient guarantees of victory. This is why the Way, which in this context means the social rationale for action, the moral/morale factor, is regarded so critically even in what would otherwise seem to be strictly tactical matters.

. . . [If] the armed forces are incapable of great success, that means they do not recognize appropriate opportunities. If the military loses the people, that means it is unaware of its own faults and excesses. If the armed forces require much effort to accomplish little, that means they do not know the right timing. If the military cannot overcome major problems, it is because it cannot unite the hearts of the people. When the armed forces have a lot of regrets, it is because they believed in what was dubious. When warriors cannot see fortune and disaster before these have taken shape, they do not know how to prepare.

Disorientation, disaffection, inefficiency, disunity, delusion, lack of foresight—these are basic problems that undermine successful collective effort. Understanding why they happen is as important as recognizing them when they happen.

If warriors are lazy when they see good to be done, are doubtful when the right time to act arrives, get rid of wrongs but cannot keep this up, that is the way to stagnation. When they are honest and decent even though ambitious, polite even when favored, strong though yielding, flexible yet firm, this is the way to thrive.

If you travel the path to stagnation, even heaven and earth cannot make you flourish. If you practice the way to thrive, even heaven and earth cannot make you perish.

An ancient Taoist saying goes, "My fate depends on me, not on Heaven." Strategists did not believe in predestination and did not encourage people to consult fortune-telling books and hope for the best. They taught people to examine their own situations and their own actions, and to take conscious responsibility for their own behavior and its consequences.

23

JUSTICE IN COMMANDERS

Commanders must be just; if they are not just, they will lack dignity. If they lack dignity, they will lack charisma; and if they lack charisma, their soldiers will not face death for them. Therefore justice is the head of warriorship.

Justice also means duty. Commanders who are not just and do not command justice lack dignity because those under their command will not fear to be unruly.

Commanders must be humane; if they are not humane, their forces will not be effective. If their forces are not effective, they will not achieve anything. Therefore humaneness is the gut of warriorship.

If commanders are not humane, their forces will not be effective because there will be no bond of loyalty between them. The troops of a leader who is not humane will lack motivation to fight loyally for the cause.

Commanders must have integrity; without integrity, they have no power. If they have no power, they cannot bring out the best in their armies. Therefore integrity is the hand of warriorship.

Without integrity, commanders have no power because they do not back up their words with their deeds and therefore cannot inspire confidence and trust.

Commanders must be trustworthy; if they are not trustworthy, their orders will not be carried out. If their orders are not carried out, then forces will not be unified. If the armed forces are not unified, they will not be successful. Therefore trustworthiness is the foot of warriorship.

Trustworthiness cements the relationship of commander and forces, letting the forces know they can expect to be rewarded for doing well and punished for cowardice or unruliness.

Commanders must be superior in intelligence; if they are not superior in intelligence, ... their forces lack [resolution]. Therefore resolution is the tail of warriorship.

Resolution derives from intelligence through the repose of confidence in an intelligent plan of action.

[24]

Effectiveness in Commanders

This chapter is all in fragments. The next five chapters have some lacunae, but they are largely descriptive and self-explanatory. They need no elucidation, but will nevertheless yield more to reflection.

FAILINGS IN COMMANDERS

These are failings in commanders:

 1. *They consider themselves capable of what they are unable to do.*
 2. *They are arrogant.*
 3. *They are ambitious for rank.*
 4. *They are greedy for wealth.*
 5. *. . .*
 6. *They are impulsive.*
 7. *They are slow.*
 8. *They lack bravery.*
 9. *They are brave but weak.*
 10. *They lack trustworthiness.*
 11. *. . .*
 12. *. . .*
 13. *. . .*
 14. *They lack resolution.*
 15. *They are lax.*
 16. *They are lazy.*
 17. *. . .*
 18. *They are vicious.*
 19. *They are self-centered.*
 20. *They are personally disorderly.*

Those with many failings suffer many losses.

LOSSES OF COMMANDERS

These are losses of commanders:

1. *When they lose purpose in their maneuvering, they can be beaten.*
2. *If they take in unruly people and deploy them, keep defeated soldiers and put them back in battle, and presume to have qualifications they really lack, they can be beaten.*
3. *If they keep arguing over judgments of right and wrong, and keep debating over elements of strategy, they can be beaten.*
4. *If their orders are not carried out and their troops are not unified, they can be beaten.*
5. *If their subordinates are refractory and their troops won't work for them, they can be beaten.*
6. *If the populace is embittered against their armed forces, they can be beaten.*
7. *If an army is out in the field too long, it can be beaten.*
8. *If an army has reservations, it can be beaten.*
9. *If the soldiers flee, they can be beaten.*
10. ...
11. *If the troops panic repeatedly, they can be beaten.*
12. *If the course of a military operation turns into a quagmire and everyone is miserable, they can be beaten.*
13. *If the troops are exhausted in the process of building fortifications, they can be beaten.*
14. ...
15. *If the day is coming to an end when there is yet far to go and the troops are eager to get there, they can be beaten.*
16. ...
17. *... the troops are afraid, they can be beaten.*

18. *If orders are repeatedly modified and the troops are dilatory, they can be beaten.*

19. *If there is no esprit de corps and the troops do not credit their commanders and officers with ability, they can be beaten.*

20. *If there is a lot of favoritism and the troops are lazy, they can be beaten.*

21. *If there is a lot of suspicion and the troops are in doubt, they can be beaten.*

22. *If commanders hate to hear it when they've erred, they can be beaten.*

23. *If they appoint incompetents, they can be beaten.*

24. *If they keep their troops out in the field so long as to undermine their will, they can be beaten.*

25. *If they are scheduled to go into combat but their minds are still divided, they can be beaten.*

26. *If they count on the other side losing heart, they can be beaten.*

27. *If their actions hurt people and they rely on ambush and deception, they can be beaten.*

28. *. . .*

29. *If the commanders oppress the soldiers, so the troops hate them, they can be beaten.*

30. *If they cannot get out of narrow straits in complete formation, they can be beaten.*

31. *If the frontline soldiers and backup weaponry are not evenly arrayed in the forefront of the battle formation, they can be beaten.*

32. *If they worry so much about the front in battle that they leave the rear open, or they worry so much about the rear that they leave the front open, or worry so much about the left that they leave the right open, or worry so much about the right that they leave the left open—if they have any worry in combat, they can be defeated.*

STRONG AND WEAK CITIES

If a city is in a marshy area without high mountains or deep canyons, and yet it abuts upon hills on all four sides, it is a strong city, not to be besieged. If their army is drinking running water—that is, water from a live source—it is not to be besieged. If there is a deep valley in front of the city and high mountains behind it, it is a strong city, not to be besieged. If the city is high in the center and low on the outskirts, it is a strong city, not to be besieged. If there are joining hills within the city precincts, it is a strong city, not to be besieged.

If an encamped army rushes to its shelters, there is no large river encircling them, their energy is broken down and their spirits weakened, then they can be attacked. If a city has a deep valley behind it and no high mountains to the left and right, it is a vulnerable city and can be attacked. If the surrounding land is arid, a city is on barren ground and can be attacked. If the troops are drinking brackish water, or stagnant or stale water, they can be attacked. If a city is in a large swampy area with no large valleys, canyons, or abutting hills, it is a weak city and can be attacked. If a city is between high mountains and has no large valleys, canyons, or adjoining hills, it is a weak city and can be attacked. If a city has a high mountain in front of it and a large valley behind it, so that it is high in front and low in back, it is a weak city and can be attacked.

[Title Lost]

. . . ! When reinforcements arrive, they can be beaten too. So a general rule for military operations is that groups over fifteen miles apart cannot come to each others' rescue—how much less when they are at least thirty and up to a hundred or more miles apart! These are the extreme limits for grouping and spacing battalions.

Therefore military science says that if your supplies do not match those of opponents, do not engage them for long; if your numbers do not match up to those of opponents, do not get embroiled with them; . . . if your training does not match that of opponents, do not try to contest them where they are strongest. Once these five assessments are clear, a military force may act freely.

So a military operation . . . heads for opponents' strategic factors. First, take their fodder. Second, take their water. Third, take the fords. Fourth, take the road. Fifth, take the rugged ground; sixth, take the level ground. . . . Ninth, take what they consider most valuable. These nine seizures are ways of taking opponents.

[29]

[Title Lost]

... *The concentrated prevail over the scattered, the full prevail over the empty, the swift prevail over the slow, the many prevail over the few, the rested prevail over the weary.*

Concentrate when there is reason to concentrate, spread out when there is reason to spread out; fill up when there is reason for fullness, empty out when there is reason for emptiness. Go on the byways when there is reason to go on the byways, go by the highways when there is reason to go by the highways; speed up when there is reason to speed, slow down when there is reason to slow down. Mass in large contingents when there is reason for huge masses, group in small contingents when there is reason for small groups. Relax when there is reason to relax, work hard when there is reason to work hard.

Concentration and scattering interchange, fullness and emptiness interchange, byways and highways interchange, swiftness and slowness interchange, many and few interchange, relaxation and labor interchange. Do not confront the concentrated with concentration, do not confront the scattered by scattering. Do not confront the full with fullness, do not confront the empty with emptiness. Do not confront speed with speed, do not confront slowness with slowness. Do not confront many with many, do not confront few with few. Do not confront the relaxed when you are in a state of relaxation, do not confront the weary when you are in a condition of weariness.

The concentrated and the spread-out can oppose each other, the full and the empty can oppose each other, those on byways and those on highways can oppose each other, the fast and the slow can oppose each other, the many and the few can oppose each other, the rested and the tired can oppose each other. When opponents are concentrated, you should therefore spread out; when they are full, you should therefore be empty. When they go over the byways, you should therefore take the highways. When they speed, you should therefore go slowly. When they are many, you should therefore use small contingents. When they are relaxed, you should therefore labor.

SURPRISE AND
STRAIGHTFORWARDNESS

The pattern of heaven and earth is to revert when a climax is reached, to wane on waxing full. [The sun and moon, yin and yang,] are examples of this. There is alternate flourishing and dying out; the four seasons exemplify this. There is victory, and there is failure to prevail; the five elements exemplify this. There is birth, and there is death; all beings exemplify this. There is capacity and there is incapacity; all living creatures exemplify this. There is surplus, and there is deficiency; formation and momentum exemplify this.

So whoever has form can be defined, and whoever can be defined can be overcome. Therefore sages use what is overwhelming in all things to overcome all things; therefore their victories are unstoppable and inexhaustible. Warfare is a matter of formal contest for victory. No form is impossible to overcome, but no one knows the form by which victory is obtained.

To use what is overwhelming in all things to overcome all things means to use natural forces and intrinsic momenta to accomplish a task. This is why intelligent leadership is essential to certain victory no matter how much raw force is available.

No form is impossible to overcome because formations have inherent laws or patterns whose developments and movements can be predicted. No one knows the form by which victory is obtained in a general sense because there is no set form that will guarantee victory, and in a particularized sense because the specific form that wins in a given case prevails because of its inscrutability to the opposition.

Changes of form and victory are infinite, coterminous with heaven and earth; they could never be fully written down. Form is a matter of using whatever is superior to win. It is impossible to use the best of one form to overcome all forms. Therefore control of forms is one, but the means of victory cannot be only one.

Adaptability is a perennial keynote to strategic thinking, but if the central integrity of leadership is compromised, whether in capacity or purpose, adaptability can degenerate into pliability, fragmentation, or dissipation of energy. By the same token, if the central integrity of leadership is lacking in intrinsic strength and the leadership resorts to dogmatic ideological and authoritarian ways to compensate, flexibility of thought and action are sacrificed to stabilization of a fixed structure, finally leading to inability to safeguard the foundation of the structure no matter how stable its internal dimensions may remain.

Therefore experts at warfare see the strengths of opponents, and thereby know their weaknesses; seeing their deficiencies, they thereby know their surpluses. They see victory as clearly as they see the sun and moon; their attainment of victory is like water overcoming fire.

To respond to a form with a form is directness, to respond to form without form is surprise. Directness and surprise are endless, having distinct places. Organize your divisions by surprise strategy, control others by the five elements, battle them with . . . When the divisions are determined, then there is form; when a form is determined, then there is definition. . . .

Sameness is inadequate to attain victory; therefore difference is used, for surprise. Therefore stillness is surprise to the mobile, relaxation is surprise to the weary, fullness is surprise to the hungry, orderliness is surprise to the unruly, many are a surprise to the few. When the initiative is direct, holding back is surprise; when a surprise attack is launched without retaliation, that is a victory. Those who have an abundance of surprises excel in gaining victories.

Surprise tactics are valued to thwart accurate anticipation of your movements on the part of opponents. Continuous fluidity is needed, because "Surprise becomes conventional, convention becomes surprise."

So when one joint aches, all hundred joints are disabled, because they are the same body. When the vanguard is defeated and the rear

guard is ineffective, it is because they are in the same formation.
Therefore in battle configurations, . . . the rear should not overtake
the front, and the front should not trample the rear. Forward move-
ments should follow an orderly course, and withdrawal should re-
turn in an orderly manner.

Forces and resources are organized for maximal efficacy on the offensive and minimal vulnerability on the defensive. The art of organization, from this point of view, is to enable different units of power to
operate in concert and also independently, without these two capacities interfering with each other in practice.

When people obey rules without rewards or punishments, these are
orders that the people can carry out. When the high are rewarded
and the low punished, and yet the people do not obey orders, these
are orders that the people are unable to carry out. To get people to
fly in the face of death without turning on their heels, in spite of
poor management, is something even a legendary hero would find
hard to do; so to put this responsibility on ordinary people is like
trying to get a river to flow in reverse.

Therefore in battle formations, winners should be strengthened,
losers should be replaced, the weary should be rested, the hungry
should be fed. Then the people will only see the enemy, and won't
see death; they will not turn on their heels even though they tread
on naked blades. So when flowing water finds a course, it can even
wash away boulders and snap boats in two; when people are em-
ployed in a manner consistent with their nature, then orders are
carried out like a flowing current.

LEADERSHIP, ORGANIZATION, AND STRATEGY: HOW SUN TZU AND SUN TZU II COMPLEMENT EACH OTHER

Sun Bin the Mutilated was a lineal descendant of the famous Sun Wu the Martialist, whose *Art of War* is perhaps the best known of the classics of strategy. In 1972 a hitherto unknown version of Sun Wu's work was discovered in an archaeological find at Silver Sparrow Mountain in China's Shandong Province. This version of Sun Wu's *Art of War* predates the traditional commentaries through which this classical text is ordinarily studied. Although Sun Wu and, to a lesser extent, Sun Bin, have long been known to history, recent developments have made them both new discoveries.

An academic attempt to translate the newly discovered *Art of War* has been made, unfortunately without success, being based on the erroneous belief that the Chinese world view lacks intelligibility and predictability. Since all strategy (and language, for that matter) depends on intelligibility and predictability, a representation of strategic literature as lacking these factors is, quite naturally, inherently flawed and intrinsically misleading.

In any case, having found that academic work of no value in this connection, for purposes of comparison with Sun Bin I draw on my own original unpublished translation of the newly rediscovered text of Sun Wu's *Art of War*.

Three essential features of tactical formulations stand out in both Sun Wu and Sun Bin: leadership, organization, and strategy. Leadership is necessary to the cohesion and direction of organization, and to the election and implementation of strategy. Organization is needed to be effective on a large scale; and strategy is needed to plan the functional economy of action undertaken by the organization.

The similarities and differences between the tactical science of Sun Bin and that of his predecessor Sun Wu are clearly apparent, and follow predictable patterns. Sun Wu, the elder tactician, tends to be more summary and more abstract; Sun Bin, the successor, is inclined more toward detail and concreteness. When viewed together in their essences, therefore, the complementary designs of these two major strategists yield a fuller picture of the foundations of tactical thinking.

Leadership is without question the major issue underlying all strategic science, inasmuch as it represents direction and purpose in both ideological and practical domains. Sun Wu defines the basic pillars of good leadership in terms of five requirements: knowledge, trustworthiness, humaneness, valor, and strictness. This is a more concentrated version of the formulation given in the earlier classic, *Six Strategies*, which refers to the qualities of humaneness, justice, loyalty, trustworthiness, courage, and strategy as the "six defenses" that a leader, or an elite corps, should command and embody to safeguard agriculture, industry, and trade.

Sun Bin also emphasizes requirements in leadership similar to those enumerated by his predecessors:

> One who leads a militia with inadequate intelligence is conceited. One who leads a militia with inadequate courage has an inflated ego. One who leads a militia without knowing the Way and does battle repeatedly without being satisfied is surviving on luck.

These parameters might be summarized as knowledge, valor, wisdom, and modesty.

Sun Bin notes the dominant flaws of character in those who are lacking the essential qualities of leadership to underscore the pragmatic nature of these requirements. He also goes further into specifics to illustrate those factors of leadership that lead to success and those that lead to failure. He says,

> There are five conditions that always lead to victory. Those who have authorized command over a unified power structure are victorious. Those who know the Way are victorious. Those who

win many cohorts are victorious. Those whose close associates are in harmony are victorious. Those who take the measure of enemies and size up difficulties are victorious.

Qualities conspicuously absent in classical descriptions of good warriors and good leaders are bloodthirstiness, violence of temper, and overweening ambition. Sun Bin also said:

Those who enjoy militarism, however, will perish; and those who are ambitious for victory will be disgraced. War is not something to enjoy, victory is not to be an object of ambition.

The primary practical reason for this warning is explained by the elder master, Sun Wu:

Those not completely aware of the drawbacks of military action cannot be completely aware of the advantages of military action.

Therefore Sun Bin outlines sources of defeat in strategic operations:

There are five things that always lead to failure. Inhibiting the commander leads to failure. Not knowing the Way leads to failure. Disobedience to the commander leads to failure. Not using secret agents leads to failure. Not winning many cohorts leads to failure.

Pursuing a similar analysis of failures of leadership, the elder master, Sun Wu, in accordance with his dictum that "The considerations of the wise include both profit and harm," also outlines what he calls five dangers in military leaders, which may be summarized as follows:

Those who will fight to the death can be killed.
Those intent on survival can be captured.
Those quick to anger are vulnerable to contempt.
Purists are vulnerable to shame.
Emotional humanitarians are vulnerable to anxiety.

Typically more detailed than his predecessor, Sun Wu, Sun Bin devotes several chapters to outlining the qualifications and requirements of leadership. The various attributes of leadership are pictured as parts of the body, all of them forming an integral whole; Justice, from which derives dignity and thence charisma, is the head of warriorship. Humaneness, which encourages effectiveness, is the gut of warriorship. Integrity, as a foundation for power, brings out the best in armies, so it is the hand of warriorship. Trustworthiness, which fosters obedience, from which derives unity, is the foot of warriorship. Intelligence fosters resolution, which is the tail of warriorship.

Sun Bin also outlines failings and losses in commanders at considerable length. Failings in commanders include

> considering themselves capable of what they are unable to do, arrogance, ambition, greed, impulsiveness, slowness, cowardice, weakness, unreliability, irresoluteness, laxity, laziness, viciousness, egocentricity, unruliness.

While the function of the leader—that is, to impart order to the action of a group—naturally requires certain capacities in the person of the leader, the effective power of the leader to direct an organization also depends on the structural integrity or order of the organization. Sun Wu summarizes order in these terms: "Order involves organizational structure, chain of command, and logistics." The importance of preparing functional bases of operation is also stressed by the later master, Sun Bin: Intelligent governments and commanders with knowledge of military science must prepare first; then they can achieve success before fighting.

To achieve success before fighting is to outdo competitors in strategic advantages, including qualities of leadership and personnel, and integrity of organizational structure.

The importance of integrity in the order is made abundantly clear in the classic of Sun Wu, where he says,

> When order is consistently practiced to educate the people, then the people are obedient. When order is not practiced consistently to educate the people, then the people are disobedient. When order is consistently practiced, that means it is effective for the group.

The principle that the operative order must be consistent with the effective character and capacity of the group is also emphasized by Sun Bin, who says,

> When people obey rules without rewards or punishments, these are orders that the people can carry out. When the high are re-

warded and the low punished, and yet the people do not obey orders, these are orders that the people are unable to carry out.

The strategic importance of order is the intensive exertion of force or capacity that order makes possible. Sun Wu explains it in this way: "What normally makes managing a large group similar to managing a small group is a system of order." The facilitation of intensive exertion is forcefully illustrated by Sun Bin in these terms: "When all is in order, the battle line moves with a shocking commotion." To represent the inner cohesion of the organization, by which the integrity of the order is maintained, Sun Bin again uses the image of a body, implying that the total integrity and discipline of the whole order depends on the personal integrity and discipline of each individual in the organization: "When one joint aches, all hundred joints are disabled, because they are the same body."

The actualization of an effectively unified order is thus naturally a matter of critical concern. Primary emphasis is placed on the moral and intellectual character of leadership because this unification cannot be attained by simple fiat. According to Sun Wu, the attainment of objective organizational integrity depends on the realization of subjective organizational unity:

> If soldiers are punished before an emotional bond has formed [with the leadership], they will not be obedient, and if they are not obedient they are hard to direct. If penalties are not enforced once this emotional bond has formed, then the soldiers cannot be directed. So unite them culturally and unify them militarily; this is considered the way to certain victory.

This was the concern of the king who asked, "How can I get my people to follow orders as an ordinary matter of course?" To this Sun Bin replied, "Be trustworthy as an ordinary matter of course." The need for correspondingly effective objective order does, nevertheless, remain imperative; Sun Wu says: "Whether there is order or unruliness depends on the operative logic of the order."

In terms of organizational structure, the logic of an operation depends on the recognition and employment of individual capacities in such a way as to maximize their efficiency within the body of the whole, as noted by Sun Bin when he says, "When setting up official posts, you should do so in a manner appropriate to the individual."

The purpose of this selectivity, of course, is not to fulfill the ambitions of individuals irrespective of the welfare of the group, but to enhance the internal harmony and therefore survival value of the organization, as Sun Bin explains: On the one hand, "If their orders are not carried out and their troops are not unified, commanders can be beaten"; while on the other hand, Sun Bin also adds,

> When flowing water finds a course, it can even wash away boulders and snap boats in two; when people are employed in a manner consistent with their nature, then orders are carried out like a flowing current.

The qualifications of leadership and the requirements of order apply, moreover, to every step on the chain of command, from the top commander in charge of the whole group to the individual in charge of personal performance. Sun Wu said,

> Those who press forward without ambition for fame and retreat without trying to avoid blame, who only care for the security of the people and thus are in harmony with the interests of the social order, they are treasures of the nation.

Subordination of selfish ambition or personal vanity to the welfare of the group does not deny but rather affirms the worth of the individual, because the proper combination of teamwork and individual responsibility is what gets the job done. The same basic principles are also echoed by Sun Bin:

> Acting with integrity is a rich resource for warriors. Trust is a distinguished reward for warriors. Those who despise violence are warriors fit to work for kings.

In addition to character and organizational ability, the capacity for intelligent planning is essential to leadership. In the words of Sun Wu: "Those who do not know the plans of competitors cannot enter capably into preliminary negotiations." Skill in tactical thinking is considered normal for leaders—not a product of cunning artifice, but a natural application of intelligence to the realities of life as it is. Sun Bin explains it this way:

> Fangs and horns, claws and spurs, harmonizing when pleased, fighting when angry—these are in the course of nature, and can-

not be stopped. Therefore those who have no natural defenses plan strategically for themselves; this is the business of wise leaders.

The essence of strategic thinking, the pivot on which tactical action revolves, is situational adaptation, as indicated by the elder master, Sun Wu: "Leaders who have mastered the advantages of comprehensive adaptation to changes are those who know how to command militias."

It is this ability to adapt to changes, furthermore, that allows the warrior to remain unruffled in the midst of chaotic upheaval, as Sun Wu observes: "Masters of military affairs move without confusion, mobilize without exhaustion." In this way the actions and measures taken by the leader can be based on objective response to the situation, unaffected by subjective emotions, unfazed by the pressures of the moment, as Sun Bin says: "Let nothing seduce you, let nothing anger you." The elder master, Sun Wu, remarks: "To face confusion with composure and face clamor with calm is mastery of heart."

By remaining calm yet alert, uncaptivated and unperturbed, the leader can concentrate mental energies on essential tasks, and not be sidetracked by ambient unrest. Conversely, skillful focus also enables the leader to be that much less distracted and so much the more serene and unruffled. Sun Bin says, "When articulating direction and establishing a standard of measure, only focus on what is appropriate."

This helps to alleviate internal unrest in the ranks by relieving the minds of subordinates from unnecessary concerns; and it also serves to help maintain security by having people usefully occupied while keeping future plans in reserve, to be revealed only at the appropriate time. As Sun Wu describes it, "The affairs of military commanders are kept inscrutable by quiet calm."

The inner inaccessibility of the leader is, of course, strategic, and must not translate into aloofness and unconcern, for then it would endanger rather than safeguard the security of an organization or an operation. As Sun Bin says, "When you know soldiers are trustworthy, don't let others alienate them." Even while maintaining a hidden secrecy, the leadership must be intimately acquainted with conditions within and without the organization, as illustrated in the often quoted dictum of Sun Wu, so simple yet so telling: "Knowing others and knowing yourself, victory will not be imperiled."

The meaning of "knowing," so complex and so critical in the context of strategic thinking, may refer or allude in a given case to any one or more of numerous diverse yet more or less indirectly related phenomena, including information, misinformation, disinformation, and censorship—and, in addition, understanding, misunderstanding, illusion, and deception.

The whole science of deliberate construction of these forms and shadows of "knowledge," and the manipulation of their specific interrelationships, is crucial to tactical action at its most sophisticated level. This is the underlying fact that has given rise to the famous dictum of Sun Wu, which is itself so often misrepresented, misconstrued, and misunderstood, that "Warfare is a path of subterfuge."

Whenever either of the masters Sun involved himself in a discussion of concrete tactics in actual situations, it becomes clear that the notion of warfare as a path of subterfuge, the practice of seizing control of the opponent's very thoughts and perceptions, underlies the whole science of situational mastery and effective surprise.

Sun Wu says, "Make a show of incompetence when you are actually competent, make a show ineffectiveness when you are in fact effective."

Sun Bin elucidates,

> Let them think you lack resolve, feign lack of ability, and appear to have a defeatist attitude, so as to seduce them into arrogance and laziness, making sure they do not recognize the real facts. Then, on this basis, strike where they are unprepared, attack where they are not defending, pressure those who have slacked off, and attack those who are uncertain or confused.

One reason for the use of surprise tactics is that they are ordinarily more economical than conventional tactics, insofar as they are designed to strike at points of least resistance. To obtain the greatest advantage with the least embroilment is one of the key arts of war.

Defensive maneuvering is thus more than defensive. Not only is it a means of storing energy, it is a way to spy out the intentions and abilities of opponents. Sun Wu advises, "Even when you are solid, still be on the defensive; even when you are strong, be evasive."

Following up on this idea, Sun Bin adds: "Do not pursue opponents in flight," for that would expend precious energy and also expose one's own position and capacity.

These conservative and even defensive maneuvers are bases for attack, which like defense begins with the mental aspect of warfare. Sun Wu proposes tactics that radically minimize one's own expenditures while putting the opponent at maximum disadvantage: "Use anger to make them upset, use humility to make them arrogant." Following up on this, Sun Bin gives some further advice on a convenient way to achieve the latter effect: "Disarray troops in confused ranks, so as to make the other side complacent."

The underlying idea is to put off on the enemy as much of the burden of warfare as possible, while reserving oneself intact. This is why the moral philosophy of warfare from which these texts arise is fundamentally nonaggressive and is ethically based on response rather than initiative. From moral philosophy, this is translated directly into practical strategy, as illustrated by Sun Wu in his tactical dictum, "Tire them while taking it easy, cause division among them while acting friendly," and echoed by Sun Bin's advice: "You eat to your fill and wait for the enemy to starve; you stay put comfortably and wait for the enemy to tire; you keep perfectly still and wait for the enemy to stir."

The power accumulated by the practice of maximum economy achieved by secrecy and reserve is enhanced by the ability to compromise the power of opponents. Since a direct approach to diminishing the enemy's force would be most costly, again the scientific approach is preferred, as Sun Bin illustrates in his pivotal dicta: "Confuse them and split them up," and "Those skilled at warfare are skilled at trimming enemies down and cutting their forces apart." Strategic preference for this approach is also evident in the advice of Sun Wu, when he says, "A superior military operation attacks planning, the next best attacks alliances." These are primary ways of splitting up opponents' forces. Sun Bin adds, "Attack them as they set up a front, split them up as they organize," explaining the logic of such maneuvers in these terms:

> Those who are able to split up others' armies and control others' forces are adequate even with the smallest quantity; those who are unable to split up others' armies and control others' forces are inadequate even if they have several times the firepower.

One aspect of force splitting is the deliberate dividing of attention. This type of strategy is common and general in application, as in the advice of Sun Wu to "Strike where they are unprepared, emerge when they are least anticipating it," and the counsel of Sun Bin to "Attack where they are unprepared, act when they least expect it."

This sense of opportune time and place is, furthermore, not simply a matter of the enemy's concrete preparedness, but also a question of mental energy and morale. Sun Wu advises, "Good warriors avoid keen spirits, instead striking enemies when their spirits are fading and waning." To this may be added, pursuant to the already stipulated need to know both others and self in order to act effectively, Sun Bin's essential caveat: "Act only when prepared."

The critical discernment of power configurations, of the relationships between one's own states and those of opponents, is underscored in Sun Wu's summary of this aspect of tactical strategy: "The ancients who were skilled in combat first became invincible, and in that condition awaited vulnerability on the part of enemies." The economy of this approach is strongly emphasized in Sun Bin's suggestion that the best preparation is that which enables you to avoid embroilment in persistent hostilities: "Intelligent governments and commanders with knowledge of military science must prepare first; then they can achieve success before fighting."

Preparation sufficient to secure victory in advance requires knowledge of environmental factors. Both the elder master, Sun Wu, and his successor, Sun Bin, emphasize the importance of prior knowledge. Sun Bin says, "It is imperative to know what ground is viable and what ground is deadly; occupy the viable and attack the deadly." Here Sun Wu goes into some detail, specifying the appropriate measures to take on particular grounds:

> On a ground of disintegration, do not fight. On shallow ground, do not halt. On a ground of contention, do not attack. On a ground of intercourse, do not get cut off. On axial ground, make alliances. On deep ground, plunder. On bad ground, keep going. On surrounded ground, plan ahead. On deadly ground, fight.

The timing of an operation is as critical as the field of operation. Sun Bin says, "Fight only when you are sure to win, without letting anyone know." Concentration and targeted release of power require inward certainty and outward security for maximum efficiency, as illustrated by Sun Wu's dictum that "Crushing force is due to timing and control."

It is not enough to have the power; it must be focused and directed, as Sun Bin says: "When your forces are larger and more powerful, and yet you still ask about how to employ them, this is the way to guarantee your nation's security."

Reliance on superior force is not merely risky but intrinsically costly, since it depends on the logic of expenditure. The need to devise effective structures through which force can be concentrated and given aim is an established strategic priority, but it is complicated by the fact that even an effective formulation loses its edge once it has become routine. As Sun Wu points out, "Usually, battle is engaged in a conventional manner but is won by surprise tactics. . . . Surprise and convention give rise to each other in cycles."

Once a tactic has become habitual, its effectiveness is lost; the enemy can see through the strategy and be prepared with a counter maneuver. Thus Sun Bin warns, "Whoever has form can be defined, and whoever can be defined can be overcome." This is not only a basic principle of defensive warfare; it is also fundamental to offense, as explained by Sun Wu in these terms: "If you induce others to adopt a form while you remain formless, then you will be concentrated while the enemy will be divided."

Formlessness, which also means fluidity of form, is thus not merely defensive but is also effective as an offensive posture. Sun Bin says, "A militia is not to rely on a fixed formation," because fixation leads to exhaustion, paralysis, and loss of opportunity. Thus Sun Wu teaches,

> The consummate formation of a militia is to reach formlessness. Where there is no specific form, even deeply placed agents cannot spy it out; even the canny strategist cannot scheme against it.

This does not mean that there is no form whatsoever, but that there is no fixed form, as Sun Bin explains:

> Form is a matter of using whatever is superior to win. It is impossible to use the best of one form to overcome all forms. Therefore control of forms is one, but the means of victory cannot be only one.

The idea that fluid adaptability underlies successful strategy is made quite clear in the corresponding dictum of Sun Wu that "A militia has no permanently fixed configuration, no constant form. Those who are able to seize victory by adapting to opponents are called experts."

The need for flexibility is emphasized in strategic literature partly because variation is in the nature of things, as Sun Wu notes in remarking that "No element is always dominant, no season is always present." The ability to change tactics is not only necessary for adaptation to external changes in circumstances; it is strategically necessary in order to baffle opponents. Sun Wu brings this out when he says, "The task of a military action is to unobtrusively deceive the minds of enemies," and Sun Bin confirms that "Experts drive their enemies to their wits' ends."

Thus Sun Wu advises,

> When the enemy presents an opening, be sure to penetrate at once. Preempt what the enemy prefers, secretly anticipating him. Act with discipline and adapt to the opposition in order to settle the contest.

This fluid skillfulness is described by Sun Bin in these terms: "To respond to a form with a form is directness, to respond to form without form is surprise."

For opponents of the expert, the question of whether one uses form or formlessness, convention or surprise, ultimately becomes a formless surprise in itself. For the tactician, it is simply a matter of what will work effectively; as Sun Wu says: "Do not mobilize when it is not advantageous, do not act when it is not productive, and do not fight when not imperiled."

After all factors have been considered, and the logic of the operation is clear, the decision to mobilize can be approached with intelligence. Then, if strategic necessity calls for it, subterfuge is the essence of the art of war. As Sun Wu says, in his colorful description of tactical surprise, "At first you are like a virgin girl, to whom the enemy opens his door. Then you are like a jackrabbit on the loose, which the enemy cannot keep out."

The prominence of subterfuge and deception in the techniques of classical strategists such as Sun Wu and Sun Bin often gives the impression of thoroughgoing ruthlessness. What must be remembered is that tactical action, as understood by these ancient thinkers, is not only considered from a material point of view, but also from psychological and philosophical points of view. Thus strategy is legitimately conceived in the aftermath, and in the reflection, of moral and ethical consideration.

This critical factor is immediately evident in Sun Wu's own introduction to the subject: "War is a national crisis; it is necessary to examine the grounds of death and life, and the ways to survival and extinction." The premise that warfare is justified by its moral ground, not by its outcome, is often overlooked by those who focus only on strategy per se without keeping the ethical dimension of the context ever present in the background.

This moral and ethical basis underlying the tradition of Sun Wu and Sun Bin can be found fully expressed in the classic *Six Strategies*, which is a basic source book for all the great works of this type. This classic is attributed to a sage of the twelfth century B.C.E., a teacher of kings from whose vast body of work derive the main sources of Chinese culture and civilization.

It is in the voluminous *Six Strategies* that both ethical and pragmatic aspects of statecraft and strategy can be clearly seen, foreshadowing the later teachings of Sun Wu and Sun Bin on strategic factors of leadership, order, and command.

The original teachings of the *Six Strategies* on the subject of leadership include the whole person, from character, mentality, attitude, and conduct as an individual, to manners and techniques proper to professional management and leadership skills:

> Be calm and serene, gentle and moderate. Be generous, not contentious; be openhearted and evenminded. Treat people correctly.
>
> Don't give arbitrary approval, yet don't refuse out of mere contrariness. Arbitrary approval means loss of discipline, while refusal means shutting off.
>
> Look with the eyes of the whole world, and there is nothing you will not see. Listen with the ears of the whole world, and there is nothing you will not hear. Think with the minds of the whole land, and there will be nothing you do not know.
>
> If you are lazy even when you see there is good to be done, when you are hesitant even though the time is right, if you persist in something knowing it is wrong, this is where the Way halts. When you are flexible and calm, respectful and serious, strong yet yielding, tolerant yet firm, this is where the Way arises.

When duty prevails over desire, this results in flourishing; when desire prevails over duty, this results in perishing. When seriousness prevails over laziness, this results in good fortune. When laziness prevails over seriousness, this results in destruction.

Earlier mention was made of the so-called six defenses listed in the *Six Strategies*, which are analogous to Sun Wu's parameters for leadership. These "six defenses" are actually qualities and capabilities of capable commanders: humaneness, justice, loyalty, trustworthiness, courage, and strategy. The *Six Strategies* also lists ways of choosing people for these six defenses:

Enrich them and see if they refrain from misconduct, in order to prove their humaneness.

Ennoble them and see if they refrain from hauteur, in order to prove their sense of justice.

Give them responsibilities and see if they refrain from autocratic behavior, in order to prove their loyalty.

Employ them and see if they refrain from deceit, in order to prove their trustworthiness.

Endanger them and see if they are unafraid, in order to prove their courage.

Burden them and see if they are unflagging, in order to prove their strategic approach to problems.

The principles of order elucidated in the *Six Strategies* are, like the principles of leadership, forerunners of the concepts of organization utilized by both Sun Wu and Sun Bin.

Some of the most powerful of these are the diagnostic principles by which defects in a system can be identified. Among these are the so-called Six Robbers and Seven Destroyers.

The Six Robbers are:

Officials who build huge mansions and estates and pass their time in entertainment, to the detriment of the integrity of leadership.

Workers who don't work, but go around getting into others' business, disrupting order.

Officials who have cliques that obscure the good and wise and thwart the enlightened.

Ambitious officers who independently communicate with leaders of other outfits, without deference to their own leaders.

Executives who disregard rank and look down on teamwork, and are unwilling to go to trouble for employers.

Strong factions who overpower those who are weak and lacking in resources.

The Seven Destroyers are:

Those who lack intelligent tactical strategy but are pugnacious and combative out of ambition for rewards and titles.

Self-contradicting opportunists, pretenders who obscure the good and elevate the bad.

Those who put on the appearance of austerity and desirelessness in order to get something.

Those who pretend to be eccentric intellectuals, putting on airs and looking on the world with aloof contempt.

The dishonest and unscrupulous who seek office and entitlement by flattery and unfair means, who display bravery out of greed for emolument, who act opportunistically without consideration of the big picture, who persuade leaders with tall tales and empty talk.

Those who compromise primary production by needless luxury.

Those who use supposed occult arts and superstitious practices to bewilder decent people.

Because selection and employment are considered part of the overall task of management, the question arises as to why there may be no effective results even if the leadership tries to promote the worthy. The answer provided by the *Six Strategies* is that in such cases, promotion of the worthy is more form than reality, going on the basis of vulgar popularity or social recommendation and not finding really worthy people:

If the leadership considers the popular to be worthy and the unpopular to be unworthy, then those with many partisans get ahead, while those with few partisans fall behind. If so, then crooks will be everywhere, obscuring the worthy; loyal administrators will be terminated for no wrongdoing, while treacherous bureaucrats will assume rank by means of false representation.

THE *SILVER SPARROW* ART OF WAR

SUN TZU

TRANSLATOR'S INTRODUCTION

In 1972, a number of fragments of *The Art of War* were discovered at an archeological site at Silver Sparrow Mountain in China's Shandong Province. In addition to extensive remnants of Sun Bin's lost *Art of War* (published in this volume as *The Lost Art of War* by Sun Tzu II), archeologists found previously unknown fragments of Sun Tzu's *The Art of War*. Unfortunately, much of this material was found in such physically deteriorated condition (having been entombed for more than two thousand years) that there are many lacunae. Some fragments are so disjointed as to be useless. There are, however, some comparatively intact elements of this newly discovered material that illustrate certain facets of Sun Tzu's strategic thinking, including political factors.

In *The Questions of Wu*, the king of Wu questions Sun Tzu about ruination and survival. Sun Tzu replies that ruination is a result of inadequate land distribution, overtaxation, bureaucratic hypertrophy, arrogance in the ruling class, and aggressiveness in the military. In contrast, Sun Tzu continues, survival results from adequate land distribution, minimal taxation, frugality in the upper echelons, and enrichment of the general populace.

In *Four Adaptations*, Sun Tzu explains the statements that there are roads not to be followed, armies not to be attacked, citadels not to be besieged, land not to be contested, and orders of the ruler not to be followed. The roads not to be followed are those along which shallow penetration into enemy territory leaves uncertainty as to what is ahead; those along which deep penetration into enemy territory does not allow for consolidation of gains all along the way; those along which movement is not advantageous, yet stalling would result in captivity. Armies not to be attacked are those that do not seem strong enough to avoid defeat, and yet in the long run may be expected to have surprise formations and skillful tactics. Citadels not to be besieged are those that could be taken, and yet, even if taken, would be no help in making progress and would also be impossible to defend afterward. If one's force is insufficient, Sun Tzu continues, a citadel will surely not be taken; but even if a citadel would surrender if besiegers had advantageous conditions, and even if no loss would ensue if conditions were not favorable for a siege, under these conditions a citadel is not to be attacked. Land not to be contested refers to wilderness where soldiers cannot live off the land. Orders not to be followed are those that contradict the foregoing four adaptations.

In *The Yellow Emperor's Defeat of the Red Emperor*, Sun Tzu recounts the tactics used by the semimythological Chinese cultural hero Huang Di, "The Yellow Emperor," in rising to ascendancy over neighboring tribes. When Huang Di attacked tribes to the south, east, north, and west, in each case he kept the shady sides of mountains to his right, followed strategic routes, kept natural barriers to his back, and thus destroyed his opponents and annexed their territories. Then he let the people rest, allowing the cereal crops to ripen, and declared amnesty.

[1]

STRATEGIC MEASUREMENTS

War is a national crisis; it is necessary to examine the grounds of death and life and the ways to survival and extinction. Thus you measure militias in terms of five parameters, comparing them in terms of strategic measurements to find out the real situation. First is guidance. Second is climate. Third is ground. Fourth is leadership. Fifth is order.

Guidance is what induces popular accord with the rulership, so the people are willing to follow it to death and follow it in life, without opposition.

Climate refers to darkness and light, cold and heat, the structure of the seasons.

Ground may be high or low, near or far, treacherous or easy, broad or narrow, deadly or viable.

Leadership is a matter of knowledge, trustworthiness, humaneness, valor, and strictness.

Order involves organizational structure, chain of command, and logistics.

All leaders have heard of these five things; those who know them prevail over those who do not. That is why we make comparisons in terms of strategic measurements—to find out the real situation. Which civil leadership has guidance? Which military leadership has ability? Whose climate and grounds are advantageous? Whose order is enforced? Whose forces are stronger? Whose officers and soldiers are better trained? Whose rewards and punishments are clearer?

In this way I know who is going to win and who is going to lose. If leaders listen to my strategy, their military actions will be victorious. Then I will stay. If leaders do not listen to my strategy, their military actions will be failures. Then I will leave. One can assess advantages through listening, then take up an appropriate posture or make an appropriate disposition to bolster one's exterior.

To take up a posture or a disposition means to manipulate strategy according to advantage. Warfare is a path of subterfuge. That is why you make a show of incompetence when you are actually competent, make a show of ineffectiveness when you are in fact effective. When nearby, you appear to be distant, and when distant, you appear to be nearby.

Seducing opponents with prospects of gain, take them over by means of confusion. Even when you are solid, still be on the defensive; even when you are strong, be evasive. Use anger to make them upset, use humility to make them arrogant. Tire them while taking it easy, cause division among them while acting friendly. Attack where they are unprepared, emerge when they least expect it.

This means that the victories of warriors cannot be told of beforehand.

Those who figure out how to win before doing battle have the majority of advantageous plans, while those whose schemes prove to be failures even before battle have fewer advantageous plans. Those with many such plans win, those with few such plans lose; there is no need to even mention those with no such plans. When I view a situation in this way, it becomes evident who will win and who will lose.

[2]

COMBAT

A general rule for military operations calls for a thousand chariots, a thousand leather-covered wagons, a hundred thousand armored troops, and provisions for several hundred miles. Thus internal and external expenses, including the needs of ambassadors and advisors, materials such as glue and lacquer, and maintenance of vehicles and armor, costs a thousand pieces of gold a day; only thus can you mobilize a force of a hundred thousand troops.

In actual combat, what is important is to win; go on too long, and you blunt your troops and snap your edge. Besiege a citadel, and your strength is depleted; keep an army in the field too long, and the resources of the nation will be insufficient. When you blunt your troops, snap your edge, deplete your strength, and exhaust your resources, rivals will arise to take advantage of your predicament. Then it will be impossible to effect a good ending, even with knowledge.

Therefore in military affairs we may hear of being clumsy but swift, while we never see the skillful prolonging an action. This is because a nation never benefits from prolonging a military action.

So those who are not completely aware of drawbacks of military action cannot be completely aware of advantages in military action.

Those who use militias skillfully do not draft conscripts twice or ship provisions over and over; taking necessities from the nation and feeding off opponents, the army can thus be sufficiently fed.

The reason that nations are impoverished by their armies is that those who send their armies far away ship goods far away, and when goods are shipped far away, the farmers grow poor. Those who are near the army sell dear, and because of high prices money runs out. When the money runs out, there is increased pressure to appropriate things for military use. Exhausting the heartland, draining the households, this takes up seventy percent of the peasants' expenses. As for the expenses of the government, the ruined chariots, the horses rendered useless, the armor and weaponry, the oxen and transport vehicles take up sixty percent.

This is why a wise leader strives to feed off the enemy. The amount of the enemy's food you eat is equivalent to twenty times that amount of your own food; the amount of the enemy's fodder you use is equivalent to twenty times that amount of your own fodder.

So what gets opponents killed is anger, what gets you the advantage over opponents is the spoils. Thus, in a chariot battle, when your side has captured at least ten chariots, award them to the first to make a capture; change the flags and use the chariots together with yours, treating the soldiers well and providing for them. This is called overcoming an opponent and growing even stronger.

So in a military operation what is important is to prevail; it is not good to prolong it.

Thus a leader who commands a militia knowledgeably has the fate of the people in his hands; the safety or danger of the nation is up to him.

[3]
Planning Attack

The general rule for military operations is that keeping a nation intact is best, while destroying a nation is next; keeping a militia intact is best, destroying a militia is next. Keeping a battalion intact is best, destroying a battalion is next. Keeping a company intact is best, destroying a company is next. Keeping a squad intact is best, destroying a squad is next. Therefore one hundred percent victory in battle is not the finest skill; foiling others' military operations without even fighting is the finest skill.

Thus a superior military operation attacks planning, the next best attacks alliances; the next attacks armed forces, the lowest attacks citadels.

The rule for attacking a citadel is that it is only done out of sheer necessity. It takes three months to prepare the equipment and another three months to construct earth mounds against the walls of the citadel.

When a military leader cannot contain anger and has his men swarm the citadel, this kills a third of his soldiers; with the citadel still not taken, this is a fiasco of a siege. Therefore one who uses the military skillfully foils the military operations of others without fighting, takes others' citadels without attacking, and crushes others' states without taking a long time, making sure to remain intact to contend with the world, so that his forces are not blunted and the advantage can be complete. This is the rule for planning attack.

So the rule for military operations is that if you outnumber opponents ten to one, then surround them; five to one, attack them; two to one, fight them. If you are evenly matched, you can divide them; if you are less, you can defend against them. If you are not as good, then you can evade them.

Thus what would be firmness in the face of a small opponent will get you captured by a large opponent.

Military leaders are assistants of nations. When their assistants are thoroughgoing, nations will be strong; when their assistants are negligent, nations will be weak.

So there are three ways in which a civilian leader troubles a militia. Calling on the militia to advance unaware that it should not advance at that point, or calling on the militia to retreat unaware that it should not retreat at that point, is called fettering the militia. Civil government participating in the running of the military without understanding military affairs leads to confusion among the soldiers. Civil government sharing the responsibilities of the military without understanding military strategy leads to mistrust among the soldiers. Once your military forces are confused and distrustful, rivals will give you trouble. This is called disorienting the military and bringing in conquerors.

So there are five ways to know winners. Those who know when to fight and when not to fight are winners. Those who know the uses of large and small groups are winners. Those whose upper and lower echelons have the same desires are winners. Those who await the unprepared with preparedness are winners. Those whose military leaders are capable and not dominated by the civilian leaders are winners. These five items are ways to know winners.

So it is said that if you know others and know yourself, you will not be imperiled in a hundred battles. If you do not know others but do know yourself, you will win some and lose some. If you do not know others and do not know yourself, you will be imperiled in every battle.

[4]

FORMATIONS

The ancients who were skilled in combat first became invincible, and in that condition awaited vulnerability on the part of enemies. Invincibility is up to you yourself; vulnerability depends on the opponent. Therefore those who are skilled in combat can become invincible but cannot make opponents vulnerable to certain defeat. This is why it is said that victory can be discerned but cannot be made.

Invincibility is a matter of defense, vulnerability is a matter of offense. When you defend, it is because you are outgunned; when you attack, it is because the opponent is no match.

Those skilled at defense hide in the deepest depths of the earth; those skilled at offense maneuver in the highest heights of the sky. Thus they can preserve themselves and make victory complete.

Those whose perception of how to win is not beyond common knowledge are not the most skillful of experts. It doesn't take much strength to lift a strand of hair, it doesn't take clarity of eye to see the sun and moon, it doesn't take sharpness of ear to hear thunder.

Those considered good warriors in ancient times were those who won when it was easy to win. Thus the victories of good warriors have nothing extraordinary about them: They are not famed for brilliance, not accorded merit for bravado. Thus their victories in battle are not in doubt. They are not in doubt because the measures they take are sure to win, since they are overcoming those who have already lost.

Therefore those who are skilled in combat take a stand on an invincible ground without losing sight of opponents' vulnerabilities. Thus a victorious militia wins before ever seeking to do battle, while a defeated militia seeks victory after it has already gotten into a fight.

When those who employ military forces put the Way into practice and keep its laws, they can thereby judge the outcome. The laws are as follows: first is measure, second is capacity, third is order, fourth is efficacy, fifth is victory. The ground gives rise to measures, measures produce capacity. Capacity gives rise to order, order produces efficacy. Efficacy gives rise to victory.

Thus a victorious militia is like a weight balanced against another weight that is five hundred times less, while a defeated militia is like a weight balanced against another weight that is five hundred times greater. Those who get the people to fight from a winning position are as though opening up dammed waters into a mile-deep canyon; this is a matter of the formation of force.

[5]

DISPOSITION AND MOMENTUM

What normally makes managing a large group similar to managing a small group is a system of order. What makes fighting a large group similar to fighting a small group is the use of emblems and signals. What enables military forces to take on enemies without defeat is the implementation of surprise tactics as well as conventional strategies. What makes a military intervention as effective as a stone thrown on eggs is discernment of openings and solidity.

Usually battle is engaged in a conventional manner but is won by surprise tactics. So those who are good at surprise maneuvers are endless as the sky and earth; inexhaustible as the great rivers; finishing, then starting again, as epitomized by the sun and moon; dying and then being reborn, as epitomized by the four seasons.

There are only five notes, but their various combinations are infinite. There are only five colors, but their various combinations are infinite. Combat dispositions are either conventional or extraordinary, but the various combinations of convention and surprise are endless. Surprise and convention give rise to each other in cycles, like a beginningless and endless circle—who can exhaust them?

The fact that the velocity of rushing water can reach the point where it can sweep away boulders is due to momentum; the fact that the strike of a bird of prey can attain a crushing force is due to timing and control. Thus those skilled at combat make sure their momentum is closely channeled and their timing closely controlled. Their momentum is like drawing a catapult, their timing and control are like pulling the trigger. In the midst of confusion, they fight wildly without being thrown into disarray; in the midst of chaos, their formations are versatile, so they cannot be defeated.

Rebellion arises from orderliness, cowardice arises from bravado, weakness arises from strength. Whether there is order or unruliness depends on the operative logic of the order. Bravery and cowardice depend on the configurations and momentum of power. Strength and weakness depend on formation.

Therefore, those who are good at maneuvering enemies mold them into specific formations, to which the enemies may be sure to conform. Give opponents an opportunity they are sure to take, maneuvering them in this way, then wait in ambush for them.

For these reasons, those who are skilled in combat look to disposition of force and momentum; they do not put the onus on individual people. That is why they can choose people yet put their trust in momentum. To rely on momentum is to get people to go into battle like rolling logs and rocks. By nature, logs and rocks remain still on even ground and roll when the ground is steep; they remain stationary when square, they roll when round. Thus the momentum of people who are good at combat is like rolling round rocks down a high mountain, because of the disposition of force.

6

VULNERABILITY AND SUBSTANTIALITY

Generally speaking, those who have taken up their position on a battlefield first and await the enemy there are fresh, while those who take up their position on a battlefield last and thus rush into combat are wearied. Therefore skilled warriors bring others to them and do not go to others.

What effectively induces enemies to come of their own accord is the prospect of gain; what effectively prevents enemies from coming is the threat of harm. So to effectively tire a rested enemy, starve a well-fed one, or stir up a calm one, is a matter of going where the enemy is sure to give chase.

Those who travel hundreds of miles without fatigue can do so by traveling uninhabited lands. Those who always take what they besiege do so by attacking where there is no defense. Those whose defense always stands firm defend where attack is certain.

Therefore a good attack is one against which an enemy does not know where to defend, while a good defense is one against which an enemy does not know where to attack. Be subtle, subtle even to the point of formlessness; be mysterious, mysterious even to the point of soundlessness: Thus you can control the enemy's fate.

To advance unstoppably, strike at openings. To retreat elusively, move too fast for the enemy to catch up with you. Thus, when you want to fight, the way to let an enemy have no choice but to fight with you, even though he is secure behind high ramparts and deep moats, is to attack where he is sure to go to the rescue. When you don't want to fight, to make an enemy unable to fight with you even if you are only defending a line drawn in the ground, divert his aim.

Thus, if you induce others to adopt a form while you remain formless, then you will be concentrated while the enemy will be divided. When you are concentrated and thus united, whereas the enemy is divided into ten, you are attacking with ten times his strength, so you are a large contingent while the enemy is in small groups. If you can attack small groups with a larger contingent, then you will have fewer to fight against at a time.

Your battleground should be unknown, because if it is unknown, then the enemy will have to post many defensive positions, and when the enemy has to man many defensive positions, then you will have fewer people to fight against at a time.

Thus when they are manned in front, they are undermanned in the rear; when they are manned in the rear, they are undermanned in front. When manned at the left, they are undermanned to the right; when manned at the right, they are undermanned to the left. When they are manned everywhere, they are undermanned everywhere. Those who are undermanned are those who are on the defensive against others; those who have plenty of personnel are those who cause others to be on the defensive against them.

Therefore, if you know the ground of combat and the day of combat, you can go to battle hundreds of miles away. If you do not know the ground of combat or the day of combat, then your left flank cannot help your right flank, your right flank cannot help your left flank, your forward wing cannot help your rear guard, and your rear guard cannot help your forward wing. How much less can they help each other when there is a distance of miles!

According to my calculations, although the enemy has many troops, still that hardly increases their chances of victory! That is why I say victory can be achieved; even if the enemy is numerous, they can be made to not fight.

Thus you plot against them to discern winning and losing strategies, you work on them to discern their patterns of action. You induce them to adopt specific formations to discern deadly and viable grounds, you skirmish with them to discern where they are sufficient and where they are lacking.

So the consummate formation of a militia is to reach formlessness. Where there is no specific form, even deeply placed agents cannot spy it out; even the canny strategist cannot scheme against it.

When you plan victory for the masses based on formation, the masses cannot discern it; everyone knows the form of your victory, but no one knows the form by which you achieved victory.

This is why a victory in battle is not repeated; adaptive formation is of endless scope.

The formation of a militia is symbolized by water. Water travels away from higher places toward lower places; military victory is a matter of avoiding the solid and strikings at openings. The course of water is determined by earth, the way to military victory depends on the opponent.

Thus a militia has no permanently fixed configuration, no constant form. Those who are able to seize victory by adapting to opponents are called experts.

No element is always dominant, no season is always present. Some days are shorter, some are longer; the moon wanes away and then reappears.

7

Armed Struggle

The general rule for military operations is that the military leadership gets the order from the civilian leadership to assemble an army, gather troops, and mass at the front.

Nothing is harder than armed struggle.

The difficulty of armed struggle is making a circuitous route into the most direct way, turning problems into advantages.

Thus when you take a circuitous route—thereby leading on opponents with the prospect of gain—leaving after others but arriving before them, then you are the one who knows strategic use of circuitousness's directness.

Thus armed struggle can be profitable and can be perilous.

If you mobilize the whole army to fight for the advantage, you will be too late; if you leave the army behind to fight for advantage, then equipment will be lost.

Thus if you rush off with your armor in storage, marching double time day and night to fight for advantage too far away, then your top command will be captured; the strongest will get there first, laggards later, and as a rule only one in ten will make it at all.

If you struggle for advantage at a considerable distance, your vanguard commander will be felled, and as a rule only half your force will ever get there. If you struggle for advantage at a somewhat lesser distance, then two out of three will get there.

Therefore an army will perish if it has no equipment, no food, or no reserves.

So those who do not know the plans of competitors cannot enter capably into preliminary negotiations; those who do not know the lay of the land cannot maneuver a militia; those who do not use local guides cannot gain the advantages of the terrain.

Therefore a military force stands on deceit and moves according to advantage; division and combination are the means of adaptation. When it moves swiftly, it is like the wind; when it moves slowly, it is like a forest; when it raids, it is like fire; when it is still, it is like a mountain. Inscrutable as the darkness, it moves like thunder rumbling. To plunder an area, it distributes its troops; to broaden territory, it parcels out defense of the critical positions. Action is taken after weighing strategy.

The first side to know how to make strategic use of circuitous and direct routes is the one to win; this is a law of armed conflict.

A classic on military order says, "Gongs and drums are used because words cannot be heard; pennants and flags are used because soldiers cannot see each other." Thus gongs and drums are mostly used in night combat, while pennants and flags are mostly used in day combat.

Gongs, drums, pennants, and flags are means of unifying the people's ears and eyes. Once the people are unified, then the bold cannot push ahead alone, while the timid cannot fall back alone. This is the rule for employing a large group.

Thus the armed forces may have their spirit taken away, while the generals may have their heart taken away. In this connection, in the morning spirits are keen, in the afternoon spirits fade, in the evening spirits wane away. Therefore good warriors avoid keen spirits, instead striking enemies when their spirits are fading and waning. This is the mastery of mood. To face confusion with composure and face clamor with calm is the mastery of heart. To stay close to home to face those who come from far away, to face the weary in a condition of ease, to face the hungry with full stomachs is the mastery of strength. Not to stand in the way of an orderly march and not to attack an impeccable battle line is the mastery of adaptation.

So rulers for military operations are not to face high ground, not to get backed up against a hill, not to pursue a feigned retreat, not to attack fresh troops, not to chase after decoys, not to try to stop an army on the way home, to leave a way out for a surrounded army, and not to press a desperate enemy. These are rules for military operations.

[8]

ADAPTING TO ALL CHANGES

The general rule for military operations is that the military leadership gets the directive from the civilian leadership to assemble the army and mass the troops.

Do not camp on rugged ground. Establish diplomatic relations on open, accessible ground. Do not tarry on isolated ground. Where you may be surrounded, plan ahead. Where the situation is deadly, fight.

There are some roads that are not to be taken. There are some armies that are not to be attacked. There are some citadels that are not to be besieged. There are some territories that are not to be contested. There are some government directives that are not to be accepted.

Therefore military leaders who have mastered the advantages of comprehensive adaptation to changes are those who know how to command militias. If military leaders have not mastered the advantages of comprehensive adaptation to changes, then even if they know the lay of the land, they cannot take advantage of it. If they govern the military but do not know the art of adapting to all changes, even if they know of various advantages, they cannot get people to operate effectively.

Therefore the considerations of the wise include both profit and harm. Because they consider profit, their work is reliable; because they consider harm, their problems can be resolved.

So what inhibits competitors is the possibility of harm, what keeps competitors occupied is work, what sends competitors running is the prospect of gain. Thus a rule of military action is not to depend on enemies not showing up, but rather rely on having means of dealing with them; don't depend on enemies not attacking, but rather rely on having your own invulnerability.

Thus there are five dangers in military leaders. Those who will fight to the death can be killed. Those who are intent on survival can be captured. Those who are quick to anger are vulnerable to contempt. Purists are vulnerable to shame. Emotional humanitarians are vulnerable to anxiety. These five things are excesses in military leaders; they are disastrous for military operations. These five dangers are what overturn armies and kill commanders, so it is imperative to examine them.

[9]

MANEUVERING FORCES

Whenever you position your forces, size up your opponents. When you cut through mountains, keep to the valleys; camp on high ground, looking toward the light, and don't fight uphill. This is how to maneuver in the mountains.

When you cut across bodies of water, you must distance yourself from it. When invaders come across water, don't meet them in the water; let half cross before you attack them, and you will get the advantage. When you are going to do battle, do not meet invaders near water. Camp on high ground, looking toward the light, and do not face the current of a river. This is how to maneuver around bodies of water.

When you cut through salt marshes, just hurry to get out as fast as you can, without stopping at all. If you skirmish in a marsh, stick by the water and grasses, with your back to clusters of trees. This is how to maneuver in marshland.

On plains, take up your position in level spots with high ground to the right and the back, deadly ground in front and viable ground behind. This is how to maneuver on level terrain.

It was the advantage of these four ways of maneuvering that enabled the Yellow Emperor to overcome four rulers.

Generally speaking, armies prefer high ground to low ground, sunlight to shade. Take care of their health and take up positions in places that can support you, so that the soldiers do not fall ill. This is considered the way to certain victory.

When you come to hills or embankments, position yourself on the sunny side, keeping them to your right and your back. This is advantageous for battle, being helped by the lay of the land.

When it rains upriver, the water will be frothing; do not cross until it settles. Whenever you cut through a natural ravine, a natural enclosure, a natural prison, a natural trap, a natural pitfall, or a natural cleft, be sure to get out of there as soon as possible, because you should not be near them. I stay far away from them, so that the enemy is nearer to them than I; I face them, so that the enemy has his back to them.

If there are canyons and ravines nearby the army, or ponds, reeds, mountain forests, or thickets, it is imperative to search them thoroughly, again and again, because these are places where ambushers and interlopers lurk.

When enemies are nearby yet quiet, they are relying on a natural fastness; when they are far away yet provoking a fight, they want you to move forward. If they have occupied level ground, that is because it is advantageous.

The movement of trees signals advance; blinds in the undergrowth are there to mislead.

Birds rising up signal bushwhackers; animals being startled mean someone is taking cover there.

Dust rising high and sharp signals chariots coming; low and wide means infantry is coming. Scattered wisps mean firewood is being brought. If there is little dust, and they are coming and going, that means they are setting up camp.

Those who speak humbly yet increase their preparations are going to advance; those who talk tough and move forward aggressively are going to withdraw. When light vehicles come forth first and stay by the flanks, they are setting out a battle line.

Those who seek peace without a treaty are scheming; those who rush around arraying forces are expecting reinforcements. Those who half advance and half retreat are trying to draw you in.

When they brace themselves up as they stand, it means they are starving; when those whose job it is to draw water are the first to drink, it means they are thirsty. When they do not move on an obvious advantage, it means they are tired out.

Birds gathering mean a place is deserted. Calls in the night indicate fear. Unrest among the troops means the commander is not respected.

When signal pennants are disturbed, that means disorder; when emissaries are irritable, that means they are fatigued. When they feed their horses grain while they eat meat, when the troops have no canteens and do not return to camp, they are desperate.

Murmurings, shirking, and whispering indicate loss of the group. Repetitious rewards signal an impasse, repetitious punishments signal frustration. Those who are violent at first and then wind up fearing their people are inept in the extreme.

Those who come in a conciliatory manner want to rest. When a militia confronts you angrily but puts off engagement, and yet does not leave, you must watch carefully.

A militia is not helped by large numbers, but by avoiding violent aggressiveness. It is enough to consolidate your strength, size up enemies, and win people. Only those who thoughtlessly slight opponents are sure to be captured by others.

If soldiers are punished before an emotional bond [with the leadership] has formed, they will not be obedient, and if they are not obedient they are hard to direct. If the soldiers have formed an emotional bond and penalties are not enforced, then they cannot be directed. So unite them culturally and unify them militarily; this is considered the way to certain victory.

When order is consistently practiced to educate the people, then the people are obedient. When order is not practiced consistently to educate the people, then the people are disobedient. When order is consistently practiced, that means it is effective for the group.

10

THE LAY OF THE LAND

The lay of the land may offer no resistance, or it may hang you up, or it may get you into a standoff, or it may be constricting, or it may be precipitous, or it may be vast and far-flung.

When you can go and opponents can come, that means the lay of the land offers no resistance. On land that offers no resistance, position yourself first on high sunny ground, where there are the best supply routes, and it is advantageous in case of a battle.

When it is possible to go but hard to return, that means the lay of the land hangs you up. When the terrain causes hang-ups, you will win if you launch an attack on an unprepared enemy, but if you launch an attack against a prepared enemy and do not win, you will have trouble returning, to your disadvantage.

When it is of no use for you to act and it is of no use for your enemy to act, this is called a standoff. Where the lay of the land has you in a standoff, do not rise to any bait the enemy might set forth; withdraw instead, to lure the enemy half out, whereupon you can attack to your advantage.

On constricting terrain, if you occupy it first, be sure to fill it up to await the enemy. If the enemy occupies it first, do not pursue if the enemy fills the narrows. Pursue if the enemy does not fill the narrows.

On precipitous terrain, be sure to take up your position on a high and sunny place to await the enemy. If the enemy occupies it first, withdraw and leave; do not pursue.

On far-flung terrain, when forces are equal and it is hard to start a fight, it is unprofitable to do battle.

These are six ways of adapting to the terrain, which is the ultimate responsibility of the commander and must be examined.

So a militia may rush, may slack, may fall, may crumble, may be disorderly, or may be losers. These six are not natural disasters; they are the fault of the commanders.

Those who have equal power but who strike ten with one are in a rush. When the soldiers are strong but the officers are weak, there is slackness. When the officers are strong but the soldiers are weak, they fall. When high officers are wrathful and uncontrollable, and when they encounter an enemy they fight on their own out of resentment, and the commanders do not know their abilities, they crumble. When the commander is weak and not authoritative, instructions are not clear, officers and soldiers are inconstant, and battle lines are formed every which way, this is disorder. When the commanders are unable to assess enemies, take on many opponents with few troops, weakly attack stronger opponents, and have no special forces in their militias, they are losers.

These are six ways to defeat. This is the ultimate responsibility of military commanders and must be examined.

The lay of the land is a cooperating factor in a military operation. The way of superior commanders is to size up the enemy so as to ensure victory, assessing the qualities and dimensions of the terrain. Those who know this and use it in battle are sure winners; those who do not know it and yet engage in combat are sure losers.

Thus if military science indicates certain victory and yet the civilian leadership declares there shall be no fight, it is all right to insist on fighting. If military science indicates failure, and yet the civilian leadership calls for a fight, it is better not to fight.

Therefore [military leaders who] press forward without ambition for fame and retreat without trying to avoid blame, who only care for the security of the people and thus are in harmony with the interests of the civilian leadership, are treasures of the nation. Such leaders view their troops as babes in arms; that is why the troops are willing to enter deep valleys with them. They look upon their soldiers as beloved children; that is why they are willing to die with them. But if the leaders are so nice to the soldiers that they cannot command them, if they are so sentimental that they cannot enforce orders, if they let the soldiers misbehave and cannot govern them, as if they were spoiled children, then these leaders are not to be employed.

If you know your soldiers are ready to strike and do not realize the enemy is not properly vulnerable, you have half a chance of succeeding. If you know the enemy is vulnerable to a strike but do not realize your soldiers are not in proper condition to strike, you have half a chance of succeeding. If you know the enemy is vulnerable and your soldiers are ready to strike, and yet you do not realize the lay of the land militates against battle, you have half a chance of succeeding.

So masters of military affairs move without confusion, mobilize without exhaustion.

Thus it is said, "Knowing others and knowing yourself, victory will not be imperiled; by knowing the ground and knowing the climate, victory can be complete."

11

NINE GROUNDS

According to the laws of military operations, there is ground of disintegration, shallow ground, ground of contention, ground of intercourse, axial ground, deep ground, bad ground, surrounded ground, and ground of death.

A ground of disintegration is where local powers fight among themselves on their own territory.

Shallow ground is where you penetrate enemy territory, but not deeply.

A ground of contention is one that would benefit you if you got it and would also benefit your enemies if they got it.

Ground of intercourse is that over which you can go and others can come.

Axial ground is that which is surrounded on three sides by competing interests and would enable the first to get it to win the world.

Deep ground is when you penetrate enemy territory so far that many of their cities and towns are behind you.

Bad ground is mountain forests, defiles, marshes, and places generally difficult of passage.

Surrounded ground is where the way in is narrow and the way out is tortuous, so even in large numbers you are vulnerable to attack by a small band.

A ground of death is where you will live if you battle quickly and die if you do not battle quickly.

On a ground of disintegration, therefore, do not fight.

On shallow ground, do not halt.

On a ground of contention, do not attack.

On a ground of intercourse, do not get cut off.

On axial ground, make alliances.

On deep ground, plunder.

On bad ground, keep going.

On surrounded ground, plan ahead.

On deadly ground, fight.

Those known as skilled warriors of old could make it so enemies' vanguard and rear could not contact each other, large and small contingents could not rely on each other, the high and low ranks would not help each other, the leadership and the followers could not control each other, soldiers left and could not be reconvened, and troop[s] were not orderly when assembled. When it was advantageous, they acted; otherwise, they did not.

It may be asked, how do you face an oncoming enemy who is massive and well ordered? First deprive him of what he likes, and he will listen.

The true condition of military action is that its essential factor is speed, taking advantage of others' shortcomings, going by unexpected routes, attacking unguarded spots.

The general pattern of invasion is that deep penetration results in total concentration, such that defenders cannot win. Glean from rich fields, and the armed forces will be adequately fed. Be careful of their health and do not strain them; consolidate energy and build up strength. In maneuvering troops, calculate strategy so as to be unpredictable. Put them where they have nowhere to go, and they will die before giving up. In the face of death, how can warriors not exert their strength to the utmost? When warriors are in extreme peril, they have no fear; when they have no way out, they are firm. When they have gotten in deeply, they stick to it; when they have no choice, they will fight. Thus they are watchful without being trained, enlist without being drafted, are won over without promises, are loyal without being forced. Prohibit soothsaying, eliminate what is dubious, and they will stay to the death.

Our warriors have nothing extra, but not because they dislike goods; their lives are up, but not because they dislike longevity. On the day the order is issued, the soldiers weep; tears wet the chests of those who are sitting, tears stream down the faces of those lying down. Cast into circumstances where they have no way out, however, they show legendary bravery.

Thus skillful military operations are like a swift serpent. Strike at the head, and the tail whips around to lash back; strike at the tail, and the head whips around to lash back; strike at the middle, and both head and tail whip around to lash back.

It may be asked whether a militia can be made to be like that swift serpent. The answer is that it can. The people of Wu and the people of Yueh dislike each other, but when they are in the same boat they will help each other like right and left hands.

So it is that tethered horses and buried wheels are not adequately reliable; the principle of order is to even out bravery, as though it were uniform. When firmness and flexibility are both successful, this is a matter of the pattern of the ground. Thus one who commands a militia skillfully achieves such cooperation that it is like commanding a single individual who has no choice.

The affairs of military commanders are kept inscrutable by quiet calm, kept orderly by uprightness and correctness. They are able to keep the soldiers and officers in the dark, so the people will not know anything; they change their operations and revise their plans, so no one can discern them. They change where they are staying and take remote routes, so that no one can think ahead. When they lead the soldiers toward an aim, it is like climbing up to a high place and throwing away the ladder; when they lead them deep into the territory of competitors and unleash their energy, it is like herding sheep, who are driven this way and that without knowing where they are going.

Mastering the armed forces and putting them in dangerous straits are called the business of generals. It is imperative to examine the variations in the terrain, the advantages in contraction or expansion, and the principles of human psychology.

The general pattern of invasions is that they are concentrated when they penetrate deeply, diffuse when their penetration is shallow. When you campaign in foreign countries, that is to be on isolated ground.

That which is accessible from all sides is axial ground. A penetrating incursion is called deep ground, while a slight incursion is called shallow ground. That which is impassible behind and constricted ahead is surrounded ground. Where there is no way out is deadly ground.

Therefore, on grounds of disintegration, I would unify their wills. On shallow grounds, I would have them keep in touch. On grounds of contention, I would follow up quickly. On grounds of intercourse, I would make sure of my defenses. On axial grounds, I would solidify my alliances. On deep ground, I would ensure a continuous supply of food. On bad ground, I would forge ahead. On surrounded ground, I would stop the gaps. On deadly ground, I would show them there is no way to get out alive.

So the psychology of warfare is to resist when surrounded, fight when there is no other choice, and go along in extremes.

Thus it is that those who do not know the plans of competitors are incompetent to enter into preliminary negotiations; those who do not know the lay of the land are incompetent to maneuver armed forces; and those who do not employ local guides are unable to take advantage of the ground. A militia that lacks knowledge of even one of these things is not the militia of an effective rulership.

The militia of an effective rulership is such that when it attacks a large country the citizens there will not rally, and when it threatens enemies, they can't even get their allies to join them.

So if you do not set your communications in order throughout the world and do not develop worldwide power, but try to intimidate opponents, relying on your own personal authority, the result will be that your strongholds can be taken and your domain can be overthrown.

Give out rewards that are not in the rules, and set forth orders that are not in the code, maneuvering the armed forces like employing a single individual. Get them going on concrete tasks, without talking about it; get them going after advantages, without telling them of the dangers. [Han version: Get them going by prospects of harm, without telling them about prospects of gain.] Cast them into perdition and they will survive; plunge them into deadly situations, and then they will live. Only when people have fallen into danger do they have the ability to create the outcome.

Therefore the task of a military action is to unobtrusively deceive the minds of enemies. Herd enemies all in one direction, and you can kill the commander hundreds of miles away. This is considered skillful accomplishment of the task.

So on the day of mobilization, borders are closed and passports rescinded; emissaries are not allowed to get through. The affair is treated with rigor at headquarters in order to execute the task.

When the enemy presents an opening, be sure to penetrate at once. Preempt what the enemy prefers, secretly anticipating him. Act with discipline and adapt to the opposition in order to settle the contest.

So at first you are like a virgin girl, to whom the enemy opens his door. Then you are like a jackrabbit on the loose, which the enemy cannot keep out.

12

FIRE ASSAULT

In general, there are five ways of using fire for offensive purposes. First is to burn human beings. Second is to burn stores. Third is to burn equipment. Fourth is to burn warehouses. Fifth is to burn squadrons.

To set fires you need the proper basis, and the proper basis requires elementary tools. There are seasons and days for setting fires; the seasons are when the weather is dry, and the days are when it is windy.

In any fire assault, it is imperative to follow up on the crises caused by the five kinds of fire. When fire is set on the inside, follow it up quickly from the outside. When fire breaks out, if the soldiers remain calm, do not attack; intensify the fire to the extreme, then follow up if possible, stop if not.

If fires can be set outside, do not wait until you get inside; set the fires when the timing is right. When the fires are set upwind, do not attack downwind. When wind persists through the day, it stops at night.

In general, armed forces should know there are adaptations of the five kinds of fire assault and observe them scientifically. Thus those who support an assault with fire are clear, while those who support an assault with water are strong. Water can be used to isolate, but not to pillage.

To fail to reward the meritorious after victory in battle or a successful siege is ill-advised; it gets you the reputation of stinginess. So it is said that an enlightened leadership considers this and a good commander carries it out. They do not mobilize when it is not advantageous, do not act when it is not productive, and do not fight when not imperiled.

Rulers should not go to war in anger, commanders should not battle out of wrath. Act when it is useful; otherwise, do not. Anger can switch back to joy, wrath can switch back to delight, but a ruined country cannot be restored and the dead cannot be revived. Therefore intelligent rulers are prudent in these matters and good commanders are alert to these facts. This is the way to keep the country safe and the armed forces intact.

13

EMPLOYING SECRET AGENTS

When you mobilize an army of a hundred thousand and go on a thousand-mile expedition, the expenses of the commoners and the contributions of the government amount to a thousand pieces of gold a day. There is internal and external disquiet, people collapse in the roads, and seven hundred thousand families are unable to do their work. To hold out for years in the struggle for one day's triumph and yet be stingy with rewards and ignorant of the conditions of the enemy is extremely inhumane; this is not the mark of a leader of men, a helper of a government, or a triumphant chief.

So what enables intelligent rulers and good commanders to move in such a way as to overcome others and accomplish extraordinary achievements is advance knowledge. Advance knowledge cannot be obtained from supernatural beings, cannot be had by analogy, and cannot be found out by calculation; it must be obtained from people who know the enemy's condition.

Thus there are five ways of employing secret agents. There are local informers, inside agents, double agents, doomed agents, and agents who have to stay alive. When the five agents are operating simultaneously and no one knows their routes, this is an effective organization of supreme value to a ruler.

Local informants are agents recruited from among the local people. Inside agents are recruited from among others' officials. Double agents are recruited from among enemy spies. Doomed agents are those who are deliberately misinformed so that they will transmit misinformation to the enemy. Agents who have to stay alive are those who are to report back.

Therefore, no one in the armed services is appreciated as much as the secret agents, no awards are richer than those given to secret agents, and no business is more secret than espionage. Only the wise can use secret agents, no one but the humane can employ secret agents, and none but the subtle can get the truth from secret agents. Subtle indeed, subtle indeed! Secret agents can be useful everywhere.

When an item of intelligence is heard before it has been reported by an agent, both agent and the one to whom it was told die.

Whenever there is an armed force you want to attack, a citadel you want to besiege, or a person you want to kill, you must first know the identities of the defending commanders, their associates, their visitors, their gatekeepers, and their chamberlains. Make sure your agents find out all of this.

You must find out enemy agents who have come to spy on you, so that you can bribe them and get them on your side, so you can use them as double agents. The knowledge thus gained enables you to recruit and employ local informers and inside agents. The knowledge thus gained enables you to get doomed agents to report misinformation to the enemy. The knowledge thus gained enables you to employ agents who are to come back alive in a manner conforming to expectations.

It is imperative for rulers to know about the five kinds of secret agent. This knowledge depends on double agents, so double agents should be treated well.

When the Yin dynasty arose in ancient times, Yi Yin was in Xia; when the Zhou dynasty arose, Lu Ya was in Yin. So only enlightened rulers of wise commanders who can use the highly intelligent as secret agents are sure of great success. This is essential for military operations, the basis on which the armed forces act.

Sources

The Art of War, by Sun Tzu, translated by Thomas Cleary. Boston: Shambhala Publications, 1988. Copyright © 1988 by Thomas Cleary.

Mastering the Art of War, by Zhuge Liang and Liu Ji, translated and edited by Thomas Cleary. Boston: Shambhala Publications, 1989. Copyright © 1989 by Thomas Cleary.

The Lost Art of War, by Sun Tzu II, translated with commentary by Thomas Cleary. San Francisco: HarperSanFrancisco, 1996. Copyright © 1996 by Thomas Cleary.

The Silver Sparrow Art of War, by Sun Tzu, translated by Thomas Cleary. Boston: Shambhala Publications, 2000. Copyright © 2000 by Thomas Cleary. [Published originally in this volume.]

The Collected Translations of Thomas Cleary

THE TAOIST CLASSICS

VOLUME ONE

Tao Te Ching
Chuang-tzu
Wen-tzu
The Book of Leadership and Strategy
Sex, Health, and Long Life

VOLUME TWO

Understanding Reality
The Inner Teachings of Taoism
The Book of Balance and Harmony
Practical Taoism

VOLUME THREE

Vitality, Energy, Spirit
The Secret of the Golden Flower
Immortal Sisters
Awakening to the Tao

VOLUME FOUR

The Taoist I Ching
I Ching Mandalas

CLASSICS OF STRATEGY AND COUNSEL

VOLUME ONE

The Art of War
Mastering the Art of War
The Lost Art of War
The Silver Sparrow Art of War